W9-BPR-087

EGYPT

7000 YEARS

OF ART

AND HISTORY

BONECHI

Editorial project: Casa Editrice Bonechi
Editorial management: Giovanna Magi
Picture research: Giovanna Magi, Sonia Gottardo
Graphic design and cover: Sonia Gottardo
Computer layout: Alessandro Calonego, Teresa Donato
Texts: Giovanna Magi, Patrizia Fabbri
Editors: Federica Balloni, Patrizia Fabbri
Translations and revised texts: Eve Leckey
Drawings: Sauro Giampaia, *pp. 10 below, 25, 27, 71;*
Stefano Benini, *fold out and pp. 10 centre, 66, 102-103, 116, 140, 144, 152, 157, 167, 188, 192, 196, 236;* Alessandro Bartolozzi, *pp. 170-171;*
A. C. Carpiceci, *p. 46 below.*

© Copyright by Casa Editrice Bonechi, via Cairoli 18/b,
Firenze - Italia
E-mail:bonechi@bonechi.it

Collective work. All rights reserved.
No part of this publication may be reproduced, stored or transmitted in any form or by any means, whether electronic, chemical or mechanical, by photocopying or other means including cinema, radio, television and any information storage and retrieval system without the express written permission of the publisher.
The cover, layout and all elements by the graphic artists of this publication are the work of Casa Editrice Bonechi graphic artists and as such are protected by international copyright, and in Italy by the provisions of art. 102, law no. 633 regarding the rights of authors.

Printed in Italy by Centro Stampa Editoriale Bonechi.

The photographs belong to the archive of Casa Editrice Bonechi.

Other archives:
Gianni Dagli Orti: *pp. 5, 8 left and below, 9 left, 12, 13 all, except above right, 14 below, 20 above right and below, 22 all except below right, 28 above, 30, 33 below right, 34 left, 44 first above, 49 third and fourth from top, 50 above, 52, 57, 58-59 above, 61 above left and below, 63, 65 below, 69 below left and right, 70, 71, 72 below, 73 second right from top and below left and right, 74 below left and right, 74-75 above, 75 below right, 76 left, 77 centre and below right, 78 above, 79, 81 above, 83, 84, 85, 86, 87, 88, 111 below right, 129 above, 138, 139 below, 146, 147, 148 above right and below, 149 below, 150, 151 above, 152, 153, 154, 155 below left, 171 below, 177 above, 180 above, 184 above, 187 above, 195 above and below left, 244 below, 253;*
Andrea Jemolo: *pp. 3, 6 below, 7, 19, 22 below right, 24 above right, 27, 28 below, 29, 47, 92 above, 93 above, 110-111 above, 142, 198, 211, 214 above, 247;*
Andrea Ghisotti: *pp. 254, 255 all except fifth left from above and below left, 256 above, 257 above;*
Leonardo Olmi: *pp. 255 fifth left from above and below left;*
Andrea Pistolesi: *pp. 260 above, 261 above;*
Ghigo Roli: *pp. 256 centre, 261 below, 262;*
Griffith Institute, Oxford: *p. 143 below left and right;*
Istituto del Papiro, Syracuse: *p. 14 the three photos above left;*
The Art Archive/Bibliothèque des Arts Décoratifs Paris/Dagli Orti: *p. 165 above;*
© 1990 Foto Scala Firenze: *pp. 248 below, 250;*
TIPS Images/Guido Alberto Rossi: *pp. 16 above, 42, 64, 112;*
Mario Tosi: *pp. 157, 158, 159, 168, 169 below, 172, 173, 174, 175, 176 above, 180 below, 232, 233, 234, 235;*
©Unesco/Nenadovic: *p. 237 centre and below;*
Licensed by the Trustees of the British Museum: *p. 9 right, Rosetta Stone ©British Museum.*

The publisher apologies for any omissions and is willing to make amends on being informed by the holders of rights.

www.bonechi.com

Exclusive Distribution of Egypt

ISIS EGYPT

CAIRO - 52. EI Daher Str. Tel. 00202 - 5910125

ALEXANDRIA - 28, Abuwan Str. Moharam
Beik Tel. 00203 - 3914356

ISIS EGYPT

EGYPT
7000 YEARS
OF ART AND HISTORY

PLANETA EGYPT

To modern eyes the peoples of ancient Egypt seem like representatives of some higher civilization whose roots lay in another world. While populations elsewhere, still in their infancy, were groping their way out of the stone age, generating cultures that were on more or less the same level in all regions of the world, the Egyptians seem to have been born already mature. They soon broke through the barriers of what, six thousand years ago, was thought humanly possible, almost as if it were the consequence of experiences sustained in some other extraordinarily civilized world. What happened here on the shores of the Nile was unprecedented and unique, an adventure which evolved at dizzying speed, creating works of art and science far beyond the prospects of the time. Even now, the building of the pyramid of Khufu (Cheops) in a period when iron and the wheel were unknown, remains an inexplicable mystery. We are still more baffled when we realize that even before the Great Pyramid rose, the Egyptians had the techniques and organization required to harness the floods of the Nile along thousands of kilometres and turn swampland and the desert itself into a new earthly paradise.

The fact that other peoples developed at much slower rates, some remaining in the Neolithic period almost up to modern times, reinforces the feeling that the peoples of "planet Egypt" anticipated the history of the world by two thousand years, with an impulse of such force that it can still be felt five thousand years later. The arms used in this colossal conquest were water and fire – the Nile and the Sun. These arms were not wielded, but were forged and cultivated by those ancient peoples so that the destruction wrought by water and fire should render propitious the fertility of the earth, and thus the very life of Egypt. Mankind collaborated with Isis and Osiris to recreate life, to make the land look like paradise once more, a terrestrial paradise which is linked to the celestial paradise. Egypt is not the Promised Land, but it is the land that man creates by his labour, day by day, year by year, in endless cycles where the Created and Creator fuse into one. There is no longer a sharp distinction between the gods and man; the gods are in the midst of men; their features are those of man, or of the animals which surround him in the sky or on the earth; their hands are invisible and infinite, as infinite as the rays of the sun. Water and cosmic fire, death and resurrection, human and divine essence are present in every clod of Egyptian earth.

The Nile and the Sun trace two boundless rings which permeate the universe of this and of the other world, they are the path along which the new man of "planet Egypt" finds the future, and the very reason for his eternal quest.

Those of us who live now, two thousand years after Christ, can still find that ineffable equilibrium between the elements of water and the elements of fire by relaxing on a sailboat in Upper Egypt. We can once more discover the invisible bridge that will take us to the source of our history and experience the same emotion that touched the hearts of our ancestors seven thousand years ago when, at the beginning of the year, they heard the song that accompanied the rising waters of the Nile: *"Come water of life which springs from heaven. Come water of life which springs from earth. The sky burns and the earth trembles at the coming of the Great God. The mountains to the west and to the east open, the Great God appears, the Great God takes possession of the body of Egypt".*

THE LAND OF THE PHARAOHS

ORIGINS

Although much of the history of Egypt is still based on various hypotheses and suppositions its beginnings lie in the Palaeolithic period when the appearance of the Nile Valley was quite different to that of today. The river covered almost the entire region and this, combined with a much damper climate than that of today, created a vast swamp that stretched as far as the Delta. Towards the end of the Palaeolithic era, the climate began to change and as a result the Nile changed its course, eventually becoming that of today. The slow but progressive transformation of the surrounding area into desert meant that life became concentrated along the fertile banks of the river. In the Neolithic period, about 10,000 years before the birth of Christ, two quite distinct populations of different origins were present: the first was African from the centre of the continent, while the second was Mediterranean from the heart of Asia. Yet there was still a third race - people who may have come from the legendary Atlantis and who reached the Nile Valley after travelling across Libya. Thus two civilizations developed: one remained in the north of the country around the Delta, establishing *Merimda,* the first settlement, while the second group remained in the south where the major town was *Tasa.* Thus, even in the earliest times, the population of Egypt was split, and despite the later unification of the country, this territorial division survived in the *nomes* of which Upper Egypt had 22 and Lower Egypt 20. This was the dawn of the Egyptian civilization, the period that the Egyptians were to call the "time of the god", the time when King Osiris sat on the throne of the country. According to legend it was Osiris who succeeded in bringing the two groups together, but this unification did not in fact, last long and Egyptian history can really only be thought of as beginning around 3200 BC.

THE UNION

The history of Egypt really begins therefore with king Narmer, often identified as the mythical Menes who succeeded in uniting the two kingdoms and founded the first of the thirty-one dynasties that alternated on the Egyptian throne until 332 – the year in which Alexander the Great conquered the country. An implacable and ferocious king, he is portrayed in the famous *Narmer stele,* 74 cm. high, dated about 3100 BC, that was found in Hierakonpolis (now Elkab) a sacred city in the prehistoric kingdom of Upper Egypt. On one side of the stele, which is actually a simple schist palette for cosmetics, the pharaoh is represented brandishing a cudgel in one hand and grasping his enemy by the hair with the other as he lies already defeated on the ground. On this side of the stele, the king wears the conical crown of Upper Egypt, and on the other side he is seen standing before numerous beheaded enemies, wearing the crown of Lower Egypt. The symbol of royalty, there were in fact three crowns: the white crown of the south, the red of the north and the double crown formed by the combination of these, symbolising the united kingdom. The symbol of Upper Egypt was the vulture, and that of Lower Egypt the cobra.

The Gebel al-Arak, a dagger from the predynastic period, with an ivory handle carved with battle scenes. Paris, Louvre Museum.

THE OLD KINGDOM

The Old Kingdom began around 3200 BC and is considered by many to represent the most splendid period of the entire Egyptian civilization. When the capital was moved from Abydos to Memphis, the main town of the first nomes of Lower Egypt, the kingdom also became known as the Empire of Memphis. During this period civil and religious laws were established and writing and artistic styles developed. The 3rd Dynasty began with Djoser who built the pyramid of Saqqara, the first large stone structure in Egypt. He also appointed a prime minister who could substitute him and assisted with the administration of the kingdom which was now by necessity rather complex and quite extensive. The next dynasty, the fourth, began with Sneferu who conceived a new way of building pyramids with flat sides. For sheer architectural grandeur however, he was surpassed by three other pharaohs of his own dynasty: Khufu, Khafre and Mankaure who were responsible for the famous complex

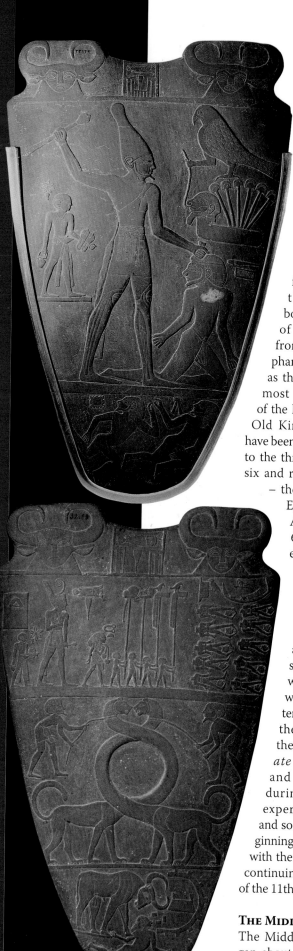

at Giza. Unfortunately little is known about them, though Khufu lead several military campaigns towards Sinai. The fifth dynasty originated in the city of Heliopolis. The god Ra himself was said to have fathered the first three pharaohs, born of a wife of one of his priests, and from then on all the pharaohs were known as the "son of Ra". The most important figure of the last dynasty of the Old Kingdom seems to have been Pepi II, who came to the throne at the age of six and ruled for 94 years – the longest reign in Egyptian history. At the end of the 6th Dynasty, however, central power was weakened by the nomarchs, the administrative officials who fought among themselves for control, while the pharaoh was unable to intervene or suppress them. This lead to the *First Intermediate Period*, a dark and troubled time during which Egypt experienced anarchy and social upheaval, beginning around 2180 BC with the 7th Dynasty and continuing until the start of the 11th Dynasty.

THE MIDDLE KINGDOM

The Middle Kingdom began about 2060 BC. Pharaoh Mentuhotpe reasserted power over Lower Egypt with the help of the Egyptian bourgeoisie. Commerce and trade were strengthened under his successors Mentuhotpe II and Mentuhotpe III, a commercial route was opened towards the Red Sea and the policy of expansion towards Nubia was reactivated. The 12th Dynasty began around 2000 BC and was one of the most splendid and famous in Egyptian history. The founder was Amenemhat I who favoured the cult of Amun, elevating him to the rank of principal deity. A capable administrator, under his rule Egypt experienced a period of great prosperity. He was succeeded by his son Senusert I who shared the throne with his eldest son in order to ensure continuity of the dynasty, a practice that was adopted by his successors. However, we know little of Amenemhat II and Senusert II except that they developed trading links with Phoenicia and drained the region around Fayyum. In contrast, one of the most important pharaohs of Egypt was Senusert III who, in four military campaigns, finally colonized Nubia, advanced as far as Palestine and built numerous fortresses along the border with Sudan. With the 12th dynasty, the Middle Kingdom came to an end and was followed by the *Second Intermediate Period*, still today one of the most obscure in Egyptian history, fraught with problems and dominated by the invasions of foreign peoples of Semitic origin, known as *Hyksos* a corruption of the Egyptian word *Hekakhasut* meaning the "heads of foreign countries". These peoples invaded the fertile plain of the delta, fortified the city of Avaris and made it their capital. With their much superior military power, the Hyksos easily defeated the weak Egyptian government and for a century were supreme rulers. Eventually a group of Egyptian princes succeeded in creating a coalition with other dynasties of Upper Egypt and together they initiated the re-conquest and liberation of the country, a process that continued until 1622 BC, when Ahmose, founder of the 18th dynasty, drove the enemy into southern Palestine, once more uniting Egypt under his rule.

THE NEW KINGDOM

In 1580 BC, during the New Kingdom, Egyptian power triumphed over the entire known world of the day. This was an epoch of both military power that was no longer based on defence but on conquest, and of the greatest artistic and cultural splendour. Thebes was still the capital and the priests of the god Amun were increasingly influential. The successors of Ahmose, Tuthmosis I and Tuthmosis II were primarily interested in military campaigns and conquests, but not so queen Hatshepsut. She removed her young nephew Tuthmosis III from the throne, proclaimed herself regent and reigned on her own for 22 years during which time she wore a beard and dressed in male clothes. After the death of his aunt, Tuthmosis III reclaimed his throne, cancelled the name of his usurping aunt from all the monuments and reigned for 34 years, one of the most splendid periods in Egyptian history. In 1372 BC the throne passed to Amenhotep IV, who has passed into history not only as a poet-king, but also as a heretical and schismatic leader. Worried by the priests of Amun, who had all but created a state within the state, he replaced the religion of Amun with that of Aten, a sun god represented by a disc, who could be worshipped without intermediaries thus enabling him to close the temples and disband the priesthood. He abandoned Thebes and founded a new capital, Akhetaten ("the Horizon of the Aten") now called Tell al-Amarnah. Finally he changed his own name from Amenhotep which meant "Amun is happy" to Akhenaton "pleasing to Aten". However, the schism would not survive its instigator.

The crown passed to the youthful Tutankhaton who, convinced by many, including the beautiful Nefertiti ("the beautiful one has come", the sister-bride of Akhenaton) eventually returned to Thebes, reinstated the cult of Amun and changed his own name to Tutankhamen. At the age of 18 he died unexpectedly and is principally renowned for the fascinating discovery of his tomb by Howard Carter in 1922. As Egypt slipped gradually into a state of anarchy, power passed to the military leaders: Horemheb, Ramesses I (a professional soldier), Seti I who continued the policy of expansion towards the east, and lastly Ramesses II, known as Ramesses the Great, who concentrated all his energies on defeating the Hittite army. He succeeded in at least halting them in an epic battle at Kadesh, which ended with neither side clearly the victor. During the 67 years of his reign, this pharaoh gave expression to his might with colossal monuments at Luxor, Karnak and Abu Simbel. His son Merneptah succeeded him and the slow, inexorable decline of the Egyptian empire began. The already precarious internal equilibrium broke down with anarchy from within and the arrival of Indo-European populations in Libya, Asia and the entire Mediterranean area, during the end of the second millennium.

The *Third Intermediate Period* began in 1070 BC with the 21st Dynasty whose capital was at Tanis. The next dynasty saw power in the hands of Libyan kings and later Ethiopian rulers (the capital was moved to Napata in Sudan). This was followed by the era of Persia and Sais and under the 27th Dynasty the Persians of Cambyses conquered Egypt for the first time. In 332 the Egyptians sought the aid of Alexander the Great who was seen as their liberator and was declared a "son of Ra" by the oracle of Luxor. He founded the new city of Alexandria, destined to become the cultural capital of the ancient world, and here he was buried in 323 BC. On his death, the Ptolemaic period began and the process of hellenization can be traced to this time. The two centuries that preceded the birth of Christ saw the continuing decline of Egypt, increasingly crushed by the growing power of Rome and eventually becoming merely one of its colonies. Finally, with the death of Theodosius in 395 AD, Egypt became part of the Eastern Roman Empire and a pall of sand seems to have descended over the past, almost as if to obliterate all memory of it.

Two examples of predynastic palettes from the Egyptian Museum in Cairo: the "Narmer palette" (both sides) the first on which a pharaoh's name appears written in hieroglyphs. Below, the "Libyan palette".

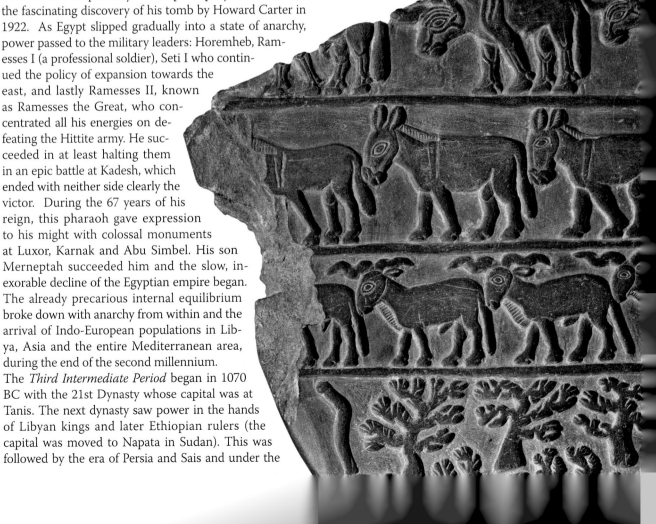

HIEROGLYPHIC WRITING

For centuries, one of the most fascinating mysteries of history concerned Egypt's unusual and complex method of writing, and more particularly once interest in the magnificent past of this ancient civilization was rekindled throughout the world. Scholars had always been eager to decipher the writing. But it was not until 1799 when a French captain named Bouchard was directing the fortification of the St Julian Fortress just over 4 kilometres outside the city of Rosetta that workmen suddenly discovered a slab of stone which would become famous in the history of archaeology and would provide the key to deciphering hieroglyphic writing – the Rosetta Stone. Following various historic events, it became the property of the English and is now one of the most important items in the British Museum. On one side of the stone, a slab of hard black basalt, is a lengthy inscription in three languages, with the texts in sequence. The first of the three inscriptions, had 14 lines and was written in hieroglyphs. The second had 32 lines and was in demotic script (from the Greek *demos* meaning 'people'), a style of common, everyday writing as opposed to hieratic writing (from *heirs* meaning sacred) which was reserved for priests and sages. The third inscription, of 54 lines, was in Greek and was therefore comprehensible. Once translated it proved to be a religious decree in honour of Ptolemy Epiphanies and concluded with the formal order that "this decree, engraved on stone in three forms, hieroglyphic, demotic and Greek should be sculpted in all the most important temples in Egypt." Beginning work more or less at the same time, two scholars have the merit of deciphering the stone – the Englishman Thomas Young, and the Frenchman François Champollion –both of whom saw their efforts crowned with success. However, rather than his rival, Champollion should be considered the real interpreter of hieroglyphic writing. Young used his intuition but Champollion applied scientific methods progressing so far with his re-

A portrait of François Champollion.

search that, on his death in 1832 he had completed an entire grammar and a dictionary.

What then was this form of writing that the Greeks called hieroglyphic (from *hiero glyphicà*, meaning "sacred signs")? The ancient Egyptians called their written texts "the words of the gods" and indeed, it was traditionally

Turin, Egyptian Museum: fragments of minerals used in making colours.
The natural pigments were crushed in the mortar and then stored in specific containers.

The famous "Rosetta Stone". The text, written in three languages, made it possible to decipher hieroglyphs. It is now in the British Museum.

A blue majolica statue of the god Thoth (Paris, Louvre Museum) from the tomb of Amen-hir-Khopshef (Valley of the Queens). A moon god, he is usually represented in human form with the head of an ibis and is the wisest of the gods, the inventor of writing and thus patron of the scribes, often portrayed with an ink bottle and palette in his hand.

believed that writing had been taught directly to man by the god Thoth at the time when Osiris ruled on earth. Over the centuries writing in fact maintained this sacred characteristic and was thought to have magical powers.

Those who were capable of inscribing the 300 signs that formed Egyptian writing (each indicating a sound or object) were held in great consideration.

The ancient Egyptians engraved the hieroglyphs on the stone walls of temples or painted them inside burial chambers, or traced them with rush pens on rolls of papyrus, the forerunner of today's paper.

The names of kings and queens were enclosed in a frame which archaeologists have called a "cartouche". The names of Cleopatra and Ptolemy, engraved within their cartouche on the Rosetta Stone, provided the clue for Champollion to begin his lengthy task of deciphering and interpreting.

MUMMIFICATION

Another characteristic element in Egyptian civilization that has stimulated the interest of scholars was, without doubt, the unusual method of preserving corpses and transforming them into mummies, a technique that was believed to be divine in origin and was traced back to Horus, the son of Osiris and Isis.

The term 'mummy' derives from the Arab word *mumiya* or *mumyai* which, according to Abd el-Latif a 12th-century Arab traveller, meant 'bitumen' or 'mixture of pitch and myrrh' – a compound much used in working with corpses and in which, in Europe too, there was a flourishing trade during the middle ages. In ancient times a distinction was made between natural and artificial mummies the former being those that had been preserved intact without having undergone any particular treatment. Indeed still today it is thought that the perfect embalming techniques used by the ancient Egyptians were responsible only as a secondary factor for the spectacular state of preservation of the corpses; the principal reason would appear to be the extremely dry climate of Egypt and the total absence of bacteria in the air and the sand. In any case, the mummification of the bodies took place according to a quite precise, and probably standardized, ritual. The body of the deceased was entrusted to the hands of specialists, who began the embalming by using a hook to extract the brain through the nostrils. The skull was then filled with a mixture based on liquid bitumen, which hardened as it cooled. The eyes were removed and later replaced with enamelled orbs. Using an extremely sharp stone, an incision was made on the left side of the body and the viscera were extracted.

Only the heart was left in place. After being treated with boiling bitumen, the stomach, liver, lungs, and intestines were wrapped and then sealed in four canopic jars of clay, limestone, alabaster, other stones, or metal, depending on the social standing of the dead man; the heads depicted on the stoppers of each jar - one human, one a jackal, one a hawk, and one a baboon - symbolized the four attendant spirits of the dead. The jars were placed together in a single container, near the mummy. The internal cavities of the corpse were carefully washed with palm wine, dried using a powder of aromatic plants, and finally filled with ground myrrh or with perfumed wood sawdust. Thus prepared, the body was immersed in a bath of natron (natural sodium carbonate) where it remained for seventy days. At the end of this period, during which the flesh and muscles were completely dissolved in the natron solution, all that remained was the skin attached to the bones. The hair of the men was cut short, while that of the women was left in all its splendid length. At this point, the corpse was wrapped with narrow bindings impregnated with resin on the lower side; wrapping began with the separate fingers, then the hand, and

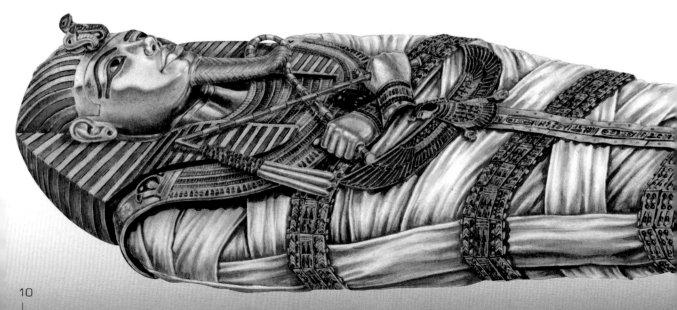

finally the arm; then the foot and leg, and so on. Work on the head was more meticulous. A cloth similar to muslin was used in immediate contact with the skin. The figure was covered with several layers of bindings, which adhered so perfectly that if they had been removed in a piece, a plaster cast made from them would have been an exact portrait of the dead man. The entire body, lying supine, with the hands crossed on the breast or with the arms stretched out along the sides, was then again wrapped in bindings for its entire length. The corpses of the pharaohs merited a precious shroud or a golden case on which were embossed the features of the dead man. The mummies in the museums of Cairo and Alexandria and in other countries are almost perfectly preserved. The oldest known mummy is that of Sekkeram-Saef, a son of Pepi I (6th Dynasty) discovered at Saqqara in 1881 and housed in the Egyptian Museum of Cairo. The skill of the

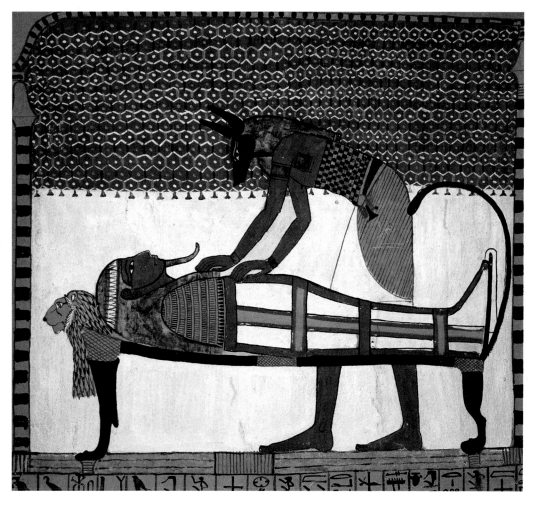

One of the most fundamental moments of the funeral rites is seen on a wall of the tomb of Sennedjem in the Valley of the Artisans; the priest, wearing the mask of Anubis, touches the heart and stomach of the mummy to wake it and accompany it to the other world.

embalmers has thus transmitted the images of the great pharaohs across the centuries: we can still recognise in the shrivelled head of Tuthmosis III (who many consider to be the pharaoh of the biblical exodus of the Jews) the characteristic family nose and the thick eyebrows; and x-ray has shown that the great pharaoh, Ramesses II clearly suffered from toothache.

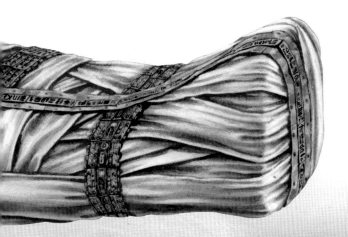

Reconstructions of the mummy of the pharaoh Tutankhamen and of the canopic vases in which the internal organs of the deceased were kept.

THE "LAND OF THE GODS"

The ancient Egyptians often called their country by the name of *Ta Neteru* or Land of the Gods, and always believed Egypt to be a divine nation whose first rulers were gods. The great variety and number of divinities worshipped by the ancient Egyptians – the *Pyramid Texts* count about two hundred between gods and mythological events – should not lead us to presume that this was a polytheistic people: like all the great religions, theirs was substantially monotheistic.

The adoration of the gods that began in the predynastic period and continued through later Egyptian history remained largely unchanged until the 5th century AD. Undoubtedly, the most characteristic aspect of the way in which divinities were represented in ancient Egypt is the combination of human and animal elements – or more exactly, of human bodies with animal heads.

Adoration of the divine forces in animal form began in the prehistoric era, as is proved by the care with which many animals were entombed.

Veneration of the gods in human form first appeared in about 3000 BC and slowly gained ground. The clothing of the gods and goddesses is quite uniform: a short loincloth for the first and a long, clinging dress with shoulder straps for the second.

All hold in their hands the general attributes with which they dispense eternal life and salvation, while the specific attributes of each god or goddess are by and large found above, or in place of, their heads.

In the predynastic era, each village, even the tiniest community, had its own local deity. When Egypt was divided into various nomes or districts (twenty-seven according to Strabo, thirty-six according to Diodorus Siculus, and forty-four for the ancient Egyptians themselves, though in reality 42 altogether), a certain divinity attained pre-eminence over the other local gods in each nome.

The country was thus divided into different 'divine factions'. However, from the most ancient of times, Egyptian religion embraced the concept of the triad.

A triad was generally made up of the most important local god plus two associated deities; this most common form permitted the inclusion of a feminine element or a young god, son of the primary divine couple.

PAPYRUS

An important element of everyday life in ancient Egypt was the papyrus, a perennial plant, similar to reeds or rushes, with a stem that grows from 2 to 5 metres in height, ending in a wide, umbrella-shaped bloom at the top. The white and spongy pith of the stalk was cut into thin strips which were laid on a board and stuck down at the edges. Another layer was placed over this in the opposite direction, then dampened and left to dry in the sun. This formed a sheet which was pressed and then scraped to make it smoother and thinner. The sheets were then joined to each other to obtain a long strip that could be rolled up, and on which scribes could write in a series of columns.

The fascinating traditional method of treating papyrus to make paper is still practised and continues even outside its birth-place, Egypt, for example as is seen in the photos on the left, from the interesting Papyrus Institute in Syracuse.

Right, from the tomb of Nefer and Kahay at Saqqara, a scene of men bent under the weight of papyrus stems; below, the mythological papyrus of Imenemsauf (Louvre Museum, Paris) with the four sons of Horus and the weighing of the heart before Thoth, portrayed as a baboon.

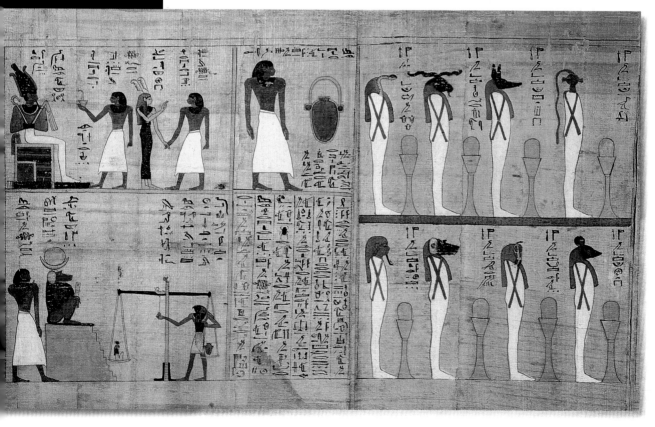

A view of modern Cairo, stretching along the banks of the Nile, that shows the lofty Cairo Tower (below, from an impressive angle), a powerful symbol of the city looking to the third millennium.

The pre-dynastic period in Egypt was characterized by confederations with political heads or kings who resided in a capital. The capital of Lower Egypt was Buto and of Upper Egypt, Nekhen, and with the subsequent union of the Two Lands under Narmer, the city of Memphis became the first capital of unified Egypt. Over the centuries, the capital moved several times until 332 BC when, with the arrival of Alexander the Great, it was transferred to Alexandria, on the west of the Nile Delta, where it remained throughout the Ptolemaic and Roman periods. With the introduction of Islam in Egypt, a succession of capitals was founded with a clearly military function, which later united to create a single city. In 969 the new city of *Al-Qahirah* (The Victorious), now known as Cairo, was founded and thereafter became the capital of Egypt and centre of Islam. The new city developed rapidly: during the Ayyubid period the Citadel was built and the construction of a great wall to surround al-Qahirah was begun. Building and urbanization flourished in Cairo under the Mamluks (from 1250 to 1517), and was continued by the Ottomans who also favoured important trading activities. During the reign of Muhammad Ali and his successors the city continued to develop. After the revolution of 1952, the economic boom of the 1960s resulted in a sharp rise in the population. At present the great city has over 16 million residents in the metropolitan area, and is the most populous city in Africa as well as an important political, cultural and economic centre of the Middle East.

CAIRO AND THE NILE

The capital is divided in two by the Nile which flows from the south after passing through Nubia, Aswan, Luxor, Abydos, Tell al-Amarna, and Memphis. It then divides into two branches forming the Delta before it enters the Mediterranean. There are four islands in the section of the Nile that flows through Cairo, two of which are inhabited. On the biggest island there are many international hotels and important buildings as well as gardens, sporting clubs, museums and the famous Cairo Tower.

Modern Cairo

It is said that Egypt is the Gift of the Nile, and this is indeed true. Since the dawn of history, great civilizations developed along its banks. The Nile flows through the heart of Cairo at one of its major stretches. Grand buildings and international hotels flank the two banks, giving modern Cairo a new image.

Among the important buildings overlooking the Nile are the Egyptian TV and Broadcasting Organisation and that of the League of Arab Nations. Five main bridges have been constructed to connect different parts of the capital and to overcome the problem of heavy traffic which is a major concern in most capitals of the world. There are five *universities* in Cairo. The oldest and most famous of the Islamic world is al-Azhar. The other four were founded in the early 20th century.

There is also an Academy of Arts where cinema and theatrical arts, ballet, and music are studied.

Cairo has a number of museums, the most important of which are the **Egyptian Museum**, the **Coptic Museum**, the **Islamic Museum** and the **Agricultural Museum**. The *Zoological Garden* of Cairo is one of the largest and oldest in the world. However, there are also the *Andalusian Garden*, the *al-Urman Garden*, the *Ezbekieh Garden*, *al-Huriyyah Gardens*, and the *Japanese Garden* of Heluan.

The *Cairo Tower* at al-Gazirah is considered a true symbol of modern Cairo. Built in reinforced concrete in 1957 by the architect Naoum Shebib, it is a 187 metre-high cylinder, and the upper part is in the form of the lotus flower. On the 14th floor there is a revolving restaurant, and from the terrace on the 16th floor a magnificent panorama over Cairo and its suburbs may be enjoyed.

More views of the modern city with the majestic skyscrapers that rise along the riverside, and the Cairo Tower.

RAMESSES II

In 1279 BC, at the age of 25, the son of Seti I, Ramesses II "beloved of Amun" came to the throne of Egypt (below, a black granite bust now in the Egyptian Museum of Cairo, portraying the new sovereign as a young man). A brilliant future awaited him, earning him the title of "The Great", as grandeur and excess were the hallmarks of all aspects of his life: his reign was one of the longest in Egyptian history (some 67 years), he had eight wives (including Nefertari, whom he loved the most) and more than one hundred children; his name is connected with epic battles, such as the Battle of·Kadesh where, in 1275 BC, with considerable difficulty, he succeeded in blocking Hittite expansion; he built more monuments and temples to the gods than any other pharaoh; and he had images of himself erected everywhere – these were not just simple statues, but veritable colossi of amazing size (right, the gigantic granite statue from al-Achmunein, today in the Egyptian Museum of Cairo, where Ramesses II is represented wearing the double crown of Upper and Lower Egypt). His architectural activity was incessant and even lead him to found a new capital, Pi-Ramesses, "The House of Ramesses", on the delta, described as "fascinating and wealthy" where the vegetation was luxuriant and the houses glistened with blue as they were decorated with tiles coloured sky-blue. Before long, however, only the ruins remained of this city, built by Jewish slaves who laboured in the brickworks. But the fame of Ramesses II himself was to prove more lasting – he died at the age of 90, leaving the throne to his thirteenth son, Merneptah, by then almost 60 years old.

AUGUSTE MARIETTE

Born in Boulogne in 1821, Auguste Mariette became an assistent at the Louvre and was subsequently appointed as leader of a mission sent to Egypt to acquire ancient papyri and Coptic manuscripts. Mariette possessed great intuition and sharp observation and in 1851, while excavating in the area of Saqqara, he discovered the Serapeum, the hypogean necropolis of the sacred Apis bulls. Thanks to the importance of this discovery, Mariette was appointed Director of Egyptian Antiquities and Inspector of Archaeological Excavations by the viceroy, Said Pascia. His wonderful achievements lead to the creation of the Museum of Cairo and he is buried in its garden.

The imposing building which now hosts the Cairo Egyptian Museum at al-Tahir Square was designed by the French architect, Marcel Dourgnon, winner of an international competition.

Today the Museum hosts the most important collection of Egyptian art in the world.

There has been European interest in Egyptian antiquities since the beginning of the eighteenth century: the Napoleonic campaign of 1798, the discovery of the Rosetta Stone the following year and above all the publication of the 18 volume *Description de l'Egypte* between 1809 and 1816, not only represented a scholarly description and historic study of Egyptian civilization but also encouraged the appetite of those who had already begun to collect ancient objects. Amongst the first to start collecting these antiquities were the consuls of various European countries. These collections were then sold in Europe and made up the original nucleus of Egyptian collections in various European museums such as those of Turin, Paris, London and Berlin.

The artistic and archaeological heritage of Egypt thus suffered serious losses: the situation was, in fact, so serious that in 1830 the renowned scholar, Champollion, asked Pasha Muhammad Ali to create a system that would safeguard the preservation of the monuments. The former leniency appeared to have ended in 1834, when a museum was founded on the banks of Lake Ezbekiah and all the objects began to be catalogued. This first collection was soon transferred to a more suitable site in the citadel of Cairo, yet the items were still so few that it was possible to fit them all into one room! The Archduke Maximilian of Austria saw these objects during a visit to Cairo in 1855 and asked the Pasha Abbas to give him some items: the Pasha gave him everything in the room and so the first original Egyptian Museum of Cairo can today be seen... in Vienna!

Fortunately, on the 1st June 1858, Auguste Mariette, a di-rector of the Louvre Museum who had also been sent to Egypt to collect antiquities, succeeded in being appointed *Mamour*, the Director of Excavations. The considerable pressure on Khedive Said to preserve Egyptian monuments, and the support of the influential consul general and important French businessmen, secured Mariette the use of the former headquarters of a river navigation company at Boulak, a small port near Cairo.

Mariette moved there and founded the first National Museum in the entire Middle East. The official opening was on 18th October 1863 and in 1891 the collections were moved to the Palace at Giza and finally in 1902 to their present location.

One of the finest masterpieces in the Egyptian Museum of Cairo is this head of queen Hatshepsut (18th Dynasty) in painted limestone. Originally part of a statue from Deir el-Bahri, the queen is portrayed in the style of Osiris with details of the face skilfully emphasized with sophisticated delicacy.

Three of the splendid jewels that decorated the mummy and tomb of Tutankhamen: above, pectoral shaped like a temple with the vulture goddess Nekhbet and Wadjet, the cobra goddess protecting Osiris; left, pectoral with symbols of the sun and moon; below, pectoral shaped like a scarab made of gold and inlaid with lapis lazuli, cornelian, turquoise and green feldspar, found in the Treasury.

The famous gold mask of
Tutankhamen. The cobra and
the vulture clearly indicate
that he was ruler of the two
lands as the vulture Nekhbet
and the serpent Wadjet,
seen together on his forehead,
were the symbols of the two
divinities that protected
Upper and Lower Egypt
respectively.

More treasures discovered in the Tomb of Tutankhamen and now exhibited in the Egyptian Museum in Cairo: left, one of the eight fans buried with the pharaoh; below, the golden base of the intermediate sarcophagus with an engraving of the goddess Isis-Nut; below right, the magnificent wooden throne entirely covered in gold and set with semi-precious stones and glass paste; below left, a small head portraying Tutankhamen as a boy, rising from a lotus bud, found in the entrance to the tomb of the boy pharaoh.

When opened on discovery by Howard Carter in the early 20th century, the antechamber of Tutankhamen's tomb contained about 700 items, mostly of magnificent workmanship and gleaming with gold. Two of the finest are the twin statues of regal appearance bearing a mace and staff, crowned by an urea of gilded bronze, the left leg forward according to the canons of traditional Egyptian noble statuary, which stood as guardians of the sovereign's eternal sleep (right). They represented the "ka" of the pharaoh, his double that detached itself from the body and accompanied him in the other world. There were also three large funerary beds (below right is the finest of these, formed by two cows with elongated horns in the shape of a lyre, holding the solar disc). In addition there were a splendid throne, exquisitely-made seats, a small wooden sanctuary completely covered in gold, and an elegant little chest decorated with tempera painting on plaster (below). 61 cm. long, 43 wide and 44 high, it has magnificent hunting scenes on the top and elaborate battle scenes on the sides, all revealing supreme and skilful care for detail and sophisticated decoration.

Also found in the tomb of Tutankhamen were a magnificent and rare sculpture of the pharaoh standing in a boat about to throw a harpoon (opposite page, left); a splendid regal diadem that was around the head of the mummy, beneath the gold mask (opposite page, above); the three large sarcophagi in which the mummy of Tutankhamen lay (opposite page, below, the third sarcophagus – radiant in its stupendous finery and sophisticated human features). This page, splendid jewels that belonged to the boy pharaoh: a scarab bracelet (below), a chain with pectoral showing three scarabs (right), and the cloisonné collar with falcons' heads (below).

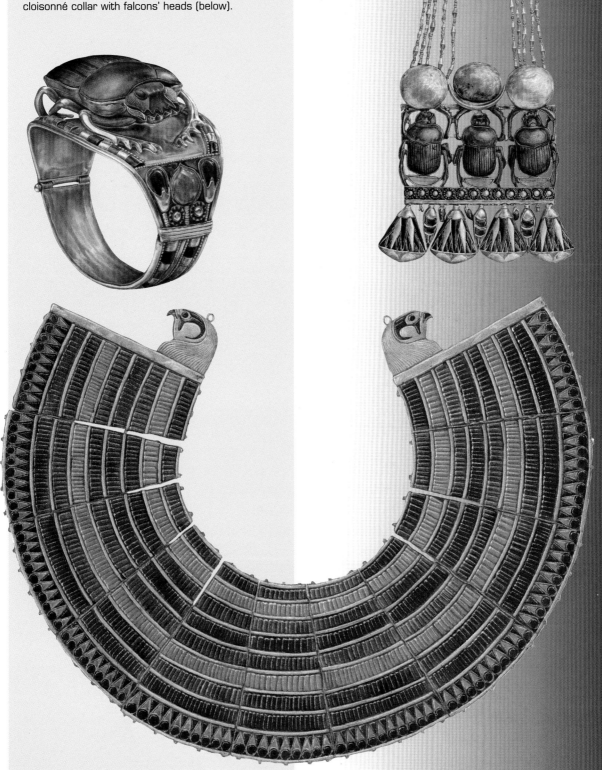

Opposite page, the great wooden chapel covered
with gold inscribed with hieroglyphs, almost 2 metres
high, 1.5 in length and 122 cm. wide surmounted by
a row of glass paste urea holding the solar disc, that
held the canopic vases of the pharaoh (the vertical
section below provides a reconstruction illustrating the
arrangement). Four female statues of the goddesses
who protected the four vases stand clasping the sides
of the chapel.

This page, right, the elegant alabaster container that
held the four canopic vases, which are really miniature
sarcophagi, containing the internal organs of the
pharaoh, whose features were reproduced on the lids
of the four compartments.

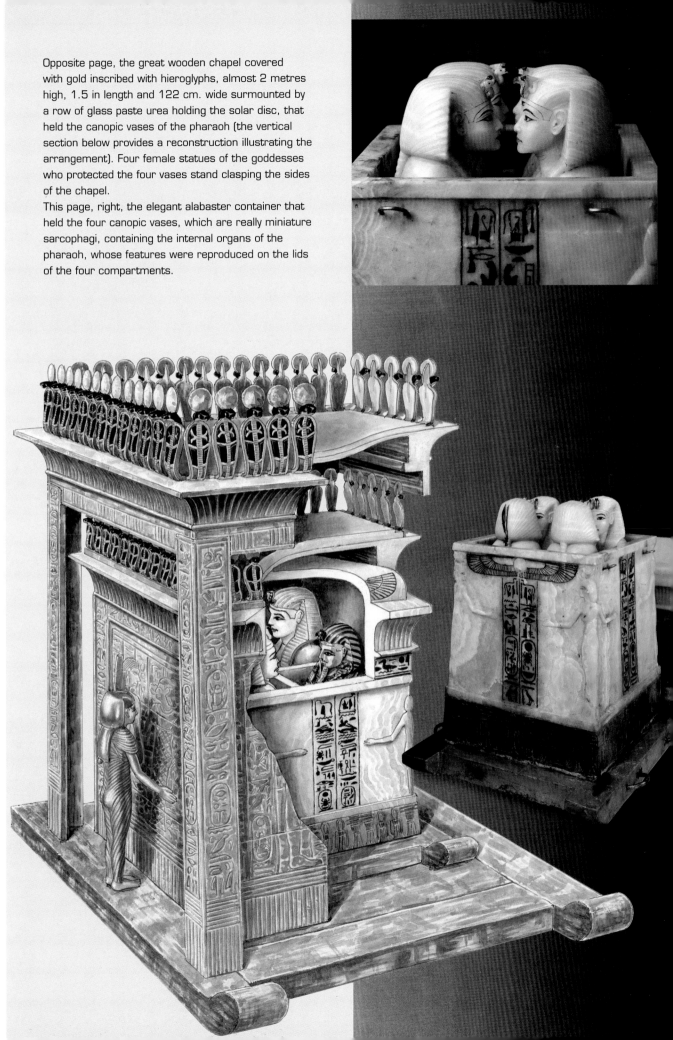

Opposite page, right, a perfume bottle of polished alabaster found between the first and second funerary chapels; below, a painted wood figure of Anubis lying on a glided sedan shaped like a pylon, found almost like a silent guard at the entrance to the Treasury.

This page, two more gems of ancient Egyptian art that are exhibited in the Egyptian Museum: left, a figure of Akhenhaton in the act of offering, from Tell al-Amarnah and dating from the 18th Dynasty; below, the magnificent and richly decorated sarcophagus of queen Ahmose Merit-Amon, from Thebes (18th Dynasty).

Found in 1897
in the temple of
Hierakonpolis,
a centre for the
worship of the falcon
god Horus, this head
is one of the most
perfect examples
of goldsmith's art
during the Memphis
period. The body,
which must have
been made of copper,
has unfortunately
not survived. Made
of beaten and
chased gold, with
oxydian eyes, it is
crowned by two long
stylized feathers,
below which is the
imperious regal
cobra. The ancient
Egyptians considered
the brilliance and
splendour of gold to
be the attributes of
a divine material and
therefore, by its very
nature, destined to
adorn and enhance
the statues of kings
and gods.

This statue in painted grey sandstone portrays the pharaoh Mentuhotpe I and comes from what must have been the marvellous funerary complex of the grand temple dedicated to him at Deir el-Bahri. Of the 11th Dynasty, Mentuhotpe I was a wise and far-sighted sovereign who, during his long and happy reign, put an end to the troubled First Intermediate Period, re-establishing his royal power over Lower Egypt and, with the help of the Egyptian bourgeoisie, finally limiting the dangerous rebellions of the ambitious nomarchs. Part of a group of eight situated in a leafy area in front of the great temple, the style of the statue is quite rough and the colouring somewhat elementary. It was perfectly preserved as it was wrapped in cloth and in ancient times was partially buried in a hole dug in the rock, almost as if it were a substitute for the body of the king.

Both man and god, in this powerful statue made from black diorite, the pharaoh Khafre, half brother and successor to Khufu, is portrayed seated on the throne, his right hand closed in a fist. Engraved on the sides of the throne are the symbols of the two lands over which the pharaoh reigned supreme: the lotus of Lower Egypt is, in fact, entwined with the papyrus, symbol of Upper Egypt. A small falcon, symbolizing the god Horus, spreads his wings around Khafre's neck in a clear sign of protection. Interestingly, the block of black stone from which the statue is made comes from a quarry in distant Nubia, almost 1000 km further to the south of the place where it was actually made.

From Saqqara, this attractive
little figure in painted limestone
represents a scribe seated
in the traditional position
and dates from the 4th
Dynasty. It is of particular
interest as it is the first
example of a sculpture
portraying a trade.

It was normal in
Egypt that the mastabas of
officials and relations of the pharaoh should
be built around the royal pyramid so that they
would join him on his last journey towards
the other world. Thus, beside the pyramid of
Sneferu at Maydum, in the tomb of his son
Ra-Hotep, this exquisite statue of the young
prince with his beautiful wife Nofret was found.
Discovered in 1871, the figures combine a high
degree of stylization with the most delightfully
natural and realistic pose and form.

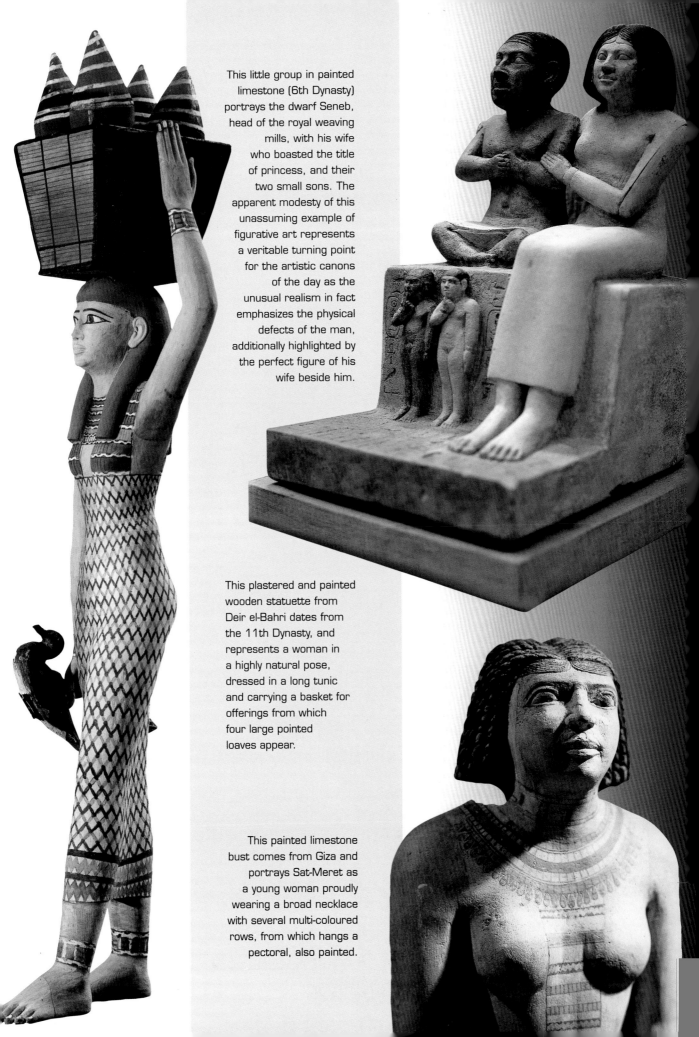

This little group in painted limestone (6th Dynasty) portrays the dwarf Seneb, head of the royal weaving mills, with his wife who boasted the title of princess, and their two small sons. The apparent modesty of this unassuming example of figurative art represents a veritable turning point for the artistic canons of the day as the unusual realism in fact emphasizes the physical defects of the man, additionally highlighted by the perfect figure of his wife beside him.

This plastered and painted wooden statuette from Deir el-Bahri dates from the 11th Dynasty, and represents a woman in a highly natural pose, dressed in a long tunic and carrying a basket for offerings from which four large pointed loaves appear.

This painted limestone bust comes from Giza and portrays Sat-Meret as a young woman proudly wearing a broad necklace with several multi-coloured rows, from which hangs a pectoral, also painted.

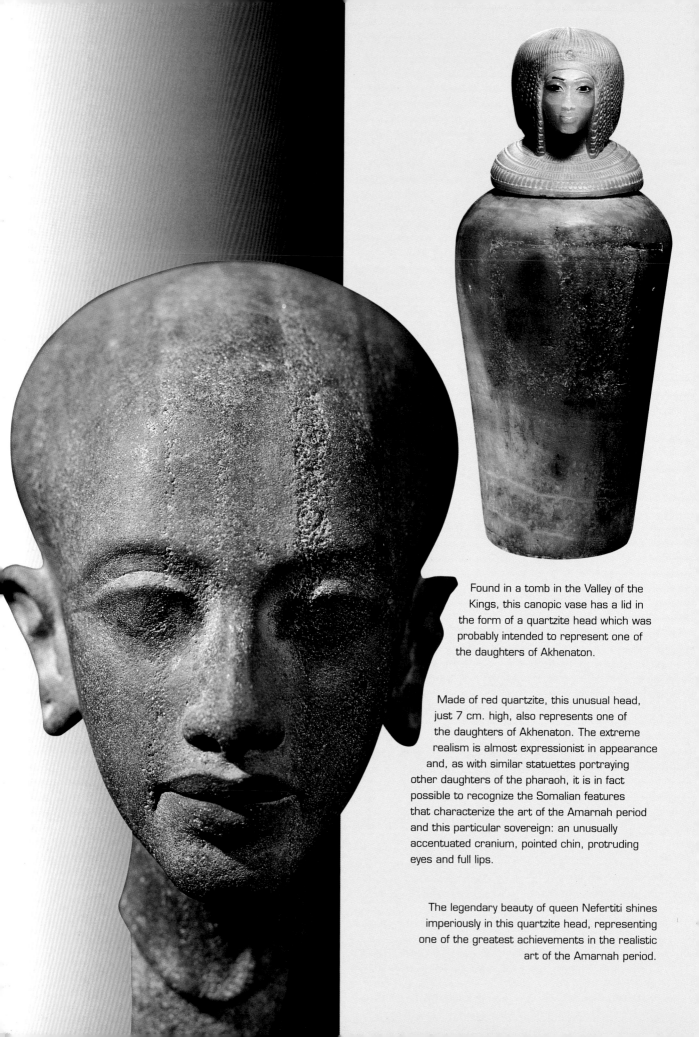

Found in a tomb in the Valley of the Kings, this canopic vase has a lid in the form of a quartzite head which was probably intended to represent one of the daughters of Akhenaton.

Made of red quartzite, this unusual head, just 7 cm. high, also represents one of the daughters of Akhenaton. The extreme realism is almost expressionist in appearance and, as with similar statuettes portraying other daughters of the pharaoh, it is in fact possible to recognize the Somalian features that characterize the art of the Amarnah period and this particular sovereign: an unusually accentuated cranium, pointed chin, protruding eyes and full lips.

The legendary beauty of queen Nefertiti shines imperiously in this quartzite head, representing one of the greatest achievements in the realistic art of the Amarnah period.

The Coptic Museum was founded in 1910 in Old Cairo beside the Babylon fortress. This site was chosen because of its associations with the beginnings of Christianity in Egypt.

The museum is surrounded by six ancient churches of particular importance: *al-Moallaka, St. Sergius, St. Barbara, Mari Girgis, The Holy Virgin Convent* and *the Church of Qasriat al-Rihan*, which was destroyed by fire in 1975. The Coptic Museum contains a collection of the most ancient Coptic objects from churches, palaces and Coptic homes. The collections belonged to Marcus Simaika. The museum has two pavilions and a courtyard where Coptic architectural elements are exhibited. The older pavilion was erected in 1910 and the new one in 1947. The old pavilion features balconies (*mashrabia*) and wooden ceilings brought from ancient Coptic palaces, as well as fountains, stucco and mosaic windows, marble and limestone pillars. The museum, effectively reopened in 1984 after extensive restoration, consists of 29 rooms exhibiting frescoes, wood carvings, metal work, pottery and glass work, tapestry, papyrus, manuscripts, stationery, icons and ivory sculptures.

There is also a *library* with 7000 books, volumes and manuscripts, the majority of which are in the Coptic language.

At the entrance to the Coptic Museum, is a fountain covered with a wooden cupola, in typical "Mashrabiah" style supported by four marble pillars. A lamp hangs from the centre of the vault with 366 small lights representing the number of days in the year. In a niche behind the fountain there is a fresco representing *Christ in Glory*, surrounded by four angels and the archangels Michael and Gabriel. Below the fresco is an image of the *Virgin and Child*.

Tis is one of the most important muse-ums in the city. Situated in Bab El Khalk Square, the museum was inaugurated in 1903 and houses some genuine masterpieces of Islamic art.

Of the *majolica* items more than 68 different decorative styles can be identified, ranging from encrustation to perforated designs. Some designs represent Coptic symbols such as the fish, as well as Islamic geometric designs. There are also majolica items of the Mamluk era, bearing mottoes and slogans of their troops and dating to the 16th century. This room also contains an Ottoman-style fireplace that dates back to the 18th century. The rugs hanging on the walls are in different Turkish styles; the room also contains stones reproducing the decorations of the Ibn Tulun Mosque, dating from the 12th century.

Also displayed are Persian and Turkish turquoise porcelain (17th and 18th centuries), as well as vases from Samarkand showing Chinese influence (12th century), and Chinese porcelain from Mamluk mosques.

On the left, two images showing the exterior and one of the rooms inside the interesting Coptic Museum, with one of the columns from the Monastery of the Patriarch at Saqqara.

This page, on the right, a room in the Museum of Islamic Art; below right, a splendid bronze carafe, and on the left one of the fifteen copies of the Koran kept in the museum, dating from the Omaijadi dynasty.

Muhammad Ali Mosque

The Muhammad Ali Mosque has become a symbol of the city of Cairo. It was built by Muhammad Ali (1769-1849) who was born in Cavalia, Greece, and was of Albanian origins. He was a soldier in the troops that were sent to Egypt to free the country from Napoleon's occupation and took part in the battle of Abou Qir on the 25th of July 1799. In 1801 he was the commander of the Albanian troops in Egypt. In 1805 the Egyptians revolted against Khurshid Pasha and Muhammad Ali succeeded to the command. The mosque was built in 1830 in two parts: the mosque and the courtyard. The court measures 52x54 m. and is flanked by four corridors formed by mar-

ble columns surmounted by small domes. In the centre of the court is the fountain for ablutions (where Muslims wash before going to prayer, five times a day). The clock tower on the west side of the fountain is made of perforated copper. The clock was a present from King Louis-Philippe of France to Muhammad Ali Pasha in 1845. The Greek architect, Yusuf Bushnak lived in Turkey and took as his model the Byzantine style of St Sophia in Istanbul, a church later transformed into a mosque. Each side of the square-shaped mosque is 41 metres in length. Resting on four square pillars, the central dome, 21 m. in diameter and 52 m. high, is surrounded by 4 half-domes and the *quiblah* dome that faces towards Mecca. On the western side

of the mosque stand two cylindrical minarets in the Ottoman style, each 84 m. high.

The Mosque of Ibn Qalawun

East of the Mosque of Muhammad Ali stands the Mosque of Sultan al-Nasir Ibn Qalawun who was one of the sultans of El Mamalik al-Baheria. The mosque was constructed in 1318 and rebuilt in 1335. At the western entrance is an engraved inscription bearing the date of its first construction. Another engraving over the northern portal shows the date of the second construction. The mosque is composed of an enclosed courtyard surrounded by four arched walls known as *iwans*. The main side is the *quiblah* formed by 4 corridors

Some of the most important mosques in Cairo: from the left, the Mohammad Ali Mosque, the tomb of the pasha and the fountain for ablutions; the Al-Rifaii Mosque, showing the Mosque of Sultan Hasan on the left (above, an attractive view of the entrance).

flanked by 4 rows of columns The other *iwans* each have two corridors with two rows of columns.

In the centre of the *quiblah* iwan there is a large *mihrab* covered with fine marble and decorated with mother-of-pearl. The dome of the *mihrab* rests on granite columns with wooden stalactites. It is decorated with green mosaic and consequently is known as the "Green dome". The mosque has two minarets in different styles and their domes are adorned with mosaics of exceptional beauty.

Joseph's well (Bir Yusuf)

Behind the mosque is a spiral well 90 metres deep with two different levels. The upper one is 50 metres deep and the lower 40 metres. This well was used to provide the citadel with water during war. Water was raised by means of a *sakiah* (a water wheel worked by oxen). Fresh water arrived through a channel that was dug into the citadel walls. Traces of this channel can still be seen today.

The Mosque of Sultan Hasan

This is one of the most beautiful and famous monumental mosques in Cairo. It was built by Sultan al-Nasir Hasan (the nineteenth Turkish Sultan to have governed Egypt and the seventh son of the Sultan al-Nasir Ibn Qalawun) whose reign was beset by many conspiracies. The mosque was built exactly opposite the Citadel of Salah al-Din. Building began in

1356 and was completed in 1363 by prince Bashir Agha. This mosque is considered one of the greatest works of Islamic architecture; it covers an area of 7,907 square metres and the entrance is 37.80 m. high. This is a school-mosque (*madrasa*) for the four rites of Islam. The courtyard is almost square in shape; each side is about 32 metres in length and is overlooked by a tall *iwan*. Each *iwan* is roofed with a tunnel-vault with a stone arch. Experts consider the arches of the main *iwan* to be a miracle of construction. On the right of the *minbar* (pulpit), is a wooden door covered with bronze. The two doors on either side of the *quibla* wall lead to the *tomb chamber* of the Sultan and are covered with bronze and gold silver inlay. The tomb chamber is 21 square metres and 50 metres high. The walls are covered with marble to a height of 8 metres. The Mosque of Sultan Hasan has two minarets, one of which is 82 metres high and is considered one of the highest Islamic minarets, although it is two metres shorter than the minarets of the Muhammad Ali Mosque which was built 500 years later.

Al Rifaii Mosque

This famous mosque was built by a woman, Princess Khushyar, the mother of Khedive Ismail who opened the Suez Canal and was an energetic renovator of the city of Cairo.. Completed in 1912, it stands to the north of the Sultan Hasan mosque. The site, chosen by Princess Khushyar, was the residence of the Al Rifaii family, which dates back to Imam Ahmed Al Rifaii, renowned for spiritualism and their ability to master snakes and vipers. The mosque is named after the Al Rifaii family. The building covers an area of 1,767 square metres. It is flanked by four massive columns supporting the pointed arches that divide the mosque into 3 porticos. On either side of the large dome are two marble columns, one white and the other dark green. The mosque houses the tombs of the royal family of Egypt from Khedive Ismail Pasha and his mother, Princess Khushyar, up to King Faruk.

The Mosque of Sulayman Pasha

Also known by the name of *Sariya al-Gabal* this mosque is situated on the north west side of the Citadel. Built by prince al-Mortaadi Magd al-Khelafa, it was the first mosque in Egypt to be constructed in the Ottoman style. In 1528 it was restored by the Mamluk Sulayman Pasha al-Khadim. It consists of two sections: the eastern part, designated for prayer, is surmounted by a cupola surrounded by half-domes richly ornamented with painted designs and verses from the Koran in a different style. Externally, the domes are covered with green mosaic. In the western section, consisting of an open courtyard, is an inscription bearing the name of the builder and date of construction. The court is surrounded by 4 *iwans* with coloured cupolas 16 metres high.

Ibn Tulun Mosque

This is one of the most important mosques in Cairo and one of the

An impressive image of the façade of the Al-Rifaii Mosque.

Ibn Tulun Mosque, showing the severe and classical elegance, also evident in the lofty minaret, with an external stairway twisting around the tower.

most impressive Islamic monuments. It was built between 876 and 879 by Prince Ahmad Ibn Tulun, the founder of the Tulun dynasty.

He founded the third Islamic capital of Egypt, al-Qataii, on the Yuchkour hill, around his enormous mosque south east of Cairo. The mosque was built to the same plans as the mosque of Samarra in Mesopotamia.

The mosque is square in shape and measures 162.5x161.5 metres. At the centre is a large courtyard, also square and measuring 92.5x91.80 metres. The courtyard is surrounded on all sides by galleries and the *quiblah* is in the largest of these.

An outer courtyard (called a *ziyadat*) surrounds the mosque on three sides and is built with bricks to protect it from fire and water.

The arches of the galleries (*riwaks*) rest on brick capitals covered with a thick layer of plaster supported by pilasters, forming interwoven arches at each corner. There are 129 windows in the walls of the mosque made of plaster with filigree decoration representing geometric and floral designs. The minaret is 40 metres high and the external staircase is a spiral like that of the Samarra mosque.

It seems that the architect of the mosque was a Christian from Syria who also built the tower of the aqueduct that served al-Qataii.

It is said that when he heard Ahmed Ibn Tulun wanted to build his mosque without sacking Christian churches to steal their columns, he alone claimed he could satisfy the prince's wish.

Al-Azhar Mosque

This is the most famous mosque in Cairo and in the Islamic world, where students from all over the world can come to complete their academic and theological studies. It is also the oldest Islamic university, in existence since 975, as well as the first Fatimid mosque in Cairo and the most important centre for teaching the Arabic language.

Gawhar al-Siqilli began construction of the mosque in 970 AD, during the reign of the Fatimid Khalif al-Muizz li Din Allah.

Completed in 972 AD, the mosque then consisted of three *iwans* surrounding the court, the largest of which was the *quiblah iwan*, composed of five galleries. The building was enlarged and restored mainly during the Mamluk period. It has a surface area of 12,000 square metres, and was the first monument built by the Mamluks just a year after having conquered Egypt.

One of the minarets was built by Sultan Qayt-Bey in 1458; on its left, the second minaret has 16 sides compared to other minarets that have eight sides only.

The World of the Pyramids

"The World of the Pyramids" is an apt name for the series of necropoli which lie along the western bank of the Nile, stretching from the ancient city of Leopolis almost as far as Herakleopolis. Over eighty pyramids, in a continuous chain fifty kilometres long, lie to the north and south of Memphis. Surrounded by a myriad of mastabas, or oblong tombs with sloping sides and a flattish top, a great many of the pyramids have smooth sides while a few are stepped. Almost at the end of this series of monuments stand the great pyramids of Giza.

Almost five thousand years ago, the Giza plateau, on the west bank of the Nile (the region of the dead), became the royal necropolis of Memphis, the capital of the pharaohs of the 4th Dynasty. The Giza site lies about 15 kilometres (9 miles) west of modern Cairo and covers an area of about 2,000 m² (21,500 ft²). On the southwest side, a 40 metre (130-ft) cliff descends to where a channel of the Nile once ran marking the borderline between fertile land and the desert. The site of Giza is the only one of the *Seven Wonders of the Ancient World* to have survived to our day; the others (the Pharos of Alexandria, the Colossus of Rhodes, the Mausoleum of Halicarnassus, the Temple of Artemis at Ephesus, the Statue of Zeus at Olympia, and the Hanging Gardens of Babylon) have long since disappeared, destroyed by man and by time. Giza however still hosts the tombs of three pharaohs of the 4th Dynasty – the **pyramids of Khufu**, **Khafre**, and **Menkaure** – and the **Sphinx**, the "Father of Terror". The fascination of these stones and the air of mystery that has emanated from them since ancient times, has deeply affected the minds and souls of scientists and archaeologists, writers and poets, paint-

ers and soldiers over the ages. Not even Napoleon was immune to their seduction. On 21 July 1798, when his soldiers were about to engage in battle with the Mamluk army whose troops stood arrayed before the hazy geometry of the pyramids, Napoleon turned to them and, indicating the monuments, exclaimed, "Allez et pensez que du haut de ces monuments quarante siècles vous observent!" ("Soldiers! From atop these pyramids, forty centuries look down upon you!") The three pyramids are located in rela-

A - MORTUARY COMPLEX OF MENKAURE

1) Pyramid
2) Three subsidiary pyramids
3) Mortuary temple
4) Causeway
5) Valley temple

B - MORTUARY COMPLEX OF KHAFRE

1) Pyramid
2) Subsidiary pyramid
3) Mortuary temple and solar barks
4) Causeway
5) Valley temple

C - MORTUARY COMPLEX OF KHUFU

1) Great Pyramid
2) Pyramids of the Queens and Bark Pits
3) Mortuary temple
4) Causeway

D - EASTERN NECROPOLIS

E - WESTERN NECROPOLIS

F - SPHINX

G - SPHINX TEMPLE

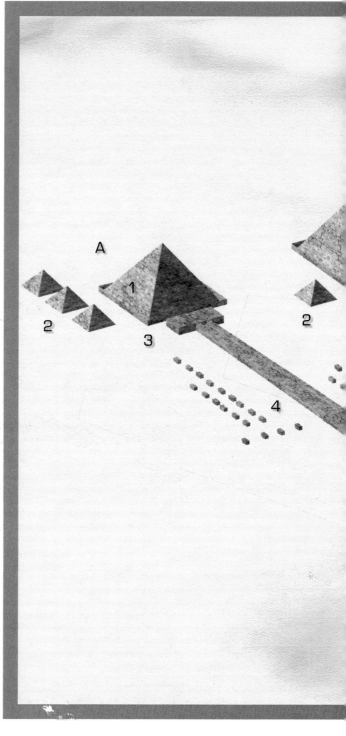

tion to the four cardinal points on a diagonal axis from northeast to southwest, so that none of the pyramids ever blocks the sun of the others. This perfect alignment has led to theories that the ancient Egyptians, experts in astronomical measurements, took the positions of certain stars into consideration in their construction plans. According to the archaeologist Robert Bauval, the three large pyramids of Giza are actually meant to be in an alignment corresponding to the three stars in the belt of the Orion constellation. The pyramids are built mainly of limestone and granite – the former from the quarries of

Tura, across the Nile from Memphis, and the latter from Aswan. Unfortunately, in the 13th century local inhabitants began removing the precious facing from the limestone blocks and used them to build homes in Cairo. The pyramids are not isolated constructions: each is part of a funerary complex made up of a *mortuary temple* (or upper temple) to the east of the pyramid, a *causeway* – a sort of ceremonial route – and a *valley temple*. The valley temple symbolized the entry of the pharaoh into the world of the gods: it was here in fact that the sacred ritual ceremony of "Opening of the Mouth" was performed. The valley temple of Khufu has been almost completely destroyed, but a large portion of Khafre's is instead well preserved. The funeral procession travelled the causeway to the mortuary temple and the pyramid, carrying the dead pharaoh on the sacred boat toward his place of eternal rest. In the mortuary temple, the pharaoh became a divinity and as such was venerated. A common feature of all three pyramids is the *burial chamber*, almost exactly aligned with the central axis of the construction. The main pyramids of Menkaure and Khufu are each flanked by three subsidiary pyramids, while that of Khafre has only one.

The pyramid
an enigma in stone

HOW WERE THE PYRAMIDS BUILT?

Rivers of ink have flowed in the debate over the system of construction used to raise the pyramids. Architects, engineers, archaeologists, and scholars of every persuasion have expressed their ideas in merit and made their contribution to finding a solution to one of the greatest unsolved mysteries of ancient Egypt. Unfortunately, the copious iconography regarding daily life in ancient Egypt is not matched by a similar store of documentation regarding the construction of the most important monuments of Egyptian architecture.
Most certainly, the stone was quarried, cut into blocks, loaded onto sleds, runners, or rollers, and dragged to the pyramid construction site.

Once there, however, there arose the problem of how to lift these gigantic stones. The most highly-credited theory is now that involving ramps: wide inclined planes, built of mud brick or sand, that gradually increased in slope and height as the pyramid went up.
The *ramp* may have been *straight* and perpendicular to the pyramid, built up to one side of it and becoming narrower at the top and longer as the pyramid grew in height. Or the ramp may have been *helicoidal*, spiralling around the structure. Concerning the construction of the pyramids Herodotus wrote, "It took ten years' […]to make the causeway for the conveyance of the stones, a work not much inferior, in my judgment, to the pyramid itself […]. It is built of

polished stone, and is covered with carvings of animals. To make it took ten years, as I said - or rather to make the causeway, the works on the mound where the pyramid stands, and the underground chambers, […]. The pyramid itself was twenty years in building. It is a square, […] built entirely of polished stone, fitted together with the utmost care. The pyramid was built in steps, battlement-wise,

Above, two stages in pyramid building showing how initially they were built in steps. Below, a reconstruction of a pyramid building site.

46

as it is called, or, according to others, altar-wise. After laying the stones for the base, they raised the remaining stones to their places by means of machines formed of short wooden planks. The first machine raised them from the ground to the top of the first step. On this there was another machine, which received the stone upon its arrival, and conveyed it to the second step, whence a third machine advanced it still higher. Either they had as many *machines* as there were steps in the pyramid, or possibly they had but a single machine, which, being easily moved, was transferred from tier to tier as the stone rose - both accounts are given, and therefore I mention both. The upper portion of the pyramid was finished first, then the middle, and finally the part which was lowest and nearest the ground."

The Machines

Obviously the machines were differently built according to the varying heights involved and the weights to lift. For blocks of around two tons that had to be lifted to a height of six metres, a machine eight metres high at most might need not much more than half an hour, so that

it would take a block six hours to be hoisted to a height of a hundred metres. With a series of machines on all sides, about two hundred blocks a day could then be unloaded on the uppermost work yard. A series of machines was not required for the fairly limited number of blocks weighing forty or fifty tons and one or two specially built pivoted levers sufficed, aided by levers and counterweights like those used later to erect the obelisks. These particular pivoted levers used for heavy loads would certainly have been of appropriate dimensions and beams of Lebanon cedar, like the masts of boats, measuring up to fifty metres in length, were employed.

The function of the pyramid

When the pharaoh died, the lengthy ritual of embalming and burial began at the temple-dwelling

of the pharaoh. Once the body had arrived with the procession of sacred boats, the purification ceremonies began at the Valley Temple and the preparation of the mummy was completed. The principal ceremony was the purification by water, comparable to that of the Sun which is reborn every morning from the *Lake of the Lily*. Purified and covered with propitiatory amulets, the mummy passed the "*Guardian of the threshold*", then began his journey of ascent, hidden from profane eyes, through the gallery, and reached the upper temple for consecration. As the body proceeded from one columned hall to the next, the number of initiates and the 'purified' who accompanied him (consisting of priests and relatives) dwindled. When it reached the large central court only the

great initiated and the pharaoh's heir continued into the "sancta sanctorum" of the mortuary temple, where the fundamental ceremony of the "*opening of the mouth and eyes*" took place. The royal heir presided over this ritual which "opened" the communication of the deceased with the after world, in front of the five chapels - the five statues of the god-king - one for each attribute given to the pharaoh at the time of his royal consecration. Officially reunited with the gods, the deceased was taken through secret ways to the subterranean chapel. Once sealed, the precious sarcophagus was set among his dearest possessions and treasures, after which the worker-priests retraced their steps, closing the marble shutters and obstructing all the passageways so that no one might disturb the pharaoh as he waited for his final

The granite pyramid stone of Huy, dating from the New Kingdom, is an example of the element that crowned the structure and was also a model of the pyramid.

ascent to the sun. The last secret ceremony was that of placing the statue of the pharaoh in the *serdab*, the small bricked cell at the heart of the mortuary temple, from which the image of the king would "see" the ceremonies and offerings made in his honour for the rest of time.

AN "ARCHITECTURAL ABSURDITY"

The oldest tombs of the pharaohs resemble the palace-castles of the First Dynasty, followed later by the stepped pyramids, and lastly, those with smooth sides. While it may be easy for us to see how the palace of the living pharaoh could become the "palace" of the deceased pharaoh (just as the house of the living prince became, with the mastaba, the house of the deceased prince), it is more difficult to grasp the relationship of the pyramid with the world of the living and with the after world. With the arrival of the pyramids, the image of a house was swept away and any connection with the real world or with tradition was abolished. It was in Djoser's time (2700 BC) with the works designed by the great architect Imhotep that this sudden, apparently inexplicable, leap ahead took place.

Indeed, in the marvellous architectural complex at the centre of Saqqara, three substantially different structural types are found: the beautiful enclosure wall which echoes the architectural traditions of the royal palaces; the stupendous massive buildings and colonnaded vestibules which represented completely new perspectives in architecture for the entire ancient world; the hermetic mass of the stepped pyramid which looms up in the centre of the complex, and for which no reference either to traditional architecture or to the architecture invented by

Imhotep himself, can be found. How can we explain the conceptual abyss between Imhotep's most important work and other structures - this apparent rejection of all architectural forms and furnishings previously attempted or invented? The abandoning of tradition becomes clearly evident on examining the construction of the pyramid. Initially the structure was a "mastaba" with a square ground plan. The pharaoh's burial chamber lies under the massive mastaba, at the end of a shaft sunk in the rock. The house-tomb was in fact twice enlarged, but still in keeping with

7) The Grand Gallery, the architectural masterpiece of ancient Egypt. It is 47 m. long and 8 m. high with a ceiling formed of massive blocks fitted together with astonishing precision.

10) The "construction chambers", a system of five small, empty compartments, one above the other and extremely low, the top one having a double-sloped roof. The first of these chambers was discovered by Nathaniel Davison in 1765, the others by Perring and Vyse in 1837. They were thought to be mainly designed to relieve the enormous pressure exerted by the overlying mass of the pyramid on the ceiling of the King's Chamber.

GREAT PYRAMID

5) Ascending passage, a little over 1 m. (3 ft) in height, leading to the Queen's Chamber.

1) Entrance to the pyramid at 25 m. (82 ft) above ground level, on the north side.

8) Three red granite "shutters" that slid vertically and hermetically sealed the burial chamber.

11) Ventilation shafts. These two ducts, which open at a height of 76 m. (249.4 ft) on the north and south faces of the pyramid, carry fresh air to the interior of the burial chamber.

9) The burial chamber or King's Chamber, 5.85 m. (19.2 ft) in height, 10.45 m. (34.3 ft) long and 5.22 m. (17.1 ft) wide, at 48 m. (157.5 ft) from ground level, completely faced in blocks of pink granite. The ceiling is composed of nine slabs each weighing 400 tons. On the west side of the chamber is the red granite sarcophagus of the king, with no cover and no inscriptions. It is 2.24 m. (7.34 ft) long and 1.03 m. (3.38 ft) high. Nothing was found inside it – neither mummy nor ornaments.

2) Sloping corridor leading down to the subterranean chamber.

4) Descending passage, probably used to permit the workers to leave the pyramid after the King's Chamber had been sealed.

MORTUARY TEMPLE

QUEENS' PYRAMIDS

CAUSEWAY

6) The Queen's Chamber or middle chamber, lying exactly on the axis of the pyramid. Measuring 6.7 m. high, 5.7 m. long and 5.2 m., it was never completed.

3) Original burial chamber, at 30 m. (98.4 ft) below ground level.

tradition. While the second enlargement was in course, the programme was abandoned for no apparent reason and the first pyramid with four steps – a great protective shell – appeared over the mastaba and subsequently three sides of this disappeared under the final six-step pyramid. The question again arises - why was the traditional tomb, that image of a living person's dwelling, swallowed up by a form that was completely new, even for the inventor himself? This is all the more problematical in view of the fact that barely a hundred years later the stepped pyramid was replaced by one with smooth sides. The leap from the stepped pyramid to the smooth pyramid is to be found in Maydūm, and is encapsulated in the original structures of the pyramid built by Sneferu, founder of the Fourth Dynasty. In terms of construction, the difference is not great. Indeed it seems almost natural that a stepped pyramid should eventually be protected by a sloping surface so as to resist the wear and tear of time: moreover the concept of flat sides is an integral part of all the great pyramids, starting with Djoser's, where the construction developed with a series of sloping flat walls around a central core (the core of the pyramid of Khufu is like a giant obelisk 146 metres high, without a point). The stylistic alteration is, however, of much greater import as one passes from an outline which has at least some tenuous relation to the architectural concepts of the time, to another where all contact with reality is lost. It should also be remembered that this latest "novelty" was not the result of a momentary caprice, but endured until the end of the Sixth Dynasty, and a magnificent example was built at the end of the third millennium. The golden age of the stepped pyramid lasted not much more than a hundred years, while that of the geometric pyramid lasted five hundred years! Whatever were the reasons that caused Khufu to attempt, this "architectural absurdity" – a macroscopic pyramid even further removed from reality than Djoser's, a costly undertaking that stretched the limits of human possibility – they must have been forceful and imperative. Since we have absolutely no precedent for this extraordinary form in earlier Egyptian works, no hint at what the stimulus might have been, the answer must be sought in the world of religion and in experiences that cannot be explained by history alone. "Spiritual pyramids" are to be found in Egyptian theology and cosmogony, in that "science" of the world before and after the "land of the Nile". These mysterious pyramidal forms have powerful echoes in the primordial tumult arising out of Chaos, the source of the great egg-lotus which opens to give birth to the sun.

There is a strong formal analogy in the pyramid shape with rays of light, a great stream diminishing to a point in infinity that transports the elected to a true Egyptian Nirvana, which is reached by crossing the bridge uniting heaven and earth. Akhenaten, the pharaoh prophet of the revealed religion, continually reproduces this pyramid of infinite arms which reach out from the sun to benefit all men, none excluded, arms outstretched almost as if to embrace mankind as a whole and carry it back into heaven. The *Pyramid Texts* themselves, which transcend history, tell us *"I have walked on thy rays as if on a stair of light to ascend to the presence of Ra.... heaven has made the rays of the sun solid so that I can elevate myself up to the eyes of Ra.... they have built a staircase leading to the sky by which I can reach the sky"*.

The Great Pyramid (as well as the Sphinx) is thus none other than a gigantic ideogram derived from the past, which signifies the staircase which *par excellence* leads to eternity.

From above, a view of the Great Gallery, the entrance to the sarcophagus chamber and two engravings by Louis Mayer (1804) in the Bibliothèque des Arts Décoratifs, Paris, showing the passage between the second and third galleries, and the sarcophagus chamber.

The pyramid of Khufu

The Great Pyramid, which the ancient Egyptians called "Khufu belongs to the Horizon", was built 45 centuries ago and is the largest at Giza. Our notions of its history come mainly from the historian and "journalist" Herodotus, who visited Egypt in 460-455 BC. He tells us that the pyramid was "twenty years in the making" and that work was continuous with groups of hundreds of men at a time working for three months; he also relates that 1,600 silver talents were spent. Herodotus talks of one hundred thousand workmen altogether but we must remember that Herodotus saw the pyramids 2700 years after their completion and in many cases he was only repeating hearsay. The estimates by today's archaeologists of the number of workers range between fifteen and twenty thousand workers. The architect was apparently a certain Hemiunu who, in building his creation, used 2,300,000 blocks of limestone averaging about 2.5 tons each, for a total weight of approximately 5,750,000 tons! The outer facing has disappeared since, from the 13th century onwards, the beautiful slabs of limestone were removed for reuse in building the homes and the mosques of the new city of Cairo, thus exposing the gigantic structural blocks underneath.

Views of the pyramid of Khufu. At the top, instead of the original crowning pyramid stone, is a flat area about 10 metres wide. Right, ivory statuette of Khufu, housed in the Egyptian Museum in Cairo.

KHUFU

The name of Khufu, the second king of the 4th Dynasty, is the ancient Egyptian name meaning "He [the god] Protects Me", the derived Greek form being Cheops. We know very little of this pharaoh; likewise, few images have come down to us. Paradoxically, all that remains of the builder of the world's largest pyramid is a tiny ivory statuette, just 7 cm. (2.76 inches) high, bearing the features of the man Herodotus described as an evil, cruel ruler who even went so far as to force his daughter into prostitution to obtain financing for construction of his monument.

KHUFU AND THE STARS

The fifth-century philosopher Proclus of Byzantium stated that the Great Gallery of Khufu's pyramid was originally an astronomical observatory that the pharaoh only later used as his tomb. This view was shared by a number of 18th-century astronomers. In any event, scholars have demonstrated that at the time of construction of the pyramids the two ventilation shafts of the Royal Chamber, which communicate with the outside, were aligned with quite specific stars: the north shaft with the star Thuban, and the south shaft with the three stars of Orion's belt. The construction and purpose of the pyramid have been explained in the most disparate ways: an astronomical observatory, a magical temple, a work by aliens or the people of the fabled Atlantis, and many others. In fact, the pyramid is a magnificent transposition of the sun's rays into stone, and today we – with all our sophisticated technology – can only continue to ask ourselves how was it ever possible to transport two and a half million blocks of stone to such heights in an age when the wheel, the pulley, and the winch were unknown.

NAPOLEON'S SECRET

Napoleon Bonaparte was one of the many visitors to have ventured inside the Great Pyramid. He entered it on 12 August 1799; the chronicles of the time recount that when he emerged, he was visibly shaken and refused to speak of his experience to anyone. It is said that even much later, as he lay on his deathbed on Saint Helena, all Napoleon would say to his faithful valet who insisted on knowing what had happened was that it was useless to tell, "since no one would believe it anyway."

fact that its plan underwent major changes and modifications during construction. And it is, of course, possible that once the Great Pyramid was completed, these three scale models were in fact used as tombs for the three queens.

The three pyramids of the queens, made of limestone blocks, that flank the eastern side of the pyramid of Khufu.

The Pyramids of the Queens

The three monuments known as the Pyramids of the Queens are located to the eastern side of the Great Pyramid of Khufu. Like the Great Pyramid, they were built of blocks of limestone and covered with a casing. They all have an inclination of 52° and a simple corridor giving access to the rock-hewn burial chamber. Standing before the eastern face of each was a mortuary temple similar to that of Khufu. Tradition has it that the *southernmost pyramid* belonged to *Queen Henutsen*, Khufu's wife and half-sister – and mother of Khafre. The *central pyramid* is attributed to *Queen Meritites*, mother of Redjedef, and the last pyramid to *Queen Hetepheres*, wife of Sneferu and mother of Khufu. During the reign of Psusennes I, a pharaoh of the 21st Dynasty, the *mortuary temple* of the pyramid of Henutsen was transformed into a chapel dedicated to the cult of Isis, the "Lady of the Pyramids." Despite the legends, the attribution of the three small pyramids to the three queens is supported only by one inscription found in this chapel; we must therefore at least consider the hypothesis that the three monuments may have had another purpose. A Polish scholar has advanced the intriguing theory that these pyramids were *models*, in about 1:5 scale, of the Great Pyramid, erected by the architects during the course of work on the principal monument; we know for a

A QUEEN AND HER TREASURE

On 2 February 1925, a few dozen metres from the pyramid of Khufu, a photographer with the archaeological expedition financed by the Harvard Fine Arts Museum of Boston, tripped while carrying his tripod and thus discovered the opening of a shaft about 30 m. (98.5 ft) deep. The expedition's archaeologist, the American George Reisner, took two years to excavate this shaft tomb, which turned out to be not the original burial place but the site of the re-entombment of Hetepheres, wife of Sneferu and mother of Khufu. Amassed haphazardly inside the tomb were the queen's burial goods, the most complete and best preserved of the Old Kingdom funerary treasures, today housed in the Egyptian Museum of Cairo. One of the pieces found in the tomb is a bed of wood and gold leaf, the same materials used for a chair, the arms of which reproduce an elegant motif of three lotus flowers. Inside the chests and coffers toiletry items were found such as implements for nail care, containers for cosmetics, and jars for perfumed oils and ointments. There is also a collection of twenty silver

bracelets with delicate butterfly-motif inlays in cornelian, lapis-lazuli, and turquoise.

The pyramid of Khafre

The measurements of this pyramid are slightly inferior to those of Khufu's, but Khafre built a little higher up the slight slope of the plateau so as to give the impression that his mortuary monument was actually taller than that built by his father. Originally 143.50 m (470.8 ft) in height, the pyramid now measures 136.40 m (447.5 ft), with 215 m (706-ft) sides. Of the three pyramids of Giza, this is the only one to have preserved some of its original Tura limestone facing on its topmost part. For a long time it was thought that Khafre's construction was solid, with no internal burial chambers, but in 1818 the Italian archaeologist **Giovanni Battista Belzoni** noticed an unusual accumulation of detritus on the north side of the pyramid, and ". . . after thirty days' work, I had the satisfaction of entering the interior of a pyramid that had always been believed impenetrable". In the central chamber he found no treasure, but only a pink granite sarcophagus "buried almost level with the floor". Using lampblack to write, Belzoni's inscription, "Discovered by G. Belzoni, 2 March 1818" is still visible on the wall. But Belzoni knew better than any other that he was not the first "discoverer" and that the pyramid had been opened and then resealed long before his time, probably in about 1200. In fact he found a number of phrases written in charcoal on the wall, in Arabic script; one of these read, "Mohammed Ahmed, quarryman, opened this with the assistance of Othman and the consent of king Ali Mohammad, from the beginning to the end."

A view of Khafre's majestic pyramid highlighting its characteristic "cap", the last part of the ancient external covering to have survived.

KHAFRE

Khafre, son of Khufu and Queen Henutsen, ascended the throne of Egypt after the early death of his older brother Redjedef, Khufu's direct successor. He reigned, it would seem, for twenty-five or twenty-six years, even though Manetho erroneously attributed him a reign of sixty-six years. The coronation name of this pharaoh means "Ra Elevates Him," and he is represented in a diorite statue found by Mariette in 1860 in Khafre's valley temple. This statue, considered one of the highest artistic expressions of ancient Egypt, shows the young pharaoh, with a young, muscular body, his face infused with an absolute, supernatural serenity, seated on a throne; behind his head sits the spread-winged falcon god Horus, embracing the nemes of the pharaoh in a gesture of divine protection.

The pyramid of Khafre rises behind the Sphinx. Right, a diorite statue of Khafre, with interesting engravings on the base representing the union of Upper and Lower Egypt.

GIOVANNI BATTISTA BELZONI

(Padua 1778-Gwato, West Africa, 1823) – Italian explorer and archaeologist. After studying engineering in Rome, Belzoni moved to England. In 1815, he was commissioned by the British Museum to travel to Egypt to collect archaeological remains. Thus not only did he bring the enormous bust of Ramesses II from Thebes, but also opened the entrance to the great temple of Abu Simbel and directed the excavations at Karnak. In 1817 he entered the Valley of the Kings where he discovered the tomb of Seti I. In 1818 he had the privilege of being the first (or almost...) to enter Khafre's pyramid.

The mortuary complex of Khafre

In front of the east side of the pyramid was the *mortuary temple of Khafre*. Unfortunately, today there remain only a few traces of the structure, among which a block of granite weighing more than 400 tons.

The facade of the temple must have been about 110 m. (361 ft) in length, with a large vestibule with 14 columns and a vast rectangular hall (also surrounded with columns) opening onto a broad porticoed courtyard.

The pits containing the solar boats of the pharaoh were dug on the north and south sides. A causeway 494 m. (540 yards) long, united this temple to the *valley temple* discovered by Mariette in 1852, which has survived in good condition. The valley temple is a solemn, austere edifice of large blocks of pink Aswan granite; the broad great hall, in the form of an inverted T, was supported by sixteen monolithic pillars each 4.15 m. (13.6 ft) high. Along the walls there originally stood twenty-three diorite and alabaster statues of the pharaoh, which have all disappeared except one found by Mariette and today on display at the Egyptian Museum of Cairo.

The perfect state of conservation of Khafre's valley temple allows us to fully appreciate the precision with which the granite blocks were positioned.

More views of Khafre's excellently preserved valley temple.

The pyramid of Menkaure

Discovered in 1837 by the Englishmen Richard William Vyse and John Shea Perring, the pyramid of Menkaure is 66 m. (216.5 ft) high and 104 m. (341.2 ft) per side. In 1500 it still boasted its beautiful exterior facing, which was gradually almost completely removed. The lower part of the pyramid is made of blocks of red Aswan granite (much of which is still in place), which contrasted with the upper portion in white Tura limestone. Herodotus described the pyramid as being ". . . covered for half its height in Ethiopian stone." The entrance to the pyramid, on the north side at about 4 m. (13 ft) above ground level, was found on 29 July 1837. Menkaure's burial chamber has a complex structure, unlike those of Khufu and Khafre; this fact reflects a series of transformations that could only have been made during the course of work. There are thus two burial chambers, one being the original and the other the definitive one. In the latter, Vyse discovered a basalt sarcophagus decorated with the typical "palace facade" reliefs, with its cover broken, containing a wooden sarcophagus and the remains of a mummified body. Unfortunately, both the beautiful sarcophagus and what might have been the remains of Menkaure were lost in 1838 when the *Beatrice* sank off Carthage as she was carrying them to England. The interior of the pyramid is quite complex. The original design called for a descending corridor from the base of the smaller original pyramid to the burial chamber; this approach was at some time abandoned, and another entrance was opened on the north side. This leads through an antechamber, the walls of which are decorated with bas-reliefs of the "palace facade" motif, to the burial chamber as originally planned. The plans were, however, again modified: underneath the original burial chamber another, much larger room was excavated (6.50 by 2.30 m. - 21.3 by 7.5 ft -, with a 4 m. -13-ft - ceiling) and was dressed with granite.

Right, corridors leading to the burial chamber inside Menkaure's pyramid and the chamber where the sarcophagus was found.

The mortuary temple of Menkaure

Unfortunately, very little remains of the mortuary temple begun by Menkaure in stone and completed in mud bricks by his son and successor Shepseskaf, although it was still intact in 1700. Some of the blocks used in its construction weigh as much as 200 tons. The temple stands on the west side of the pyramid and it had a quite complex structure with a vestibule, a rectangular courtyard, a double-colonnaded portico that led to the sanctuary, and many annexes. A *sloping causeway* united the mortuary temple with the *valley temple*, where the archaeologist George Reisner discovered, during excavations conducted in 1907 and 1908, the famous *schist triads* in which the pharaoh is associated with Hathor and other deities symbolizing Egyptian *nomes*.

The subsidiary pyramids

The three subsidiary pyramids, of which the largest is flat-sided while the other two are stepped, rise to the south of the main pyramid of Menkaure. Each was in turn flanked, also on the south, by a small mortuary temple, in mud brick with wooden columns. Even though no proof has yet come to light, it is thought that the subsidiaries belonged to the royal brides of Menkaure. Two are unknown, but the third is Khamernebtry II, whose features are those of Hathor in the triads. The measurements of the bases of these three structures are one-third those of the main pyramid. Inside one of the subsidiaries, Richard Vyse found the name of the pharaoh written in red ink.

This page, perfect views of Menkaure's pyramid, above, flanked by the subsidiary pyramids and below, by the remains of the mortuary temple. Opposite, a splendid figure of Menkaure housed in the Egyptian Museum in Cairo.

MENKAURE

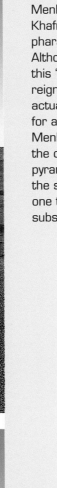

Menkaure succeeded his father Khafre and was the penultimate pharaoh of the 4th Dynasty. Although Manetho tells us that this "just and pious pharaoh" reigned sixty-three years, he actually occupied the throne for a little less than thirty. Menkaure was responsible for the construction of the third pyramid in the Giza complex, the smallest – but also the only one to still possess its three subsidiary pyramids.

The Sphinx

An integral, and very famous, part of Khafre's funeral complex is the Great Sphinx, the gigantic crouching lion with a human countenance that many believe reproduces the facial features of the pharaoh. The Sphinx, located southeast of the Great Pyramid of Khufu, is 20 m. (76.4 ft) tall and 57 m. (187 ft) long; the head, wearing the typical nemes, is 6 m. (19.7 ft) high. Some 4500 years ago the monument was modelled out of a natural knoll of limestone at Giza, containing rock of three different types. Over the centuries erosion by sand and wind have disfigured the powerful body and the enigmatic face. To legitimize his ascent to the throne, the 18th Dynasty pharaoh Tuthmosis IV recounted how the Sphinx appeared to him in a dream and asked him to dig out the sand that covered it almost completely: "Tuthmosis, my son, I am your father Khepri-Ra-Atum; if you free me from the sand that oppresses me I will make you king and you will wear on your head the White Crown and the Red Crown." Tuthmosis did as he was told, and also built retaining walls to halt the advance of the sand. To recall the event, he placed a pink granite stele, about 4 m. (13 ft) in height, between the paws of the Sphinx. The Greek term "sphinx" derives from the ancient Egyptian *sheps-ankh* (the living image). In the New Kingdom, the Great Sphinx was associated with Harmakis (Horus at the Horizon); for the Arabs it was Abu-I-haw, the "Father of Terror." In its extraordinary monumentality and mystery, the Sphinx, "half mountain and half crouching beast" (as it was defined by Pierre Loti), is a sculpture unique in all of Egyptian art.

The enigmatic, yet majestic profile of the great Sphinx, eroded by thousands of years of sand and wind but still an evocative symbol of ancient and modern Egypt.

The fascinating creature with a human face and lion's body has impressed and intrigued artists throughout history. Above left, it is seen portrayed by Jean Léon Gérôme (1824-1904), in a painting now in the Club des Diplomates in Cairo, where Napoleon Bonaparte is seen at the foot of the Sphinx. The other three 19th-century drawings showing the Sphinx and the pyramids are by David Roberts. Right, a fascinating view of the Sphinx framed by the lintels of the door to the funerary temple.

The Sphinx Temple

In front of the Sphinx, slightly to the right, are the remains of a small temple in limestone and pink Aswan granite, with two entrances and a courtyard with an interior colonnade of large rectangular pillars and an altar for offerings at the centre. Its structure is similar to that of the valley temple of Khafre, which stands alongside it. This temple may have been used for ceremonies on the occasion of the jubilee of the pharaoh - or it might actually have been dedicated to the Great Sphinx. Unfortunately, in the temple itself there is no trace of decorative detail and no texts have yet provided us with any information about it.

The Solar Boat Museum

In May of 1954, the young archaeologist Kamal el-Mallak brought to light, on the southern side of the pyramid of Khufu, two huge rock-hewn pits closed by 41 enormous blocks of limestone, bearing the cartouches of Redjedef, the son and successor of Khufu. Inside the northern trench a wooden vessel was found that had been buried there after having been dismantled into 1224 pieces; it took more than ten years of painstaking work for the archaeologists to put the gigantic three-dimensional 'jigsaw puzzle' together. Once reconstructed, the boat was placed on exhibit in the *museum* built especially for it near the pit in which it was found. The *boat*, built of cedar, sycamore, and jujube wood, is 46 m (150.9 ft) long and 6 m (19.7 ft) at the beam. Its slender form terminates at the prow and stern with mizzen masts in the form of papyrus stems. At the centre is a closed cabin, 9 m (29.5 feet) in length. The boat was equipped with six pairs of oars, from 6 to 8.5 m. length (19.7 to 27.9 ft). All the wooden elements were held together by ropes and pegs; no nails were used. The second pit has yet to be opened, but a micro-probe has revealed it to contain a boat similar to that reassembled from the pieces found in the first pit. The significance of this boat has long been the subject of debate and discussion. The pit also contained ropes, and the vessel displays marks left by the ropes in its wood; these facts have led to conjecture that the boat was actually used on water. It may have been one of the vessels used by the pharaoh during his reign, or it may even be the boat on which the body of Khufu was transported along the causeway toward his eternal resting-place. It may also have a purely religious significance, as the *solar boat* on which the soul of the dead pharaoh journeyed to join the sun god Ra in his eternal celestial navigation.

The private cemeteries at the pyramid of Khufu

East and west of the Great Pyramid are the two large private cemeteries of highly-placed court officials and other personalities at the court of Khufu who had themselves buried alongside the tomb of their king in order to remain at his side even in death. The two cemeteries, known as the **Eastern Necropolis** and the **Western Necropolis**, are made up of mastabas, aligned in two parallel rows and displaying many features in common: a false stele door, an offering chamber, and a burial chamber. Certain of these mastabas also contained the statues known as *"substitute busts"* in niches alongside the burial chamber. These sculptures represent only the head of the dead person, most certainly had a ritual function, and were characteristic only of the Old Kingdom.

Eastern Necropolis

To the east of the three secondary or subsidiary pyramids of the Great Pyramid of Khufu are the mastabas of court dignitaries and important figures in the pharaoh's retinue: the royal brides and, at their sides, the firstborn children followed by the others. The *mastaba of Khufu-Kaf*, son of Khufu and Queen Henutsen, is decorated with beautiful bas-reliefs; although they have lost their original colours, they are otherwise in a state of perfect preservation. Not far away are *mastabas of Qar* (or Meryre'nufer), a court official at the time of Pepi II (6th Dynasty), and of *his son Idu*. In both these tombs beautiful statues of the dead with

The mastabas of the Western necropolis date to the 4th and 6th Dynasties. *Iasen*, Inspector of Priests, embellished the walls of his *tomb* with paintings that illustrate scenes of rural life and fishing. The *mastaba* of *Kaemankh*, Superintendent of the Treasury, is also richly decorated. The *mastaba of Iymery*, the Prophet of Khufu, contains some of the most beautiful and best-preserved bas-reliefs to be found in the necropolis.

The tombs of the pyramid builders

The hundreds upon hundreds of masons, stone-cutters, and stone-dressers who worked on construction of the three pyramids were also given their private necropolis. About one kilometre west of Giza there have recently come to light the remains of about six hundred tombs, both large and small. Built mainly of mud brick, and mostly pyramidal in form, these burial places, like their more important neighbours, are decorated with bas-reliefs and have been found to contain statues, crockery for cooking food, and inscriptions that tell us the titles of their occupants: "Inspector of Builders," "Superintendent of the Workers," and so on. The discovery of this necropolis is important for two reasons. First of all, because it finally overthrows Herodotus' theory regarding the construction of the pyramids with its attendant image of slaves forced to work for the glory of the pharaoh under the lash and in inhuman conditions: quite the contrary, the pyramid-builders were not slaves but free Egyptian citizens who received regular wages. Secondly, the decorations offer us an interesting glimpse of the daily lives of the workers who were permitted by the pharaoh to build their tombs so near the royal sepulchres.

their families were found. On the opposite corner of the necropolis is the extraordinary *mastaba of Meresankh III*, the royal bride of Khafre. This tomb, which has for the most part retained its coloured paintings, contains – at the back of a wide niche – ten large statues of Meresankh, the pharaoh's mother Hetepheres, his daughter Shepseskau, and other women of the family. Nearby is the large *mastaba of Prince Ankh-haf*.

Previous page, the solar boat of Khufu, with the curving prow shaped like a papyrus, and the cabin in the centre. Above, the Egyptian archaeologist who discovered it, Kamal el-Mallak. This page, above, statues of the deceased sculpted into the south wall of the first room of the mastaba of Qar; below, two views of the mastaba of Idu: a detail of the false door with a figure of the deceased seated while he receives offerings, and statues of the deceased in alcoves.

The pyramid, the mastabas and the archaeological site

Splendid images of the monumental site of Saqqara dominated by the step pyramid that was the last resting place of Djoser. The most fascinating element in the pharaoh's funerary chamber is the decoration of the walls (detail below) consisting of thousands of blue and green majolica tiles representing bundles of rushes. The horizontal limestone mouldings are similar to the cords that bound the stalks of the papyrus.

Covering an area of eight kilometres, the necropolis of Saqqara is the largest in Egypt. Historically it is also the most important as all the main dynasties are represented, from the first up to the Ptolemaic and Persian eras. Rising like a citadel surrounded by pyramids and mastabas of all periods, the funerary structures of Djoser represent the ideal centre. To the north a series of quite beautiful tombs spreads out, including the pyramid of Teti and the Serapeum. Patron of the necropolis was the god Sokar (and the area is named after him) often portrayed clothed in green and with a hyena's head.

The step pyramid: a residence for eternity

Although the third dynasty actually began with the pharaoh Sanakht, of whom little is known despite a reign that lasted for eighteen years, the real founder is considered to be Djoser, a name derived from "geser" in Egyptian meaning 'sacred', and whose importance is such that his name is written in red ink in the Turin *Canon of Kings*. Djoser is Saqqara and Saqqara is Djoser: perhaps only in the case of Abu Simbel and Ramesses II has a pharaoh been so closely identified with his architectural monument. The majestic step pyramid of Djoser, at the centre of the funerary complex of Saqqara, is the oldest structure in the world entirely built of stone. Discovered in 1821 by the Prussian General von Minutoli, it was systematically explored and studied some twenty years later by the German archaeologist Lepsius. Originally it was constructed in the form of a normal 'mastaba'. The mastaba (which in Arab means bench or shelf) was the tomb of nobility and court dignitaries, rectangular in shape and with slightly inward-leaning walls. A second mastaba was added on top of the first, then a third and several more until a pyramid of six gradually diminishing 'layers' existed. This form later became formalised in the Sumerian ziggurat. As it stands today, the pyramid is 62 metres in height and the base measures 109 by 125 metres. The **burial chamber** of the pharaoh was located almost at the centre of the pyramid, at the bottom of a

THE SAQQARA NECROPOLIS

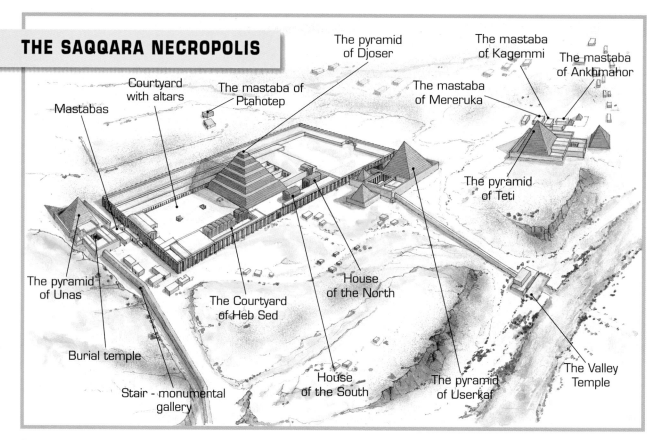

- The pyramid of Djoser
- The mastaba of Kagemmi
- The mastaba of Ankhmahor
- The mastaba of Ptahotep
- Courtyard with altars
- The mastaba of Mereruka
- Mastabas
- The pyramid of Teti
- The pyramid of Unas
- The Courtyard of Heb Sed
- House of the North
- Burial temple
- House of the South
- The pyramid of Userkaf
- The Valley Temple
- Stair - monumental gallery

Partial reconstruction of the vast and complex necropolis of Saqqara. Extending over an area 8 km long and 1 km wide, all the main dynasties are represented here, although the focal point of the entire site is without doubt the pyramid of Djoser, surrounded by important temples, courtyards, altars and buildings.

large vertical shaft 28 metres deep. From here a labyrinth of rooms, corridors, chambers and passageways protecting the eternal rest of the sovereign spreads outwards over an area of more than five kilometres. The shards of about forty thousand alabaster pots, plates, bowls and vases were found here and some four thousand have been restored to their original form. The complex of Saqqara is enclosed by a rectangular peripheral limestone wall ten metres high with 14 false doorways creating recesses and reliefs in imitation of the façade of the royal palace of Memphis.

The single real entrance of the 14 false doorways was on the south-east. Inside, instead of the courtyard one would normally expect, was a gallery formed by two rows of 20 columns over six metres high, each ribbed to appear like wood and joined to the side wall by a low "tongue" wall. The visual effect must have been striking as one passed from the relative shadow of the gallery to the brilliant light that floods the courtyard.

The south tomb

The replica of the tomb found inside the pyramid is a complete secondary funerary monument. Built to house the canopic vases of the pharaoh, it has the same architectural and decorative elements: the stairway that is 30 metres long reaching a well 28 metres deep, the crypt built of granite and the chambers decorated with blue faience porcelain tiles.

The "House of the South" and the "House of the North"

Built in the north eastern part of the courtyard, at the back of the great pyramid, these two structures are also dummies as the interiors are bricked and have no chambers. They may perhaps have been intended to symbolise Upper and Lower Egypt as, reproduced on the capitals of the columns that decorate the façade, are respectively the lotus flower for the "House of the South" and the papyrus for the "House of the North".

Visible above the entrance door of the former is the elegant frieze known as a "kheker", an imitation in stone of a roof covering made from bundles of reeds.

The entrance to the "House of the South" with the "kheker" frieze and below, a view of the "House of the North" with three engaged columns in the form of flowering papyrus.

The Courtyard of Heb Sed
(Jubilee Courtyard)

The great courtyard named for the festival of Heb Sed lies to the east inside the Djoser complex.
On the north side is the immense hulk of the step pyramid: on the east side were thirteen chapels with vaulted

Above, a view of two of the thirteen chapels that stand on the eastern side of the courtyard. Below, the white limestone statue of Djoser, clothed in the costume that he wore during the ceremony of Heb Sed, a heavy nemes on his head and with the artificial beard. Found in the serdab of Saqqara, this is the oldest full-relief and life-size sculpture of a pharaoh that has survived until today.

roofs, while the façades had three slender grooved columns. These chapels, dedicated to the jubilee celebration, have no interior and were probably dummies dedicated to the Egyptian deities.
The 'south tomb' is at the south west corner of the courtyard and has various funerary chambers which probably housed the internal organs of the pharaoh.
A chapel beside the tomb has a characteristic frieze decorated with a cobra, the pharaoh's protective symbol.
In a corner of the courtyard stand three statues of imposing size: supported by a pilaster like a caryatid, these are a rare example of the statuary of the Old Kingdom. They are much damaged, but the central one clearly represents Djoser, with the long artificial beard, the arms crossed on the breast, holding the symbols of power, and the long, adherent costume worn on the occasion of Heb Seb.

THE HEB SED OR JUBILEE FESTIVAL

During the 25th or 30th year of a pharaoh's reign the ceremony of Heb Sed took place and was, to all extents and purposes, a jubilee when the sovereignty of the ruler was again recognized and confirmed. The ceremony, which began during the first dynasty, is frequently portrayed in wall paintings and it has therefore been possible to reconstruct the event. It was celebrated on the first day of the month of *Tybi* during the season when crops were sown (Peret), and was originally held in a series of structures made of leaves and papyrus and lotus stalks. The pharaoh, Djoser, decided that the event should be more important and had stone, and therefore permanent, buildings made to accommodate it. The festival began with a great procession lead by a High Priest and was celebrated in the various chapels situated around the courtyard. Once the gods had given their consent to the pharaoh's spiritual suitability, he had then to demonstrate his physical suitability by

undergoing tests that could vary from one sovereign to another. The test may have been a bullfight, or shooting arrows to the four cardinal points, but the most common was a race running along a course indicated on the ground of the court, around the House of the North and the House of the South. At the end of the race, the pharaoh was crowned for a second time with the white and the red crowns of the two kingdoms.

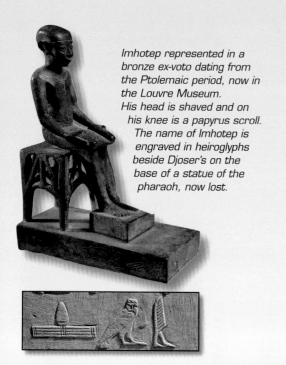

Imhotep represented in a bronze ex-voto dating from the Ptolemaic period, now in the Louvre Museum.
His head is shaved and on his knee is a papyrus scroll. The name of Imhotep is engraved in heiroglyphs beside Djoser's on the base of a statue of the pharaoh, now lost.

IMHOTEP

Imhotep is one of the great geniuses in the history of mankind. Architect, magician, philosopher, so great a doctor that the Greeks identified him with Asclepius, their god of medicine, he was without doubt the author of a Book of Knowledge which, however, has been entirely lost. Imhotep followed the family tradition: his father was Kanofer whom the pharaoh personally appointed to be in charge of all the kingdom's buildings. He learned his trade in his father's workshop, probably in Memphis, firstly carving stone vases, then becoming a sculptor and architect and subsequently rising to assume the highest offices of the state, both religious and administrative. The high priest of Heliopolis as well as grand vizier, on the base of a statue erected in honour of Djoser an engraving describes him as "first after the king".
On becoming a deity, Imhotep – whose name means "he comes in peace" – joins the triad of Ptah, to whom he is son, and Sekhemkhet.
He is represented seated, dressed in a long tunic, his head shaved and a papyrus scroll on his lap. According to Manetho, it was Imhotep who "discovered how to cut stone for the building of monuments", yet also introduced the new techniques extensively, bringing about an unprecedented artistic revolution.

The Pyramid of Userkaf

The first pharaoh of the fifth dynasty, grandson of Djedefre, Userkaf – whose name means "his ka is potent" - chose to be buried close to Djoser in the north east corner of the funerary complex. His predecessor, Shepseskaf, had chosen a masta- ba as his burial place, today known as the El-Fara'un mastaba. This was only a brief break in tradition though, as Userkaf immediately returned to the pyramid-shaped tomb. This sovereign attributed great importance to the cult of the sun and this may explain why his burial temple was built on the southern side of the pyramid, instead of the eastern, as the south is exposed to the sunlight all day long.
The pyramid, discovered by John Shae Perring and identified by Cecil Firth in 1928, is not very big (the sides are 73 and 30 metres in length and less than 50 metres high) and is badly damaged as it was used in ancient times as a quarry for building materials. Originally it was faced with enormous fine-grained limestone blocks from Tura. An immense statue of Userkaf made of pink granite was found in the court and the head is now exhibited in the Egyptian Museum of Cairo.

The Pyramid of Teti

Teti was the founder of the sixth dynasty and succeeded Unas, having married his daughter Idut.
His pyramid is to the north east of the funerary complex built for Djoser and it had three satellite pyramids, of which two belonged to the queens Khuit and Iput, the latter being the mother of the future pharaoh Pepi I.
Teti faithfully reproduced the entrance, the arrangement of the rooms and especially the decoration of the Pyramid Texts from Unas' pyramid, though here the texts also cover the basalt sarcophagus. Some of the largest, most important and attractive mastabas are found around Teti's pyramid, such as those of Mereruka and Kagemmi.

Views of the pyramid of Userkaf (below) and the pyramid of Teti (above) which is noted for the beautiful vault of the funerary chamber, decorated with stars that stand out from the blue of the sky in delicate relief.

THE MASTABA TOMB

Normally the tombs of dignitaries and nobility situated around the pyramid are shaped like a mastaba – an Arab word meaning a bench. They are rectangular in shape with slightly inward leaning walls, have an upper cornice on all sides and a "dummy" entrance door with or without an external atrium.
The sarcophagus was lowered into the shaft which lead to the underground chamber. Once the sarcophagus was arranged amongst the treasures and mementoes, the funerary chamber was sealed, the shaft was filled with stones and sand, and the entrance was bricked up. The funeral was celebrated and gifts were offered in the small external atrium in front of the dummy door where the deceased was portrayed as if participating in the rituals held in his honour. An image of the deceased was also present at the rituals and funerary banquets, standing by the false doorway or magically inhabiting his serdab in the form of a statue.

MASTABA CONSTRUCTION

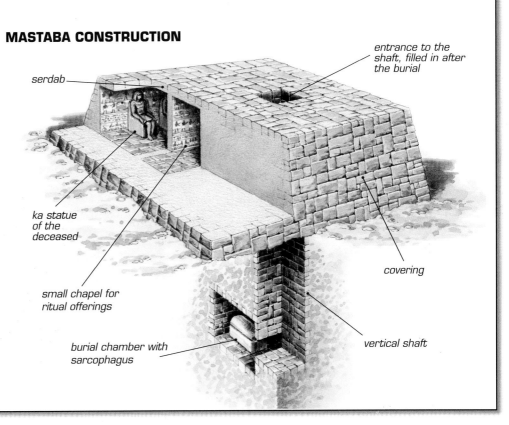

serdab

entrance to the shaft, filled in after the burial

ka statue of the deceased

small chapel for ritual offerings

burial chamber with sarcophagus

covering

vertical shaft

The Mastaba of Mereruka

This mastaba was discovered in 1893 by a French mission lead by Jacques de Morgan. It was built by Mereruka, vizier, Head of Justice, "Superintendent of the City" but also Teti's son-in-law, at the beginning of the sixth dynasty. It is the largest tomb in the area (40 metres by 24, with a surface area of 1000 square metres), contains 29 rooms and probably is a copy of Mereruka's princely palace. It is divided into three parts – apartments for the owner, for his wife, Hert-watet-khet, and for their two sons.

The walls of the tomb are painted with scenes depicting every-day life in Egypt, the professions, hunting, fishing and the animals of the Nile.

Mereruka is portrayed in many situations: on the right of the entrance as he draws images of the three seasons of the Egyptian year, or on the sacred boat with his wife who is playing a harp. There is a statue of him in a niche in the pillared votive chapel (the 13th chamber in Mereruka's area and also the main room of the mastaba).

The Mastaba of Kagemmi

This tomb belongs to another important potentate and learned High Priest of Teti's court who was also the superintendent of the pharaoh's pyramid. The building is half solid, like early mastabas, and half composed of pillared rooms, chambers and stores. The decorations of the secondary rooms are even more lovely than those in the funerary chambers that lead to the serdab. The scenes of fishing and offerings at the entrance and the engraved reliefs in the pillared room representing games and dancing, farm work and a judgement taking place in the Tribunal of Teti are all beautifully executed.

The Mastaba of Ankhmahor

Also known as "the tomb of doctors" (although Ankhmahor was not a doctor, but a priest) this is a sixth dynasty structure. The engraving showing the ritual of circumcision is famous. Still practiced in many cultures, this operation involved some risk, despite its simplicity. It was carried out by a priest who used a flint or oxidian knife and intonated magic spells during the ritual.

The Mastaba of Ti

Considering the level of artistic expression achieved here, the delicate synthesis of the forms and the harmony of the structure, this is probably the finest tomb in the entire funerary complex. It was already completed in 2600 BC when Khufu was only beginning to build the great pyramid. Ti, husband of princess Nefer-Hotep, lived at the time of the fifth dynasty.

To use a contemporary term, we could call him a VIP: "unique friend", "holder of secrets", "head of the king's works", "director of the pyramids" of Nefer-Ka-Râ and Niuser-Râ – these are only some of the inscriptions describing him in the tomb. The relief engravings here are considered to be some of the loveliest of the entire Old Kingdom. The great court has twelve pilasters and a chapel, and the most lively scenes decorating the area are those of family life, hunting and fishing. The human figure is always portrayed quite formally but at the same time with exquisite delicacy, and the sequence of painted reliefs seems to take place in front of our eyes transmitting a strong sense of movement.

The decorations of the mastabas of Saqqara, usually bas-relief, provide us with interesting information about everyday life in ancient Egypt. The mastaba of Mereruka, for example, has scenes of goldsmiths working (2) and how hyenas were domesticated (3); in the mastaba of Ankhmahor is a scene of circumcision (6) and a bas-relief in the mastaba of Ti shows the preparation of wood for boat-building (8). In Kagemmi's mastaba are scenes of dancing (5), hippopotamus hunting (4) and fishing amongst the reeds by a lake (9); a school of scribes is seen in the mastaba of Ti (10). The life-sized figures of the deceased stand against the wall looking as though they are about to detach themselves from it and enter the world of the living (1,7).

Serapeum

Located to the north east of the step pyramid, the Serapeum was formed by a long underground gallery with side chambers, each containing an enormous granite sarcophagus weighing about 60 tons where the bodies of mummified bulls were interred. These bulls were considered to be deities and on death were therefore mummified and buried in the same way as a pharaoh.

Portrayed as a bull with a solar disc between the horns, the centre of the cult of the sacred Apis bull was in Memphis. In order to be recognised as sacred, the animal had to have certain features that were known only to the priests. On the death of an Apis bull, the priests sought out another animal, the final choice being determined by numerous special characteristics (Herodotus lists some 29), including a white triangle on the forehead, a mark like an eagle on the neck and another in the shape of a crescent moon on its flank. The word Serapeum is the Latin form of the Greek *Serapeion* and derives from the fact that once the Apis

bull had become a divinity after death, it was known as *Osor Apis*, which the Greeks modified into the name *Serapis*. During the Ptolemaic period statues of Greek poets and philosophers including Plato, Homer, Pindar, Heraclitus and Hesiod were placed in the open near to the Serapeum in the area known as the hemicycle.

The Mastaba of Ptahotep

On the opposite side of the necropolis is the mastaba of Ptahotep, vizier and judge who lived at the time of the fifth dynasty and whose name means "Ptah is happy". His double tomb is shared with two members of his family. Discovered by the French archaeologist, Auguste Mariette, it is of impressive size

and was decorated with fine relief engravings, probably the work of Ankhen-Ptah, which describe, in minute detail, daily life in ancient Egypt including servants bearing gifts and men rowing a boat.

The image of Ptahotep on a seat with legs shaped like those of a lion, while with his left hand he raises a particularly elegant glass to his mouth is especially lovely.

The Pyramid of Unas

The pyramid of the ninth and last sovereign of the fifth dy-

nasty is at the south west corner of the funerary complex of Djoser.

It consists of a pyramid with a temple and causeway that leads to the valley temple.

Smaller than the other pyramids (the sides are less than 60 metres) it was already in a poor state of repair in 2000 BC when Ramesses II had it restored.

To the south of the pyramid is a 25 metre-deep shaft leading to three Persian tombs. The mummified body of the deceased, covered in gold and jewels, was preserved in one of these.

Left, the entrance of the Serapeum and below left, an Apis bull carved in limestone, also from the Serapeum (30th Dynasty) and now in the Louvre Museum, Paris; below right, the long row of sphinxes which, according to Strabo, flanked the avenue leading to the Serapeum and now also in the Louvre.
This page, the splendid decorations of Ptahotep's mastaba (above left, the figure of the deceased on a seat with legs shaped like a lion's, is particularly impressive).
Below, the pyramid of Unas and, beside, the 700-metre long processional ramp that joined it to the valley temple.

THE *PYRAMID TEXTS*

Of pre-dynastic origin, the *Pyramid Texts* are the oldest complete collection of religious writings, spells, ritual chants and all else that was necessary to ensure the protection of the other world for the dead pharaoh. The 228 inscriptions, painted in blue and written in heiroglyphs, were intended to facilitate the pharaoh's journey into eternity and cover all the walls of the chamber except at the far end where the façade of the royal palace was painted. "Ra receives your soul in heaven and your body on earth" the dead sovereign is assured. The names of important divinities of the Egyptian pantheon are mentioned for the first time in the *Pyramid Texts*, such as Amun "The Secret", Khonsu and Nefertum who was described as "the bud of a lotus flower that is held to the nose of Ra".

The walls of the burial chambers in Unas' pyramid are completely covered with long columns of texts carved in heiroglyphs and inlaid with blue pigment. These are the pyramid texts discovered by Gaston Maspero in 1881. Such texts appeared first in this pyramid and were repeated in the tombs of Pepi I, Merenra and Pepi II but ceased to be used during the chaos and anarchy of the First Intermediate Period.

The Mastaba of Nebit

Just south of the pyramid of Unas are the mastabas of Nebit and Khenut, both wives of the pharaoh and dated late fifth dynasty. Nebit's mastaba is noted for the rather rare decoration of the second chamber. The queen herself is portrayed here in the palace harem, the apartments reserved for the women, while, smelling a flower, she participates at the presentation of offerings. The tomb consists of a room with four niches that contained statues for the cult of the deceased.

The Mastaba of Idut

Discovered in 1927 by the English archaeologist Cecil Firth, this tomb was actually built for a vizier who lived at the time of the pharaoh Unas at the end of the fifth dynasty. At the time of the sixth dynasty, princess Seshseshet, better known as Idut, took over the burial chambers and entirely altered the original decorations. The mastaba has ten chambers of which only five are decorated. As well as the usual scenes of offerings, hunting and fishing, the tomb contains numerous scenes of everyday life, such as those illustrating the process of butchering a bull, where two men are seen using long knives to cut the various sections of the animal.

The Mastaba of Niankhnum and Khnumhotep

Also known as the "tomb of the two brothers", the structure was discovered below the causeway of Unas' temple in 1964 and was built during the fifth dynasty.

Below, a detail with ritual significance from the mastaba of Idut showing the foreleg of an animal destined for sacrifice being cut off.

The two brothers, possibly twins, were both priests of Ra in the temple of Niuserre and were also responsible for "care of the hands of the pharaoh". They are portrayed with their two sons at the sides of the vestibule entrance. The bas-reliefs engraved on the fine-grained limestone walls are most attractive, sophisticated and quite vivacious, such as, for example, the scene showing some young men on a papyrus skiff performing acrobatic games.

The Mastaba of Irukaptah

Entirely excavated from rock, the tomb of Irukaptah was built during the fifth dynasty. It is known as the "tomb of the butchers" as he was "Head Butcher of the Great House". Unique of its kind, the single room is decorated on the north and east walls with large painted and plastered relief figures in a standing position, representing members of Irukaptah's family who were also buried here.

The Mastaba of Nefer and Kahay

Quite small in size and similar in structure to the "tomb of the butchers", this was the burial place of Nefer, "Supervisor of the Craftsmen" and "Head of the Choristers", shared with nine other relatives including his brother Kahay. In the stele of a false door the figure of his brother Werbau is portrayed during a funeral banquet. The relief panel showing the cutting and carrying of papyrus stalks in the upper band, and a group of animals crossing a ford in the lower one, is of great charm.

Below, the massive exterior of princess Idut's mastaba. Right, from above, the exterior of the "tomb of the two brothers", the fascinating series of statues in niches in the "tomb of the butchers" and an image from the tomb of Nefer and Kahay with the deceased wrapped in a leopard skin cloth, seated at a table covered with offerings.

history the statue represents a trade. Lastly, the splendid painted limestone statue of the High Priest Ra-Nofer, 1.80 m. high, impresses with the extreme simplicity of its form.

At Saqqara discoveries are continually being made. Recently an archaeological team discovered a tomb of the 26th Dynasty with three wooden sarcophagi, each containing a mummy. The breast of one is entirely covered with turquoise coloured beads (below). On the left, the impressive limestone statue of the High Priest Ra-Nofer is of particular interest for the sophisticated detail of the wig, deeply sculpted with the fine plaiting that was typical of dignitaries.

THE DISCOVERIES OF SAQQARA

Over the centuries numerous remains have been discovered in the archaeological area of Saqqara, and among these are some of the most beautiful and important of the ancient Egyptian civilization.

In 1860 the sycamore wood statue of Ka-Aper came to light and, struck by the similarity between this ancient priest and the head of their village, the workers who discovered it gave it the nickname "Sheik el Beled". The painted limestone statue portraying a seated scribe dates from the fourth dynasty, and for the first time in

A small village in the Nile valley, Abusir is a site of great historic and architectural importance, as an Egyptian **necropolis** of the fifth dynasty was located here.

The site is of particular note as it was chosen for royal burials although not all the pyramids of this dynasty were built at Abusir; two are to be found in nearby Saqqara, slightly further south (the pyramids of Unas and Userkaf).

However, numerous pyramids made in local stone are found here and their appearance, less grandiose compared to the usual monumental structures, could be an indication of a period of economic crisis for Egypt, or even of a difficult moment for the power of the royal dynasties, coinciding with the time of their construction.

The *pyramids* of various sovereigns can be seen at Abusir, such as those of *Sahure* (with subsidiary pyramids), *Nyuserre* (with a subsidiary pyramid and two queens' pyramids), *Neferikare* (the most impressive which, with the other two, forms the upper group of monuments dominating the archaeological site, and visible even from quite a distance), *Neferefre* and queen *Khentkawes II*, wife of Neferikare.

Also quite interesting is the only mastaba here, belonging to *Ptahshepses* a high-ranking official during the reign of Sahure. Most of the papyri attributed to the Old Kingdom come from this site and provide great insight into life and economy at the time of the fifth dynasty. About a kilometre from Abusir is **Abu Ghurab** where there are remains of several *sun-temples*, also dated to the fifth dynasty whose members were devotees of the deities connected with the cult of the sun, such as Ra and Aten.

Built in local stone and less majestic in appearance, the pyramids of Abusir are, however, famous and of considerable historic importance.

Memphis

Very little remains today of the ancient capital of Menufer, called Memphis by the Greeks, the city where Phoenicians, Judeans, Armenians, Greeks, Libyans and Sudanese each had their quarter which extended over fifteen kilometres between Giza and Saqqara, with the citadel of the "white walls" at its centre – perhaps begun by the great architect Imhotep and with a wealth of temples and sanctuaries dedicated to all the gods of the ancient world. The decline began with the creation of Alexandria and by the fourth century AD it was already a mass of ruins. With the rise of Cairo the few temples left standing because they had been used as Christian churches, were demolished and the entire area became a building site for the new city. Today nothing is left but a few ruins that came to light in the excavations that began in the 19th century. The most important are those of the famous *temple of Ptah*, where the pharaohs were crowned, and a *chapel of Seti I*, both located near the present village of Saqqara.

Right, from above, the alabaster sphinx of Amun-Ofis II, 4.5 metres high and 8 metres long that once flanked the entrance to the temple of Ptah, is one of the largest in existence made from a single block; the imposing colossus of Ramesses II, one of the gigantic 13 metre-high statues that originally stood in front of the pylons of the temple of Ptah.

Although the reason is not known, Sneferu, founder of the fourth dynasty and father of Keops, again moved the royal necropolis from Saqqara to Dahshur where he built two *pyramids*, one known as the "Bent Pyramid" or "rhomboid" and the other as the "Red Pyramid". The "Bent Pyramid" owes its name to the fact that half way up, the walls change dramatically from one angle of incline (54°30') to another (43°). The pyramid also has two entrances, one on the north side and one on the west, leading to two chambers covered by a corbelled roof.

Above, the "bent" pyramid that also has a subsidiary pyramid. Below, the pyramid to the north, also known as the red pyramid. In the photograph on the left, the roof of the third funerary chamber inside the "red" pyramid, a perfect masterpiece of architecture where the stone mouldings create a gradual overhang.

It has been possible to attribute the second pyramid to Sneferu from some stone facing where his name was found written in red ink. Its name derives from the warm colour of the stone at sunset. This is the first monument to have the perfect classical, pyramidal form.

Sneferu also had another pyramid built at Maydum, known as the "false pyramid" and was thus the only sovereign to possess three altogether.

Maydum

The two most characteristic images of Maydum – the "false pyramid" and the brightly coloured geese that were part of the decoration of the tomb of Itat, now exhibited in the Egyptian Museum in Cairo.

Almost on a level with El Fayyum, towards the Nile, stands the *false pyramid*, another highly original work attributed to Sneferu, the first king of the 4th Dynasty. As it stands today, the structure is in the form of a high step from which two smaller steps rise. Its present aspect might lead one to believe that it was a solar temple, but the great quantity of debris around the base reveals that it looked quite different originally. Other steps must have jutted out from the four sides of the present base, so that the entire structure was in the form of a sharply pointed eight-step pyramid. The summit may have been somewhat like the sun temples of Abu Ghurab, built a hundred years later, with a third obelisk emerging from the truncated pyramid. It is also thought that an outer casing had been planned to turn it into a true flat sided pyramid but

that work had come to a halt shortly after beginning. The name of Maydum is also associated with quite a different item – the "Maydum geese" representing one of the oldest wall paintings of ancient Egypt still existing. The painting is tempera on plaster, 1.73 metres in length and dates from about 2700 BC. Originally it decorated the tomb of Itat at Maydum and was without doubt part of a larger composition of which it is easy to imagine the decorative detail and natural liveliness. This extremely stylized piece is now housed in the Egyptian Museum in Cairo. The colours are solid without any shading, the animals are quite symmetrical and are drawn with a sharp profile. The image is therefore abstract but still the attention to detail, the sensitivity to use of colour and a clear concern with reality and nature are highly evident.

Beni Hasan

Half way between the royal cities of Thebes and Memphis in Middle Egypt, situated on the river Nile in an area of luxuriant oases and palm groves, Beni Hasan is famous in particular for the remains of a large **necropolis** with spectacular rock-cut tombs literally excavated in a cliff face and dating from the 11th and 12th Dynasties. Most of these are the monumental burial places of the nomarchs, the Governors of the 16th (*Oryx*) *Nome* of the Middle Kingdom, who were, at this time, in competition with the pharaohs. The progressive strengthening of their power during the Middle Kingdom was a result of the decentralization of power by which they were also conferred the recognized right to an eternal resting place worthy of their rank. And indeed, the tomb-chapels of Beni Hasan are really quite exceptional, both for their extraordinary architectural structure and the quality of the *decorations* painted on stucco portraying various subjects (farming, sailing, hunting, military operations and many arts and crafts). There are altogether 39 *rock-cut tombs* in Beni Hasan (the name is derived from an Arab family who controlled this region between the 18th and 19th centuries), some of which have a portico in front.

To the south of the necropolis is **Speos Artemidos**, a rock-cut temple built by the female pharaoh Hatshepsut to the lion goddess Pakht, identified with the Greek goddess Artemis.

Tunah al-Gabal

Tunah al-Gabal is the necropolis of the city of Hermopolis, located 12 kilometres to the south-west of the remains of the city whose deity was Thoth (identified with the Greek god Hermes). The location of an interesting group of **tombs** dating from the Ptolemaic period, it represents a genuine funerary and cultural complex. Two tombs here are clearly of considerable importance: the *Tomb-Chapel of Petosiris* (literally meaning a 'Gift of Osiris') High Priest of Thoth during the reign of Philip Arrhidaeus, half brother of Alexander the Great and also his successor, consisting of a vestibule and an older chapel decorated with traditional Egyptian themes; and the *Tomb-Chapel of Isadora*, a young woman who lived in the second century and drowned in the Nile while attempting to reach her lover. There are also three *underground burial chambers* for sacred animals principally containing ibis and baboons – animals sacred to Thoth, the god of Hermopolis. Another interesting monument in this area, just a couple of kilometres from the necropolis, is a large *stele*, one of the boundary markers placed to indicate the extent of Akhetaten (al-Amarnah) the capital city built by the pharaoh Akhenaton.

Above, a view of the tomb of Knumhotep III at Beni Hasan, dating from the Middle Kingdom; right, the wooden sarcophagus of Petosiris, found in his tomb at Tunah al-Gabal, and now exhibited in the Egyptian Museum in Cairo.

Hermopolis

On the left bank of the Nile, and known in ancient times as Khmunu (City of the Eight, referring to the primeval Gods of the Ogdoad, a fundamental cosmological and theological element in Egyptian religious thought that had many devoted supporters among the priests of this region) Hermopolis was the splendid capital of the *Hare Nome* of Upper Egypt, corresponding to al-Ashmunayn near Tell al-Amarnah. For centuries a powerful religious centre, the city was particularly famous for the cult of the highly venerated Thoth, god of health and wisdom, patron of scribes and inventor of the calendar, messenger of the gods and therefore identified with Hermes, for whom the city was eventually named. Throughout the Greek and Roman periods, the city succeeded in maintaining its prestige intact by its dedication to another cult, that of Hermes Trismegistos (the thrice great), master of alchemists and initiates. The main evidence of the city's past splendour are the remains of the magnificent **Temple of Thoth**, restored by Queen Hatshepsut (1479-1457 BC), later enlarged by Ramesses II (1279-1212 BC) and often restructured until the 4th century AD. Two imposing baboons (animals sacred to Thoth) reconstructed from elements of the four colossal statues erected by Amenhotep III, still stand guard over the sacred remains and the ruins that reveal the existence of a vast *Graeco-Roman agora*. Numerous red granite columns and long arcades surround quite a large area. Today the entire ancient city is below the level of the water table, while the necropoli are situated outside the residential centre.

A detail of the cover of the sarcophagus of Djethotefankh, brother of Petosiris and a priest of Thoth at Hermopolis (4th century BC).

Tell al-Amarnah

The ruins of the mythical palace of Akhenaton, set against the stark and fascinating natural context of Tell al-Amarnah.

Between the world of the pyramids and the world of the temples and sanctuaries, including that of Thebes, lies, geographically as well as ideally and stylistically, the world of Akhenaton, the "heretic pharaoh". This brief period of just a few decades which passed so fleetingly in the history of Egypt, was certainly the result of a transcendental impulse that began with the Sphinx, matured with the event of Imhotep, and finally emerged in the pyramids. This ideal of the God-Man which flashed into the collective conscience had for centuries been latent in the intuition of a few initiates and in particular the creators of the world of the pyramids. Akhenaton's vision took on concrete form in the city of Akhetaten "Horizon of Aten" in Tell al-Amarnah.

Akhetaten

The reconstruction of the splendid capital created in 1376 BC by Akhenaton and which disappeared when its creator died, is the result of continual studies carried out since the beginning of the 20th century on the few ruins left at Tell al-Amarnah, an area about 20 km from Hermopolis (Ashmunein), 280 km south of Cairo and 350 km north of Thebes. The city stretched for almost 15 km in a long band along the eastern bank of the Nile. An extensive necropolis was gradually created in the rocky mountains behind the city (to the east and not the west as in the other large cities); in between the two was the village for the workers building the city of the living and the city of the dead. The main axis of the city was lower, nearer to the Nile and consisted of a large boulevard, 100 metres wide, known as the "Road of the Sultan" which joined the Great North Gate with the South Gate.

The "Road of the High Priest" lay almost parallel about 800 metres away while approximately 400 metres further on was the "Road of the Artisans". Effectively, the "Road of the High Priest" divided the city into two broad strips: one towards the Nile, access to which was from the "Road of the Sultan", destined for the residences of the king, the officials, the port and government services; and one towards the interior, on the East, reached from the "Road of the Artisans", where the other citizens lived. All around, at the foot of the rocky chain which stretches out behind Akhetaten like

This reconstruction illustrates well the interior of the house of a wealthy family during the Amarnah period, including the garden that was a characteristic element in residences of the well-to-do. The walls and pillars were decorated with lively geometric symbols and natural scenes. Paris, the Library of Decorative Arts: reconstruction by Benard in a lithograph by Charpentier.

a great plateau, numerous boundary stelae still exist.

The Palace of Akhenaton

A monumental *House of the Pharaoh* is located in Tell al-Amarnah. Like all the structures of this city, the house had neither the colossal size nor the massive structures capable of defying time and the elements. Its scale is human and is in harmony with the environment, as it was conceived for the temporal and spiritual life of the man and his family. The dwelling stands on a rise above the "Road of the Sultan", with three tiers of hanging gardens around it and a carriageway with a pedestrian stairway joining it to the road. Most of the area is occupied by a small park, 3500 metres square, filled with plants and flowers. Husband and wife have separate quarters, composed of a room with an alcove, a bathroom and a wardrobe. The pharaoh also had a painter's studio where brushes of palm fibre and fishbone "pencils" have been found. The daughters have six rooms around a court of their own. All the walls, the ceiling and even the paving are decorated and painted with scenes of outdoor life, with flowers, plants, domestic animals and birds.

One of the letters sent by Akhenaton to a Palestinian leader: the text is, in fact, addressed to "Intaruda, prince of Achshaph". The content of the letters so far deciphered reveals the world of Egyptian diplomacy. This was the 12th year of Akhenaton's reign and the pharaoh was gradually loosing control of his empire.

AKHENATON AND THE LETTERS OF TELL AL-AMARNAH

In 1887 an elderly peasant was walking through fields near the ruins of the village of Amarnah looking for "sebakh" (a natural nitrous manure that is used in making mud bricks), when he came across hundreds of clay tablets with unusual engraved writing. They were taken to Luxor and sold for barely ten piaster. Subsequent examination by the English archaeologist A. Sayce proved them to be genuine and the tablets were recognized as the originals and the copies of diplomatic correspondence between the Egyptian court and the governments of neighbouring Babylonia, Assyria, Anatolia, etc.
The peasant had unwittingly discovered all that remained of what we could well call the State Archive of Akhenaton.
The tablets are engraved with cuneiform characters in the Akkadian language, a mixture of the languages of Assyria and Babylonia, used in diplomatic affairs. About 350 still remain in existence.

An elegant head of exquisitely carved wood from Tell al-Amarnah, now exhibited in the Louvre Museum in Paris (18th Dynasty).

Crossing a verdant, cultivated strip about 10 kilometres wide, the site of Abydos is situated 150 km. from Luxor near to the village of al-Araba al-Madfunah, meaning literally "al-Araba the buried", and in fact the sand has almost completely covered most of the monuments. Abydos was the name that the ancient Greeks gave to the town of *This*, where the earliest dynasties had their origins, a sacred city dedicated to the cult of Osiris. Although there was also a central seat at the *sanctuary of Busiris* (the original form *Pa-Uzir* means in fact the "residence of Osiris"), the myth of Osiris had its supreme expression at Abydos, both for the construction of important monuments and for the pilgrimage that Egyptians had to make to the temple at least once in their lives. In fact, the head – the most important relic of the god – was housed in the sanctuary of Osiris. According to legend, the god Seth killed his own brother, Osiris, cut his body into pieces (thirteen according to some, 42 according to other accounts) and scattered them through the various provinces of Egypt. The goddess and wife of the victim, Isis, sought out all the pieces and gathered them together in the osireion at Abydos. The only piece missing was the penis which was swallowed by a fish in Lake Manzalah near Port Said. With the strength of her love Isis resuscitated her husband, his eyes opened and with a ray of light that shone from them, Isis conceived their son Horus. The tradition of the murder of Osiris by his brother Seth is very similar to the story of Cain and Abel in the bible.

Interesting images of daily life that can still be seen in the area around Abydos. Ancient and traditional methods continue to be used in the production of items such as the terracotta jars in the illustration above.

Above, the colonnade that forms the façade of the temple of Seti I at Abydos.

Above, an interesting view of the ruins of the temple of Abydos and below, a detail of the impressive columns in one of the hypostyle halls in the temple of Seti I.

Only a few ruins remain today of the *sanctuary* and the ancient city where all religious Egyptians sought to have a funerary chapel or at least a commemorative stele. On the other hand, the **Temple of Seti I** is very well preserved and is famous for its splendid paintings, though even in Greek times it was renowned and Strabo praised its "wonderful construction". Excavated by Auguste Mariette, the temple was built to commemorate the pilgrimage of Seti I to Abydos. Although work was continued on it by his son, Ramasses II, while he succeeded in completing the decoration, the building was never finished.

The structure is adapted to the slope of the land in such a way that the two courtyards with their respective pylons (the first of these has been destroyed) formed two terraces and the temple, in its turn, stands on another two steps. The façade consists of a typical portico with columns. The present entrance leads directly into the *first hypostyle hall*. From the *next hypostyle hall* seven doors lead to seven *chapels* dedicated – from right to left – to Horus, Isis, Osiris, Amun, Harakhte, Ptah and Seti himself. Opening off the chapel of Osiris is an area also dedicated to his cult, though the purpose of this space, with two pilasters on the right side and clearly designed to be completely inaccessible, is entirely unknown. From the second hypostyle hall a *corridor* on the left leads to other chapels dedicated to the gods of Memphis. An important feature of this corridor is that one of the rare lists of the kings, with the cartouches of Seti's predecessors is found here. Although incomplete (for political reasons some of the pharaohs were omitted), this record

has enabled us to establish the succession of kings from Menes on. Directly behind the temple are the remains of the **Osireion** or the **Cenotaph of Seti I**, built below ground level, and its interesting and unusual layout is reminiscent of the mysterious tomb of Khufu described by Herodotus. In a large room measuring 30.5 m. by 20 m. with eight square granite pillars and small chapels around it, an island was created surrounded by a canal symbolising the primordial waters, with hollows for the sarcophagus and canopic chest. On the mound that formed the island barley may have been sown symbolising the resurrection of Osiris. The two rooms with arched roofs are decorated with texts from the Book of the Dead and particularly lovely astronomical representations. To the north of Seti's temple is the much smaller **Temple of Ramesses II**. On the outside of the northern wall are scenes of the Battle of Kadesh, and the Poem of Pentaur, and enough of the ruins remain to give a good idea of the building: two pylons and two courts (the second is still quite visible) lie before

two hypostyle halls with eight pillars each and three small sanctuaries; further north are the remains of the **Temple of Osiris**, frequently modified until the 18th Dynasty.

Above left, a detail of the beautiful bas-reliefs in the temple of Seti I; above right, a scene in the south west chapel of the pharaoh offering the Zed pilaster to the goddess Isis; left, frescoes in the central chapel.

Dendera

Dendera, the Greek *Tentyra*, was sacred and noted for three sanctuaries: the first two, almost entirely destroyed today, were the **Temple of Ihy**, the young son of Horus and god of music who played the sistrum, and the **Temple of Horus**. Instead, the third, the **Temple of Hathor**, has survived almost intact together with numerous other remains that enable us to reconstruct the exact arrangement of the entire sacred area. The temple that still stands today is dedicated to the goddess Hathor, whose name (literally *Hat-Hor*) means the "residence of Horus", frequently portrayed with the features of a sacred cow or as a female figure with the head surmounted by horns. Built of granite, like most of the temples built during the Ptolemaic dynasties, the existing temple is simply the reconstruction of a much older, pre-existing temple probably dating from the time of Khufu and

Below, the façade of the chapel of Hathor, with its unmistakable columns. Right, a typical Hathor capital (cubical in shape and softened by the appearance of the face of the goddess) from the same temple and datable to the Greek period.

Above, also from the temple of Hathor, a detail of the ceiling of one of the two hypostyle halls, showing Nut creating the sun to give light to the temple; right, a view of the immense ruins of the temples of Dendera.

Pepi I. The temple has a *façade* with six columns, a splendid outer *hypostyle hall* opening on to a court covering an area of 25 by 42.5 metres and 18 m. high, with 18 columns capped by Hathor-headed capitals decorated with the face of the goddess, and an inner *hypostyle hall* or Hall of Offerings. The decorated *chapels* and *crypts* are also very interesting. A smaller temple, known as the **Sanctuary** or **Great Seat**, was also located in the interior at the most hidden and secret place in the entire temple. Here the mysteries of the birth of cosmic order from primordial chaos were celebrated. Hathor, as well as being a goddess, was protectress of dance and music. Thus every year

in Dendera on the twentieth day of the first month of the inundation, the Festival of Drunkeness took place.

Behind the Temple of Hathor, the ruins of the **Temple of Isis** can be seen; to the south west is the *sacred lake* where the mysteries of the cult of Osiris were celebrated. To the right of the façade are the brick remains of the *Sanatorium* where the sick begged the gods to cure them. Two other monuments worthy of attention are the **Mammisi** (given this Coptic name by Champollion) or *birth houses* or temples which celebrat-

ed the birth of Horus. The oldest is the Birth House of **Nectanebo I**, almost sliced in two by the west wall of the court in front of Hathor's temple, and completed during the Ptolemaic period. The other, built at the time of Augustus and decorated under Hadrian, is on the north side of the court. Between the two mammisi is a Coptic *church* of the 5th century.

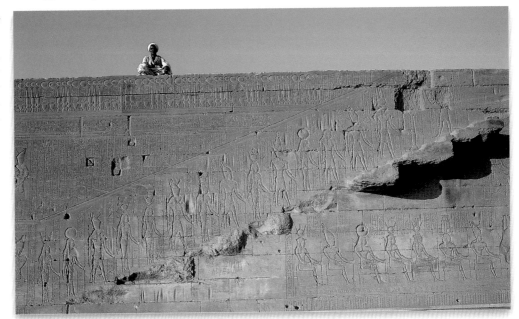

Views of Dendera: above left, one of the mammisi (birth house) seen from above; below left, another mammisi; below, a view of the ruined temples of Dendera.

Luxor

"Hundred-gated Thebes"

*A*strip of green in the midst of yellow desert, cultivated fields, against a background of red rocks (the
Libyan Chain), this is the setting for Luxor which, with
the area of Karnak, was once one of the greatest capitals
of the ancient world. And it is still a captivating city, with
its modern hotels lining the banks of the Nile, the feluccas gliding over the tranquil waters of the river, and the
small silent streets of the bazaar coming to life towards
evening with colour, light and noise.

This is the ancient, great city of Thebes, capital of the
Egyptian empire for almost a thousand years, called by
Homer in the ninth canto of the Iliad "the hundred-gated
Thebes," where "only the grains of sand of the desert sur-
passed the quantity of riches enclosed within" its walls.
The Copts called it Tapé, hence the Greek Thebai, and
our Thebes - but for the Egyptians it was Uaset, "the
dominant," and Niut, "the City", later known as Diospolis
Magna. Its present name, Luxor, derives from the Arabic
Al-Uqsur, a translation of the Latin castra - in fact, the
Romans maintained two encampments in the city.

In the Memphite period, it was a small village, site of
worship of the war god Munt, whose temples marked
the boundaries of the territory. In the Middle Kingdom,
its importance grew thanks to its geographical position
and for political reasons, and the military successes of
its princes eventually succeeded in making it a power.
Thebes reached the height of its glory during the New
Kingdom: the Thebans defeated the Hyksos invaders with
the intercession of the great god Amun, who thus became
the god of the realm and was worshipped with much ceremony in the triad with Mut and Khonsu. This was the
era of great victories and triumphs in Anterior Asia, in
Nubia, and in Libya. It was perhaps the most felicitous
of periods in Egyptian history and Thebes had no rivals:
the victorious pharaohs accumulated incredible wealth
("city where the houses are rich treasuries") from war
spoils; merchants arrived from the Red Sea, the Persian
Gulf, and even from the Sahara, via the oases routes, to
make their fortunes, as well as those of the inhabitants of
Thebes, who, it is said, reached the incredible number of
half a million in that period.

The temples, the dwellings of the gods, rose on the east
bank of the river; buildings for the cult of the dead sovereigns rose on the west bank. Beyond this row of temples,
running parallel to the river, is the imposing rock bluff
which hides the Valley of the Kings. Then, as inexorable for Thebes as for other cities, came decline. The geographical position that a thousand years earlier had favoured its rise to power now became the prime factor in
its decadence: too far from the centre of activity around
the Delta, where the Ramessides were forced to create

military posts to stem the foreign invasions, Thebes
lost its political, spiritual, and military supremacy.
The dynasties that followed came from the Delta,
and the cities of Tanis, Bubastis, and Sais took
Thebes' place as capital of Egypt. Left defenceless,
Thebes was easy prey for all and sundry: the Assyrian invasions of the 7th century, at the hand first of
Esarhaddon and then of Ashurbanipal, were devastating: the inhabitants were deported as slaves,
the statues and the treasuries were sacked, the temples were destroyed. By the Ptolemaic era, Thebes
had become a provincial backwater. Following an
attempted rebellion under Ptolemy IX Soter II and
an insurrection against Roman suppression, the
city was razed by Cornelius Gallus.

In 27 BC, a terrible earthquake gave the coup de
grace to the entire region. As Christianity spread,
the sacred significance of the temples of the Egyp-

The Nile, the feluccas, the white mosque inside the temple of Amun and its massive columns – a most typical image of the splendour of Luxor.

tian gods and the tombs of the pharaohs was obfuscated as homes, sheds, and barns were built over or abutting them. But as Thebes slowly (and literally) disappeared, Luxor took its place.

During the 1800s, Luxor was a tranquil, industrious village of Upper Egypt that drowsed peacefully while great political and social events were played out in Cairo and Suez. After 1811, when Thomas Cook opened the first travel agency, all of Egypt rapidly began to open its doors to the new tourist industry. Luxor, with its fascinating ruins, moorings on the riverfront for the dahabieh, and its climate, so mild in comparison to the European winters, soon became a vacation spot for the new tourists, the winter residence of rich Englishmen, and a compulsory stopover during the long voyages made by European officials. Luxor, with its palaces and the mysterious valley that ran along the other side of the river, soon also attracted many archaeologists, writers, and painters, who flocked to study, document, and describe

all that was still visible of the glorious past of Thebes or to discover what remained hidden in the sands. Thus Jean-François Champollion and Ippolito Rosellini, Heinrich and Emil Brugsch arrived, as well as Lady Lucy Duff-Gordon, who lived for seven years in a house built on the roof of the Temple of Amun.

Luxor also attracted another category of visitors: improvised archaeologists, seekers of antiques and treasures, collectors - with no scruples but lots of money - and the tomb raiders, ever ready to kill or betray for a handful of piasters. And with them the black market for antiques came into being, with genuine artefacts and junk, real treasures and blatant fakes. All these people, whose stories were often strangely intertwined, helped penetrate the thick veils of mystery that still surrounded ancient Egyptian civilization. Luxor, constantly expanding and with an increasing number of modern hotels, became one of Egypt's most important historical and archaeological tourist attractions.

The Temple of Amun-Ra

An imaginary reconstruction of Thebes by Hector Horeau. From the height of a pylon, the view sweeps across Karnak and its magnificent monuments: the houses of the priests, surrounded by gardens, the pylons at the entrance, the avenue of sphinxes leading to the temple of Luxor. On the left are some objects of the period: rugs, seats, jars for cooling water, boxes for the papyrus. Left, an unusual contemporary image of the majestic pylon; below, a monumental head of Ramesses II seen at the entrance to the temple.

The only evidence of Luxor's glorious past is the temple built by the ancient Egyptians to the glory of Amun-Ra, king of the gods, and which they called by the name of Southern Harem of Amun. The temple, uncovered in 1883 by Gaston Maspero, is 260 metres long and was mostly built by two pharaohs, Amenhotep III, who began it in the 14th century BC, and Ramesses II, who completed it by adding the great porticoed court with its axis shifted eastwards.

Numerous other sovereigns, including Tutankhamen, Horemheb and Alexander the Great, enriched the construction with relief sculpture, inscriptions and minor buildings.

The Temple of Luxor was linked to that of Karnak by a long *dromos* or processional avenue paved in stone and flanked by human-headed sphinxes. This street has not yet been completely excavated and work is still going on. The avenue ended at the entrance to the Temple of Luxor, at the Great *Pylon* built by Ramesses II. Its 65-metre facade is decorated with bas-reliefs of scenes from the pharaoh's military campaigns against the Hittites. On the left are the Egyptian Camp and the War Council, and on the right, the Battle of Kadesh. Below, in vertical bands of inscribed hieroglyphics, is the *Poem of Pentaur*, which celebrates the pharaoh's courage. The four large vertical slits on the facade were meant to hold flagstaffs.

Originally, the Great Pylon was preceded by two *obelisks*, *two seated colossi*, and four *standing colossi*. Today, only the left obelisk, 25 metres high, is still standing: its "twin" was taken to Paris in 1833 and erected by the engineer Jean-Baptiste Apollinaire Lebas in Place de la Concorde on 25 October 1836. The two granite colossi, fifteen and a half metres high on bases about a metre high, represent the pharaoh seated on a throne. Of the other four pink granite statues set against the pylon, one represented queen Nefertari and another, on the right and in poor condition, her daughter Merit-Amun.

The great pylon of the temple of Luxor as seen and painted by David Roberts in the 19th century, picturesquely surrounded by the mud houses of the local inhabitants, and as it is today, still preceded by the obelisk and the immense statues of Ramesses II, shown in Roberts' painting still half buried by the sand.

To the left of the obelisk is a head of Ramesses II, belonging to one of the colossi in front of the pylon.

The triumphal entrance leads into the *Courtyard of Ramesses II*, with its double row of columns with closed papyrus capitals and statues set between them. On the northwest side of the courtyard is the shrine/depository of the sacred boats. It was built by Tuthmosis III and dedicated to the triad of Amun, Mut and Khonsu.

Commemorative inscriptions and scenes of sacrifices and religious ceremonies decorate the inner walls of the court. From the left, personifications of the mining districts bearing tributes to the god Ramesses II, sacrificing to the goddess Seshat, and the inauguration ceremony of the monumental entrance with the pharaoh's children, bearing flowers, at the head of the procession. The *second pylon* is the formidable rear wall erected by Amen-

Creating a wonderful perspective, the triumphal entrance of the first pylon leads to the courtyard where the statue of Ramesses II is flanked by grand colonnades. In the background the massive second pylon, built by Amenhotep III and guarded by two more stone colossi, originally represented the entrance to the temple, followed by a grand colonnade, creating a continual, elegant and fascinating play of light and gentle shade.

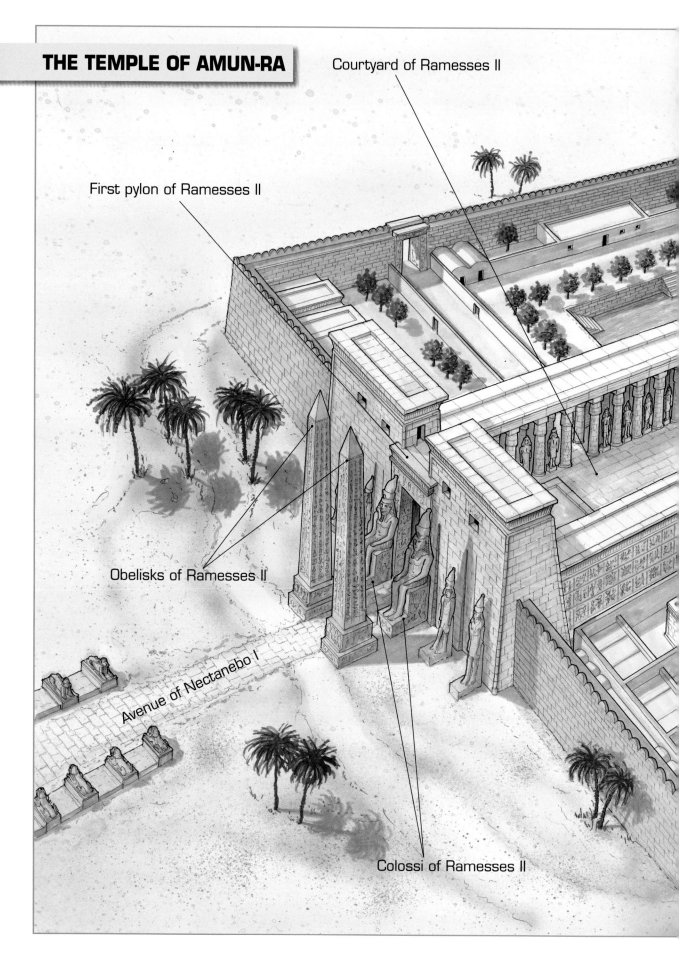

Courtyard of Ramesses II

First pylon of Ramesses II

Obelisks of Ramesses II

Avenue of Nectanebo I

Colossi of Ramesses II

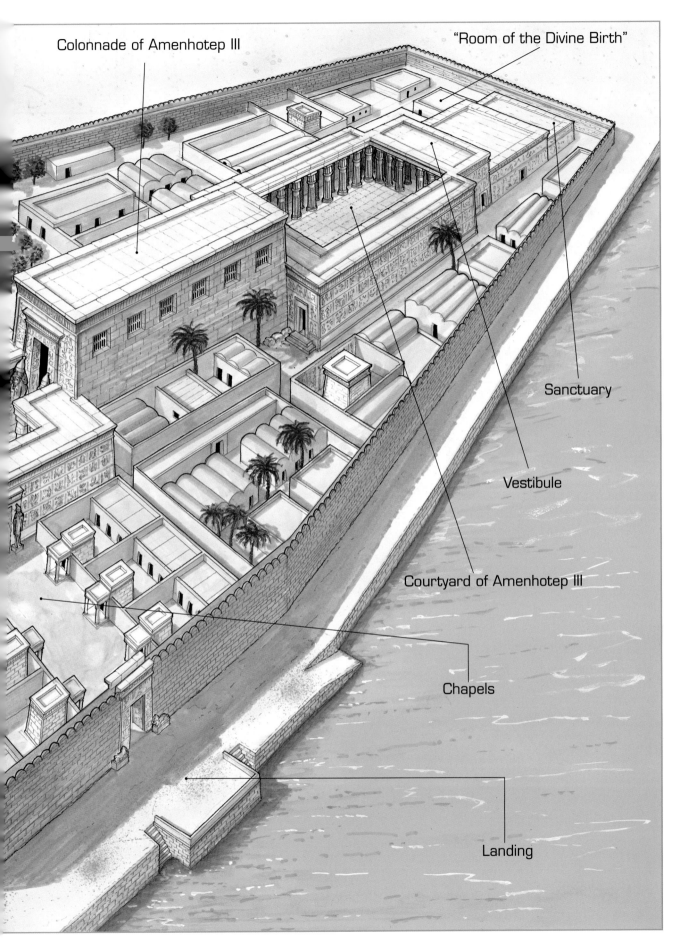

Colonnade of Amenhotep III

"Room of the Divine Birth"

Sanctuary

Vestibule

Courtyard of Amenhotep III

Chapels

Landing

103

hotep III, and was the original entrance to the temple. On the other side is a 52-metre *colonnade* of two rows of seven campaniform columns, also the work of Amenhotep III, to which the decorations, lively depictions of the great Opet portraying the procession of sacred boats being taken to Luxor from Karnak and vice versa, were added later by Tutankhamen and Horemheb.

The Opet, or Festival of the New Year, lasted somewhat over fifteen days, beginning on the nineteenth day of the second month of the inundation — that is, in late August. The ceremony reached its climax when the sacred boat of Amun-Ra, followed by those of Mut and of Khonsu, was carried by thirty priests out of the Temple of Karnak and along the entire avenue of sphinxes to the Temple of Luxor. Here the boats were closed in the sanctuary for several days, after which they were accompanied back to the Temple of Karnak by a festive crowd singing songs and performing sacred dances. At the beginning of the colonnade are two fine limestone groups of the pharaoh and a queen.

The colonnade gives access to the *second courtyard*, or *Court of Amenhotep III*, lined on three sides by double rows of bundle columns with closed papyrus capitals.

Left, another view of the surviving obelisk and the two colossal statues of Ramesses II. Below, a view of the courtyard of Ramesses II which highlights the architectural structure of the colonnades.

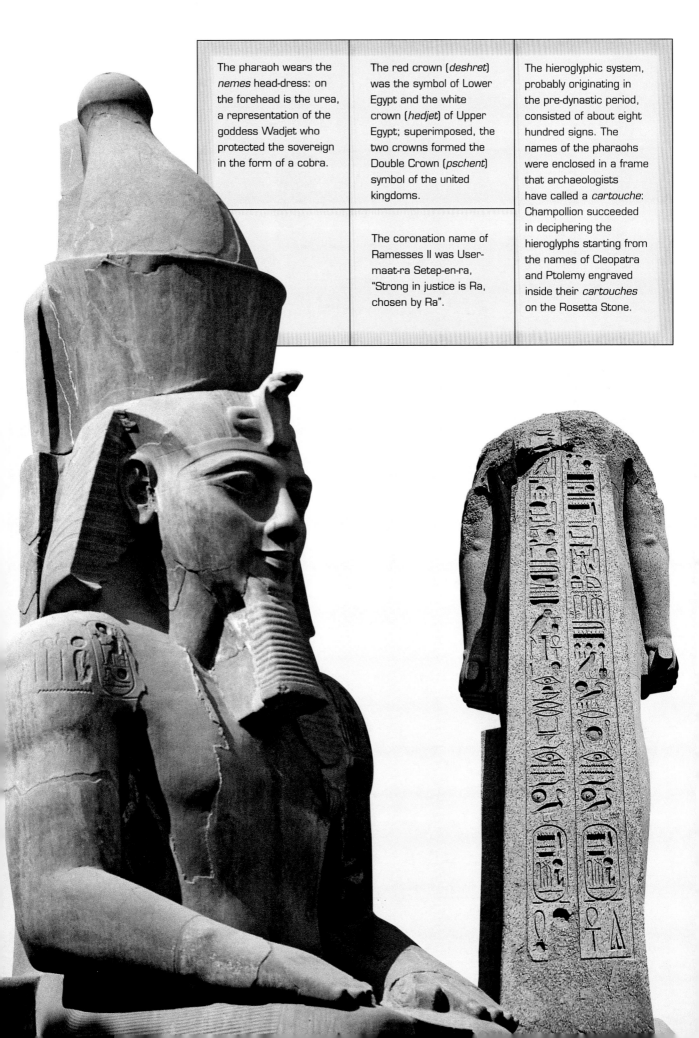

The pharaoh wears the *nemes* head-dress: on the forehead is the urea, a representation of the goddess Wadjet who protected the sovereign in the form of a cobra.

The red crown (*deshret*) was the symbol of Lower Egypt and the white crown (*hedjet*) of Upper Egypt; superimposed, the two crowns formed the Double Crown (*pschent*) symbol of the united kingdoms.

The coronation name of Ramesses II was User-maat-ra Setep-en-ra, "Strong in justice is Ra, chosen by Ra".

The hieroglyphic system, probably originating in the pre-dynastic period, consisted of about eight hundred signs. The names of the pharaohs were enclosed in a frame that archaeologists have called a *cartouche*: Champollion succeeded in deciphering the hieroglyphs starting from the names of Cleopatra and Ptolemy engraved inside their *cartouches* on the Rosetta Stone.

The fourth side is actually a transversely-placed hypostyle hall with four rows of eight columns each, in the same style as those in the courtyard: a veritable petrified forest of great effect.

Next is the *vestibule*, flanked by two rooms; the one on the left is consecrated to Mut, the one on the right, divided in two, to Khonsu and Amun-Min (in Luxor, Amun had taken the form of the ithyphallic Min).

Next is the *offering room*, with four columns and decorated with scenes of religious ceremonies in which Amenhotep appears; then the **sanctuary**, or *depository of the sacred boats*, which was transformed into a chapel running along the axis of the temple by Alexander the Great, who appears in the presence of Amun in the inner and external wall decorations.

Other rooms open off the sanctuary, including the interesting **Birth Room** with relief decorations chronicling the divine conception and birth of the king: Amun speaking with Thoth, with the pharaoh, and with the queen; Khnum fashioning two newborn figures on his potter's wheel (Amenhotep and his *ka*); Thoth announcing to Mutemuya, mother of Amenhotep III, that she has conceived; Mutemuya, pregnant, being taken before Isis and Khnum; Mutemuya on her bed, assisted by the deities of childbirth; the nursing of the infant and his presentation to Amun.

Behind the sanctuary, a room with two rows of eight columns leads to the most sacred room in the temple, known as the **Holy of Holies**, which was inaccessible to common mortals. The statue of the great Amun was kept here and only the pharaoh and the highest priests were allowed into its presence and strictly for the purpose of celebrating liturgical ceremonies.

Further views of the beautiful temple of Luxor, with the large Osiris statues of the pharaoh that have survived at least partly, though damaged, between the columns of the Ramesses II courtyard and, on the right, the colonnades of the Amenhotep courtyard showing different styles of capital (flowering and closed papyrus) and column shaft (smooth and bundle).

Louis-Marie-Julien Viaud is without doubt better known by the pseudonym under which he published his travel books: Pierre Loti. Whether amidst the ruins of the Egyptian temples or on the blazing sands of Nubia, Loti was entranced by Thebes though he sensed the gradual decline that the Western influence of the Europeans inevitably brought with it. Inside the Temple of Amun-Ra, Loti was able, for a brief moment, to forget Luxor, the noise of the river craft, the interfering clerks of the Cook Agency, and the plaster and cement of the bulky Winter Palace, and to rediscover the great and eternal Thebes. Loti stood in silent wonder before the statue of Ramesses II, overpowered by the majesty of those colossi that surrounded him, and wrote of their "proud bearing, one leg forward as though to begin a march that no force on Earth could check." The three Ramesses stand challenging time, "... their heads high, smiling... as they stride confidently into eternity."

The Luxor Museum

The arrangement of this extremely well-organised museum, inaugurated in 1975 on the Nile Corniche, reflects the most modern of criteria of museology. The works on display are few but all of great importance, mostly dating back to the 18th Dynasty. Found in excavations in the area of Thebes, they provide eloquent evidence of the city's historic and artistic grandeur. In the **garden** stand a statue of Amenhotep II from Qurna and a stele of him from Karnak.

In the **entrance** is a colossal pink granite *head* of Amenhotep III; in the rotunda is a partially-gilded wooden head of the goddess Mehet-neret discovered in the tomb of Tutankhamen; opposite the entrance, two *scribes* in granite dating from the Middle Kingdom and a pink granite head of Sesostris III.

Also on the **ground floor**: a *group* with Amenhotep III, a *statue of Tuthmosis III*, a *bust of Amenhotep II* wearing the double crown of Upper and Lower Egypt, and a *stele* narrating the victory of Ahmose over the Hyksos.

On the **upper floor**, in addition to sculptures of various sovereigns, are display cases containing jewels, amulets, cups, tomb furnishings, votive tablets, and papyrus scrolls.

One particularly elegant *canopic jar* in alabaster has a cover bearing the likeness Queen Tuya, mother of Ramesses II.

One of the most interesting exhibits is the

Wall of the Talatat, the recomposition of a wall 18 metres long and 4 metres high, from a temple built by Akhenaton in Karnak before he moved his capital to Amarnah. The 283 sandstone blocks of which it is composed were found in 1925: the temple had been destroyed and the blocks used as fill for the ninth pylon of the Temple of Amun in Karnak.

The myriad of small scenes that stud the wall offer an extremely interesting panorama of daily life: work in the fields, artisans at work, the beer factory. The scenes on the right side are more strictly religious in character and show the pharaoh and Queen Nefertiti worshipping the sun god Aten.

The **Mummification Museum** was inaugurated in Luxor in May 1997. Such a specialized collection, which complements that of the Egyptian Museum of Cairo with its enormous

number of mummies, is indispensable for the country that is foremost in the art of preserving corpses and makes available to the public the most complete information on the subject.

With a specialized *library* and a *multimedia hall* for conferences and projections for visitors, the museum exhibits the most representative archaeological finds relative to the mummification techniques used in ancient Egypt, including a huge *mummified crocodile*, 2.25 metres in length, found in the Temple of Kom Ombo, and the *mummy of Masaharta* son of Pinudjem I, from the period in which this ancient science reached the height of its development (11th century BC). The exhibits are preceded by a space providing illustrations of both the process of mummification and the various phases of the 70-day journey of the dead from the moment of death to that of burial.

Opposite, the exterior of the Luxor Museum and the room where the statues found in 1989 in the temple of Amun-Ra are displayed.
Right, the statue of Amenhotep II and the renowned and fascinating figure of the goddess Junit, found in the Amenhotep courtyard, perfectly made, with a gentle face and smiling expression.

Works of art from the Luxor Museum: above, a detail of the interesting "talatat wall", blocks of sculpted and painted sandstone found in the ninth pylon of the temple of Karnak; below from left, a cow's head in gilded wood found in the Treasury of Tutankhamen's tomb, representing Mehet-uneret; a head of Akhenaton from a group of colossal statues in the portico of the solar temple of Karnak; and the stone statue of Sesostris I.

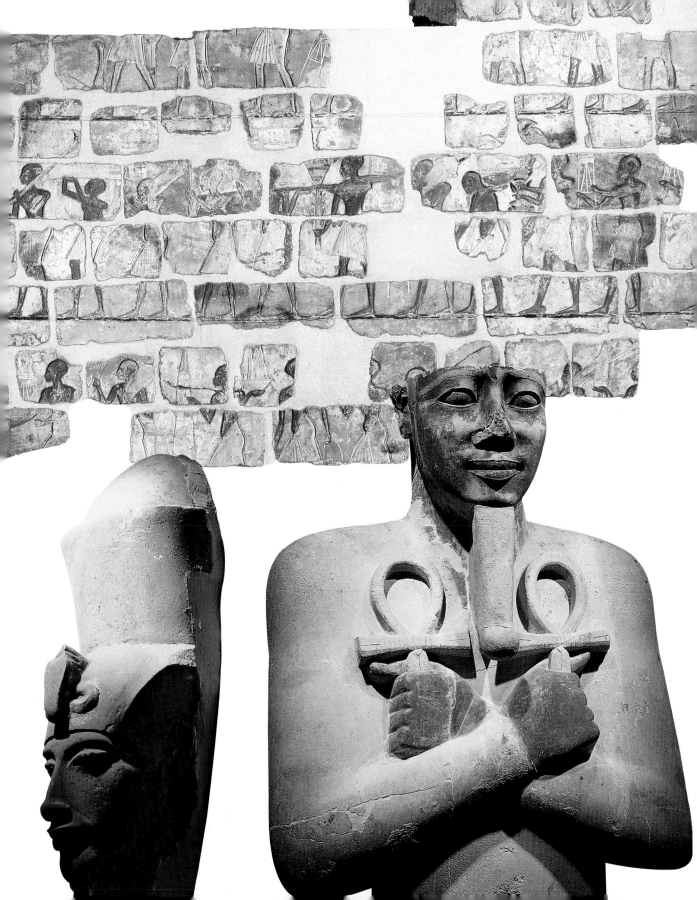

The rosy light of dawn highlights the great archaeological complex of Karnak. Clearly visible from left to right are the first pylon, the column of Taharqa, the second pylon, followed by the columns of the hypostyle hall, the obelisks of Tuthmosis I and Hatshepsut. On the far right, the columns and pillars of the Akh Menu of Tuthmosis III and the Nectanebo gate.

Above, an interesting view of the sacred area of Karnak in a 19th-century work by David Roberts.

Previous page, an impressive view of the eighth pylon of the temple of Amun at Karnak, watched over by the majestic remains of two mighty stone colossi; below, the long row of sphinxes along the avenue that leads up to the first pylon.

About three kilometres from the Temple of Luxor is the vast monumental area of Karnak, which the Greeks called *Hermonthis*. A mudbrick wall divides the archaeological site into three separate areas: the largest is the central area, of about thirty hectares, which Diodorus Siculus tells us was the oldest and which enclosed the *dominion of Amun*; to the south, still unexplored for about half of its extension (almost nine hectares) and linked to the first by a *dromos* of ram-headed sphinxes, is the *dominion of the goddess Mut*, wife of Amun and symbolically represented as a vulture; lastly, the *dominion of Munt*, the god of war, extends to the north over an area of about two and a half hectares. Each complex changed in size over the course of time and each successive pharaoh left his mark, either by enlarging the temples proper or by adding rooms and chapels. The structures of the three sacred complexes are identical: the main temple dedicated to the god stands at the centre of each enclosure alongside the sacred lake, generally square in shape and used for ceremonies. Although all three complexes are impressive, the one dedicated to Amun is of quite astonishing size.

113

Views of the avenue of sphinxes that leads to the first pylon and the great courtyard that lies beyond it. Built at the time of the 22nd Dynasty, it is more than 100 metres wide. On two sides are two long rows of seated rams that were brought here from Ramesses' II dromos of sphinxes. An animal sacred to the god Amun, the ram is seen protecting the pharaoh who is portrayed between its front legs.

The Temple of Amun

This is the largest columned temple in the world, and so architecturally complex as to provide a valid basis for study of the evolution of styles, from the 18th Dynasty to the end of the Ramesside era. A short *avenue of sphinxes* leads to the first *pylon* (the largest, 113 metres wide and 15 metres thick), the unadorned yet monumental entrance to the temple, dating to the Ptolemaic dynasty. The ram-headed sphinxes - the ram was sacred to Amun - represent the god protecting the pharaoh, who is portrayed between the animal's paws.

The temple of Ramesses III, on the right of the great courtyard may be considered a perfect example of architecture at the time of the Ramesses dynasties, with a large pylon leading to a porticoed courtyard, beyond which is the vestibule and then the hypostyle hall.

THE TEMPLE OF AMUN

Obelisk
of Tuthmosis III

Peripteral chapel

Seventh pylon
of Tuthmosis III

Hypostyle hall

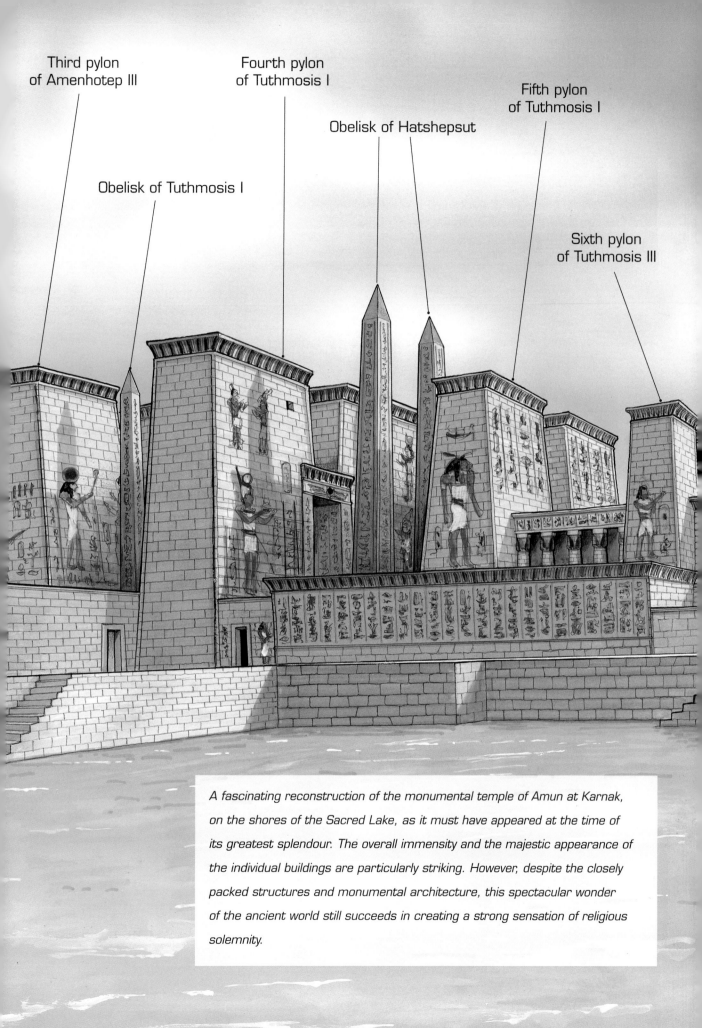

Third pylon
of Amenhotep III

Fourth pylon
of Tuthmosis I

Obelisk of Hatshepsut

Fifth pylon
of Tuthmosis I

Obelisk of Tuthmosis I

Sixth pylon
of Tuthmosis III

A fascinating reconstruction of the monumental temple of Amun at Karnak, on the shores of the Sacred Lake, as it must have appeared at the time of its greatest splendour. The overall immensity and the majestic appearance of the individual buildings are particularly striking. However, despite the closely packed structures and monumental architecture, this spectacular wonder of the ancient world still succeeds in creating a strong sensation of religious solemnity.

The *first courtyard*, called the Ethiopian Court, dates to the 22nd Dynasty. It is closed to the north by a portico of robust columns with closed papyrus capitals. At the feet of the columns are aligned the sphinxes Ramesses II had made to flank the access to the hypostyle hall. At its centre is a tall column with an open papyrus capital; it is all that remains of the gigantic Pavilion of the Ethiopian King Taharqa, 21 metres high, with a wooden ceiling, built to shelter the sacred boats. In front and to the right of the column is the entrance to the **Temple of Ramesses III**, with on three sides Osiris columns showing the pharaoh in his Jubilee garments. Set against the *second pylon* is a mutilated, colossal granite statue of Ramses II and another, 15 metres high, representing king Pinudjem.

The portal, 29.5 metres high, leads into what is considered one of the most beautiful examples of Egyptian art: the **hypostyle hall**, 102 metres wide and 53 metres long, where - in a perennial challenge to the centuries - an incredible 134 columns, each 23 metres high, rise up into the sky. The tops of the open papyrus capitals were about 15 metres in circumference: standing room for fifty peo-

Standing between the legs of the colossal figure of Ramesses II, as seen below, is the little figure of Bent Anat, daughter of Isinophre, her tender beauty still perceptible. Her presence here is not fortuitous as the young woman was the wife and daughter of Ramesses.

ple. The hall is a veritable forest of columns, and their size and the play of light and shade they create evoke a great sense of wonder. The nave, begun around 1375 BC by Amenhotep III, who conceived the space as a simple colonnade leading to the sanctuary of Amun, is higher than

Left, the colossal statue erected by Ramesses II by the second pylon still stands in all its magnificence just as it must have appeared to Pinudjem, an important priest of Amun and pharaoh of the 21st Dynasty who, in fact, usurped him.
Right, the first courtyard with the only surviving column of ten that originally surrounded the kiosk of Taharga, also reproduced in a painting by David Roberts.

the side aisles which were begun by Horemheb, continued by Seti I and Ramesses II, and finally finished under Ramesses IV. This difference in height made it possible to insert the wide openwork stone windows, known as *claustra*, which magically illuminated the interior. Beyond the hypostyle hall there once stood the obelisks of Tuthmosis I, each 23 metres tall and weighing 143 tons, of which only one now remains. Hatshepsut's obelisk is still higher (30 metres tall and weighing 200 tons) and for its construction it is said that the queen paid no heed to cost: according to the chronicles of the time, she paid as many "bushels of gold as bags of grain." Beyond the fifth and sixth pylons (respectively of Tuthmosis I and Tuthmosis III), is the unique **Akh-Menu of Tuthmosis III**, the Great Festival Hall also known as

The theatrical porticoed courtyard with Osiris columns in the temple of Ramesses III, Karnak. On the left is a detail of one of the columns which, although damaged, still show evidence of their original monumentality.

For centuries visitors have been struck by the spectacular grandeur of the hypostyle hall, a true architectural work of art and one of the most beautiful still remaining of Egyptian art. It is not surprising that David Roberts painted some fine works of this monumental forest of some 134 columns 23 metres in height, all engraved with hieroglyphs and bas-reliefs. His own diary reveals the amazement of the 19th-century traveller, "It is so far beyond anything that I have yet seen, that I cannot even think of any comparison."

the "Temple of Millions of Years." It is a fine hypostyle hall with two rows of ten columns, their shafts painted dark red in imitation of wood, and a row of thirty-two square pillars decorated with various scenes. Scarce traces of painting have come to light on some of the pillars; they are datable to the 6th century AD and reveal that this room was transformed into a church by Christian monks.

Prevous page: above, the columns of the hypostyle hall seen from the courtyard of Amenhotep III; below left, a statue of a seated pharaoh on the approach to the temple of Amun; below right, a beautiful bundled papyrus column in the small courtyard near to the sixth pylon.

Below, the pillars, still with their architrave, in the Festival Hall of Tuthmosis III and, on the right, a view of the interior.

The sacred lake

The sacred lake of Amun's dominion covered an area of 120 by 77 metres and was surrounded by various buildings: the storerooms, the priests' dwellings, even an aviary for aquatic birds. In these waters, the priests purified themselves every morning before beginning the daily sacred rites.

Above, a view of the sacred lake; left, a detail of one of the many interesting items situated around the monumental area.

Right, the sacred area of Karnak in a painting by David Roberts.

In the form of trinkets, seals or amulets, the scarab has always been a symbol of the Egyptian civilization. Jars filled with scarabs discovered in tombs of the pre-dynastic period are evidence that it was already venerated at that time. The dung beetle (scarab) was seen as an example of tenacity and precision due to its ability to roll a ball of dung held between its rear legs for considerable distances. The Egyptians thought that it was a self-generating creature, though in fact, it lays its eggs in this ball of dung, which it then buries. These characteristics identified it with the god of the rising sun, Khephri who was self-generating and rolled the sun to the beginning of its cycle through the sky from east to west. At midday it became Ra and then Atum in the evening, before sinking into the afterlife.

The gigantic granite scarab that Amenhotep III had carved to honour Atum Khepri; scenes of offerings to the sun god are engraved on the base.

The Temple of Ptah

The Temple of Ptah was rebuilt in white sandstone by Tuthmosis III on an earlier mud-brick temple of the Middle Kingdom. Today, the *vestibules* of columns with composite capitals still stand near to the northern wall of the main enclosure of Amun. The temple was subsequently restored and enlarged by Shabaka and other sovereigns of the Ptolemaic dynasty.

A *statue of the lion-goddess Sekhmet*, wife of Ptah, is in the chapel on the right. The goddess wears the solar disc and the urea on her head. Sekhmet represented the destructive power of the sun and was the goddess of war, but also the divinity who helped to heal bone fractures.

An open air museum

The excavations and research carried out continuously at Karnak over many decades have

This page, above, a view of the Open Air Museum of Karnak, with the door of the temple of Montu erected by Sesostris III; left, the Open Air Museum of Karnak again showing a pilaster decorated with an image of a pharaoh offering incense.

Previous page: above, the colonnaded vestibule in the temple of Ptah, at the north wall of the main enclosure of Amun; left, a statue of the lion goddess, Sekhmet, Ptah's bride; below, the kiosk of Sesostris I, also known as the White Chapel, one of the oldest buildings in the Karnak site and considered a masterpiece of architecture belonging to the Middle Kingdom. It was reconstructed by Henri Chevrier with seventy blocks of white limestone from Tura, found inside the third pylon.

brought to light amazing monuments and given coherence to an inestimable heritage of objects and remains, only some of which are displayed in the museums of Cairo and Luxor. In time, therefore, the need to provide sufficient and appropriate space for the appreciation of such a vast and precious wealth of antique treasures without removing them from the original context, became imperative. Thus the idea of an 'open air museum' came into being – an officially defined area entirely dedicated to both the conservation and the display of valuable elements of statuary and monumental architecture. In this veritable and spectacular "field of stones" long forgotten items and objects that for years had remained in storage were once more brought into the open to be rightfully rediscovered.

One of the most lovely exhibits of this museum is the **White Chapel of Sesostris I,** one of the oldest monuments in Karnak, with some of the finest *bas-reliefs* sculpted in the entire Middle Kingdom. When these remains were discovered

during excavations of the third pylon, Henri Chevrier was so greatly impressed by their beauty that in 1938 he decided to work personally on the reconstruction of this sophisticated chapel with pilasters. It is not known where the chapel originally stood though it is clear that Amenhotep III had it

Left, the Chapel of Tuthmosis IV.

Below and right, details of some interesting artifacts that may be seen in the Open Air Museum of Karnak: bas-reliefs, decorated pilasters, monumental ruins and a long row of statues of the goddess Sekhmet.

dismantled and that it represented one of the most important elements in the temple of Amun, evidence of the original splendour that has endured the passing of time.

The **Chapel of Tuthmosis IV** consisting originally of numerous monolithic blocks weighing several tons and now standing impressively within the museum, was one of the chapels dedicated to housing the sacred boats that were also dismantled by Amenhotep III. Although they were enormous, the various elements that formed the chapel

were dispersed or stacked up around the third pylon. For a long period its recomposition therefore seemed to be a necessary and interesting task, but one that would however, be partial and imperfect. Consequently the definitive and satisfactory rebuilding of the chapel was only completed in 1996.

Principal pharaohs of ancient Egypt

ARCHAIC PERIOD · (Thinite Period) - 3000-2660 BC

Thinite period, from the name of This or Thinis, the place of residence of the first two dynasties.

1st DYNASTY - CIRCA 3000 BC

(Horus) NARMER

Identified by many with the mythical king Menes, Narmer - king of Upper Egypt - conquered the Delta and united the two kingdoms under the new symbol of the White Crown of the South grafted onto the Red Crown of the North. He founded the 1st Dynasty and set up his capital at Abydos (ancient Thinis, which has not yet been found). The Narmer Palette commemorates this first great event in Egyptian history.

(Horus) MENES

Many tend to identify Menes with king Aha, who probably founded the city of Memphis, as well as with Narmer (see above).

(Horus) UADJI

Uadji, known as the 'Serpent King', made various expeditions into the Arabian Desert and was buried in Saqqara. His funerary stele is particularly fine.

(Horus) DEN

His reign seems to have been long and important: he officially instituted the Heb-Sed, a ceremony that tested the sovereignty of the pharaoh in the thirtieth year of his reign.

(Horus) ADJB

Adjb made several expeditions into the eastern desert and ordered the first census in Egypt. He was buried in Saqqara but a cenotaph of his is also to be found in Abydos.

(Horus) SEMERKHET

He may have usurped the crown.

(Horus) QAA

Legitimate successor of Adjb, he was the last of the 1st Dynasty pharaohs.

2nd DYNASTY - CIRCA 2850 BC

(Horus) HOTEPSEKHEMWY

Founder of the 2nd Dynasty.

(Horus) RANEB

An almost unknown pharaoh: jars with seals bearing his name on their stoppers were found in a tomb in Saqqara.

(Horus) NYNETJER

He fought against the autonomistic tendencies of Lower Egypt. He was buried in Saqqara in a gallery-tomb.

(Horus) SEKHEMIB

We know nothing of this pharaoh.

PERIBSEN

Peribsen replaced the cult of the god Horus with that of the god Seth in the cities of the south.

(Horus) KHASEKHEMUI

Defeated Peribsen and re-established order, adopting both Seth and Horus as royal divinities and instituting the seat of highest religious power in Heliopolis.

OLD KINGDOM · circa 2660-2180 BC

3rd DYNASTY - CIRCA 2660 BC

SANAKHTE

Perhaps to be identified with Nebka, Sanakhte was the founder of the 3rd Dynasty.

DJOSER

The most important of the 3rd-Dynasty pharaohs, who according to Manetho reigned twenty-nine years. The monarchy became centralized under his rule and the capital was moved to Memphis while the solar cult became the cult of the king. He extended his power southwards, reuniting Nubia and Egypt. His High Priest, the architect Imhotep, built the first great step pyramid for him at Saqqara.

SEKHEMKHET

He may have been Djoser's son and like Djoser began a funerary complex with a stepped pyramid. He was, however, unable to finish it.

KHABA

Successor to Sekhemkhet, he probably had a small pyramid built at Zawiyat al-Aryan.

HUNI

The last pharaoh of the 3rd Dynasty, he may have ordered, at Maydum, construction of the step pyramid that was later reworked by Sneferu.

4th DYNASTY - CIRCA 2600 BC

SNEFERU

He reigned for twenty-four years, during which he made many expeditions into the Sinai, Nubia, and Libya, bringing back numerous prisoners. He was also an untiring builder: his works include the first two pyramids of Dahshur and the completion of that of Maydum.

KHUFU (CHEOPS)

The reign of this pharaoh lasted twenty-three years, in the course of which he constructed the Great Pyramid of Giza. His domestic policy was essentially that of centralizing both political and religious power.

REDJEDEF (DEDEFRE)

Son and successor of Khufu, he reigned eight years. He began the pyramid of Abu Roash.

KHAFRE (CHEPHREN)

Khafre, brother of Redjedef, reigned for twenty-

six years: he was responsible for the Sphinx and the second pyramid of Giza with its mortuary temple and granite valley temple. He maintained centralized political and religious power.

MENKAURE (MYCERINUS)

The reign of this son of Khafre lasted about thirty years. He built the smallest of the three pyramids of Giza and returned some of the property which Khufu had previously confiscated from the priests.

SHEPSESKAF

Married to the daughter of Menkaure, whom he succeeded on the throne, he renewed the struggles against priestly power. As his tomb he chose not a pyramid but the Mastaba el-Fara'un in South Saqqara.

5th DYNASTY - CIRCA 2480 BC

USERKAF

Restored the worship of Ra as the royal cult. The pyramid in North Saqqara and the Solar Temple of Abu Ghurab were built during his reign.

SAHURE

He had a canal dug to Bubastis which joined the Mediterranean with the Red Sea and built a pyramid and a solar temple at Abusir.

NEFERIRKARE

This pharaoh ordered the building of several temples and a pyramid at Abusir. He definitively adopted the name of 'Son of Ra' set in a cartouche in the royal protocol.

SHEPSESKARE

All that is known is that Shepseskare reigned for seven years.

NEFEREFRE

His pyramid at Abusir is unfinished.

NYUSERRE

Breaking with the tradition of solar temples at Abusir, this pharaoh once more returned to the site of Saqqara to build pyramids.

MENKAUHOR

We know nothing except that he reigned for eight years.

DJEDKARE

This pharaoh also built at Saqqara during his thirty-two year reign.

UNAS

The interior of Unas' pyramid at Saqqara is decorated with the 'Pyramid Texts', one of the most important extant Egyptian hieroglyphic writings.

6th DYNASTY - CIRCA 2330 BC

TETI

Under Teti, art achieved its highest splendour, as in the tomb of the viziers Kagemmi and Mereruka in North Saqqara. The governors of the various provinces became hereditary princes.

USERKARE

This successor of Teti continued his policies.

PEPI I

Under Pepi I, royal power diminished as that of the princes, high dignitaries, and priests increased. He reigned for fifty years and built a powerful army of Nubian mercenaries.

MERENRE

He organized an expedition towards Upper Nubia but reigned for only five years.

PEPI II

He had an extremely long reign. He was six years old when he ascended the throne and held power until he was over one hundred. During his reign, the country became divided and the Old Kingdom came to an end.

FIRST INTERMEDIATE PERIOD · circa 2180-2040 BC

The First Intermediate Period includes the 7th and 8th Dynasties with their capital at Memphis and the 9th and 10th, with the main capital at Heracleopolis and therefore known as the Heracleopolitan dynasties. It is difficult to indicate the precise names and numbers of the pharaohs who succeeded each other during this period. In the absence of a unifed and recognized power, Asian bands invaded and plundered the Delta cities.

MIDDLE KINGDOM · circa 2040-1780 BC

11th DYNASTY (THEBAN)

ANTEF I (SEHERTANI-ANTEF)

Defeated the Prince of Heracleopolis, declared himself king, and shifted the seat of power and the capital to Thebes. He began the 11th Dynasty and, simultaneously, the period known as the Middle Kingdom.

ANTEF II

His reign lasted about fifty years.

ANTEF III

The third Antef reigned for barely five years.

MENTUHOTEP I

His name means 'the god Montu is satisfied'. He reigned for about fifty years, reuniting the country and extending power to Lower Egypt. He was supported by the middle classes who were interested in reopening trade throughout the territory. He was responsible for construction of the imposing mortuary temple with its pyramid, colonnades, and stepped podium at Deir el-Bahri.

MENTUHOTEP II

He reigned for only a few years.

MENTUHOTEP III

Reopened maritime trade with the Aegean and organized an expedition to the Red Sea. He was dethroned by a usurper.

12th DYNASTY - CIRCA 2000 BC

AMENEMHAT I

The name of this vizier of Mentuhotep III means 'Amun is at the summit'. As pharaoh, he moved the capital to Memphis, gave more power to the cult of Amun, pushed the frontiers beyond the Third Cataract of the Nile into the heart of the Sudan, and created many fortifications in the outposts.

SENUSERT (SESOSTRIS) I

This was the first pharaoh to share his power with his son to ensure the dynasty. He conducted expeditions to Nubia (to the Second Cataract), Palestine, Libya, and to the mines in the Wadi Hammamat.

AMENEMHAT II

The kingdom was extended to Megiddo in Palestine, and to Ugarit on the Syrian coast. This pharaoh also made his son co-regent.

SENUSERT (SESOSTRIS) II

He reclaimed the area of Fayyum and continued the expansion and consolidation of the empire.

SENUSERT (SESOSTRIS) III

The most important pharaoh of the 12th Dynasty: under him the power of the nomarchs was eliminated everywhere and in four campaigns he colonized Nubia, establishing the frontier at Semna. He also undertook an expedition to Sichem in southern Palestine.

AMENEMHAT III

He improved Fayyum and built the imposing residence there, which the Greeks recalled as 'The Labyrinth'.

AMENEMHAT IV

Under his weak hand, Egypt underwent a period of decadence.

SEKHEMRE

He became king by marrying the regent queen Sobkneferu, taking away part of her power. Nubia separated from Upper Egypt. He was the last pharaoh of the 12th Dynasty.

13th AND 14th DYNASTIES CIRCA 1780 BC

There are about seventy kings in these dynasties: there was general decadence in all fields, especially the political and artistic.

SECOND INTERMEDIATE PERIOD · circa 1780-1560 BC

Egypt in this period witnessed the invasions of the Hyksos, Canaanite, and Ammonite nomads, who under the pressure of the Indoeuropean peoples of central Asia invaded the fertile Delta lands and advanced as far as Assiut, devastating the land. The Hyksos introduced the wheel and the horse into Egypt - both previously unknown there - and the cult of the god Baal. Their name, in Greek form, derives from an Egyptian term which means 'Prince of Foreign Lands'. They settled in Avaris, on the Delta, and were not driven out until the 17th (Theban) Dynasty.

15th AND 16th DYNASTY HYKSOS DYNASTIES - CIRCA 1660 BC

SALITIS (SHESHI)

One of the chiefs of the Hyksos bands that invaded Egypt. He founded Avaris but set up his government in Memphis.

KHYAN

The capital was transferred to Avaris, east of the Delta.

APOHIS

He reigned for forty years. A struggle between Avaris and Thebes broke out near the end of his reign; defeated by the kings of Upper Egypt, he was the last of the so-called 'shepherd kings'.

17th DYNASTY

NUBKEPERRE INYOTEF V

The founder of the dynasty, he proclaimed himself king of Upper and Lower Egypt. He reinforced the monarchy of Thebes and rejected that of Avaris.

SUADJENRA

Suadjenra seems to have been the sixth sovereign of this dynasty; we know no more.

KAMOSE

Fifteenth and last sovereign of the 17th Dynasty, he defeated the Hyksos with a surprise attack on Avaris.

NEW KINGDOM · 1560-1070 BC

18th DYNASTY - 1552-1306 BC

AHMOSE

Brother and successor of Kamose, he destroyed Avaris and chased the Hyksos to Palestine. He reconquered Nubia as far as Abu Simbel and re-established monarchic rule throughout a unified Egypt.

AMENHOTEP I

The name of this son and successor of Ahmose means 'Amun is Satisfied'. During his reign the Egyptian frontiers reached as far as the Euphrates. He experienced early clashes with the Mitanni and the Hittites. He had no legitimate heirs and had his oldest daughter marry the son of a concubine, who succeeded him to the throne.

TUTHMOSIS I

He brought the cities of Abydos and Thebes to their greatest splendour; he had the Temple of Karnak embellished with pylons and obelisks and the Great Hypostyle Hall built.

TUTHMOSIS II

Son of the preceding monarch, he was the husband of his half sister Hatshepsut. He reigned for fifteen years, during which he crushed uprisings both at home and abroad, affirming his absolute power. He had no legitimate male descendents at his death and the son of one of his concubines was elected heir to the throne, becoming king with the name of Tuthmosis III.

HATSHEPSUT

At the premature death of Tuthmosis II, his half sister and wife became regent for the official heir Tuthmosis III, but she actually held all the royal power and took the title of pharaoh, even wearing male attire and the ceremonial beard of the Egyptian sovereigns. She sent important trading expeditions to the mysterious land of Punt, embellished and enlarged the complex of Karnak, and had the temple of Deir el-Bahri built.

TUTHMOSIS III

He was able to reign only after the death of queen Hatshepsut and, hating her memory, gave way to an unbridled revenge, cancelling her name from all the monuments of Karnak and Deir el-Bahri. He reigned for thirty-four years and under him Egypt experienced one of its most splendid periods. With seventeen military campaigns in Asia he definitively defeated the Mitanni: his victories include Kadesh and Megiddo. Egyptian frontiers included the 'Islands of the Great Circle' (the Cyclades, Crete, and Cyprus), whose customs and religion Tuthmosis did not however attempt to change. Late in his reign he advanced up the Nile to the Fourth Cataract.

AMENHOTEP (AMENOPHIS) II

This king followed his father's policies at home and abroad. He married his son and heir to the daughter of Muteniya, king of the Mitanni.

TUTHMOSIS IV

His was a brief reign, during which the alliance between Egypt and the Mitanni was strengthened.

AMENHOTEP (AMENOPHIS) III

This son of the preceding ruler reigned for about forty years. He married Ty, a Syrian princess of great beauty whose influence over the pharaoh was very strong. His reign was characterized by its great splendour; Egypt was blessed with a period of peace and prosperity and outstanding development in the arts.

AMENHOTEP IV (AKHENATON)

He ascended the throne in 1372 and passed into history as the heretic king or the pharaoh of the schism: he replaced the religion of Amun with that of Aten, the solar disk. He closed the temples, scattered the priests, abandoned Thebes, and founded a new capital, Akhetaten ('The Horizon of Aten'), now Tell al-Amarnah. And as a final gesture, he changed his name from Amenophis, which means 'Amun is Contented' to Akhenaton, which means 'Pleasing to Aten'. He married Nefertiti ('The Beautiful one has come'), an extremely beautiful Mitanni princess who greatly influenced his renewal of customs and art ('the Amarna Revolution').

SMENKHKARE

Son-in-law of Akhenaton (he married the pharaoh's oldest daughter Meritaten) and perhaps also his younger brother, in 1347 he became co-regent and then succeeded him to the throne, but died immediately thereafter.

TUTANKHAMEN

He married Akhenaton's second oldest daughter, Ankhesepaten: taking advantage of his extreme youth, the priests convinced him to return to Thebes and re-establish the supremacy of the cult of Amun. This was when the young king abandoned the name Tutankhaten and adopted that of Tutankhamen with which he passed into history. His death at only eighteen years of age is surrounded by mystery. His tomb contained the most fabulous ensemble of funerary furnishings ever found in Egypt.

AY

A high royal dignitary who was already elderly at Tutankhamen's death. He married the boy-king's widow but reigned for only four years. At his death Egypt precipitated into anarchy and misery.

HOREMHEB

An able general under Akhenaton, Horemheb was the commander-in-chief of the troops in Memphis under Tutankhamen. In foreign policy he stipulated peace with the Hittite king Mursili II; at home, he destroyed all traces of the Amarna heresy, fought administrative corruption, and adopted a policy of social reform.

19th DYNASTY - 1306-1186 BC

RAMESSES I

Ramesses was nominated vizier by Horemheb, under whom he had been a soldier. He maintained Thebes as capital of the two kingdoms and seat of the cult of Amun and at the same time elected Tanis, on the Delta, as capital of the empire. To ensure his family's power, he shared the throne with his son, who later became Seti I.

SETI I

He drove back the Hittite king Muwatalli who had advanced into the Sinai and occupied Kadesh. He was responsible for construction of the Great Hypostyle Hall in the Temple of Amun at Karnak and of the temple at Abydos.

RAMESSES II

Perhaps the greatest of the Egyptian pharaohs, Ramesses II reigned for almost seventy years, in the course of which he enriched Egypt with countless structures from Karnak to Abu Simbel. Abroad he led a series of brilliant military campaigns: it was under him that the first international peace treaty with the Hittites was signed, to be followed by the diplomatic marriage between the pharaoh and the Hittite king's daughter. Ramesses' favorite wife was Nefertari, in whose honour he had the Small Temple of Abu Simbel built. He also founded a new capital on the Delta, Pi-Ramesse ('the House of Ramesses').

MERNEPTAH

Although he was only thirteenth in the line of succession, he ascended the throne after all the other sons of Ramesses II had died prematurely. It is said that the Exodus of the Hebrews from Egypt took place during his reign.

AMENMESSES

Usurper of the throne.

MERNEPTAH SIPTAH

Married the Ramesside princess Twosre.

SETI II

This pharaoh attempted to bring a halt to the economic and administrative crisis into which the country had fallen. The Delta region was once more subject to Libyan invasions.

IARSU

With this Palestinian usurper of the Egyptian throne, the 19th Dynasty came to an end with the country still in the throes of crises and anarchy.

20th DYNASTY - 1186-1070 BC

SETHNAKHTE

Scattered the Libyan bands and returned the property his predecessor had usurped from the temples to the priests.

RAMESSES III

An extremely energetic pharaoh who put an end to the invasion of the 'Sea Peoples' and finally restored peace and prosperity to Egypt. The imposing temple of Medinet Habu bears his name.

From RAMESSES IV to RAMESSES XI

The sons and grandsons of the Ramesside dynasty followed each other on the throne, often as a result of palace conspiracies. The last of the Ramessides named Herihor, high priest of Amun, as Viceroy in Nubia: profiting from the weakness of the pharaoh, Herihor usurped the titles of Upper Egypt and soon became the only lord of the Egyptian empire.

THIRD INTERMEDIATE PERIOD· circa 1070-713 BC

21st DYNASTY (TANITE) CIRCA 1070-945 BC

SMENDES

Vizier of Ramesses XI, Smendes married a Ramesside princess and reigned at Tanis on the Delta.

PSUSENNES I

This son of Smendes also reigned from Tanis.

PINUDJEM I

High Priest of Amun, son of the preceding pharaoh.

SIAMUN

Contemporary of Solomon in Israel.

PSUSENNES II

Last king of the 21st Dynasty.

22nd DYNASTY (BUBASTID) CIRCA 945-722 BC

SHESHONQ I

This pharaoh of Libyan origin elected Bubastis as his capital (from which the dynasty he founded takes its name). He conquered Jerusalem and brought home a great deal of booty.

OSORKON I

Son of Sheshonq, he fought against the power of the priests of Thebes. During his reign Upper Nubia detached itself from Egypt and joined to Sudan creating a new kingdom with Napata as its capital.

SHESHONQ II

According to some, the son of Iuput and grandson of Sheshonq I, though others maintain he was the son of Osorkon I who he succeeded on the throne, Sheshonq II was also a high priest of Amun. However he reigned only briefly.

OSORKON II

The temple of Tell Moqdam bears his name.

TAKELOT I

Married princess Karomama, daughter of Osorkon II. Their son Osorkon was elected High Priest of Thebes.

SHESHONQ III

Egypt disintegrated and the monarchy was further weakened. The 22nd Dynasty ended in utter anarchy with the ephimerous reigns of Pami and Sheshonq V.

23rd DYNASTY - CIRCA 808-730 BC

PETUBASTIS

From Tanis, he began the 23rd Dynasty, which reigned parallel to the 22nd until 730.

OSORKON III

Renewed relationships with the Theban religious authorities, giving one of his daughters in marriage to the god Amun and instituting the function of the 'Divine Bride Votress of Amun', which was to become increasingly important later in Egyptian history.

PIANKHI

As his victory stele tells us, Piankhi set out from the Sudan to conduct a triumphal campaign throughout the land, annexing Upper Egypt to Nubia. He was the founder of the 25th or Nubian Dynasty.

24th DYNASTY - CIRCA 725-713 BC

TEFNAKHTE

Reconquered part of Lower Egypt and established the capital at Sais on the Delta. He allied himself with the bordering peoples to oppose the devastating expansion of the Assyrians.

BOCCHORIS

He made peace with the Assyrian king, paying him a tribute. At home, he persecuted the rich priestly caste and launched sweeping reforms to raise the poorer classes from their misery. The Greeks recorded him as a just and generous king.

THE LATE PERIOD
circa 713-343 BC

25th DYNASTY (NUBIAN) - 713-664 BC

SHABAKA

In 713 he conquered the entire Nile Valley and,

according to tradition, sent his predecessor Bocchoris to the stake.

SHABATAKA

This son of Piankhi succeeded in repressing a revolt led by Hezekiah, King of Judah.

TAHARQA

Took over power after having his nephew and predecessor, Shabataka, assassinated. Under his rule the Assyrian king Ashurbanipal conquered Lower Egypt and annexed it, together with Middle Egypt, as a single province of the Assyrian empire. Taharqa took refuge at Thebes.

TANUTAMUN

Last king of the Nubian Dynasty and son of Shabataka. When the Assyrians devastated and sacked Thebes in 661, the pharaoh fled to Napata.

26th "SAITIC" DYNASTY - 664-525 BC

PSAMTIK I

Conquered the Delta with the aid of the Assyrians and re-established the monarchy in Egypt with Sais as capital.

NECHO II

Dedicated his energies to the creation of a great fleet which probably succeeded in circumnavigating Africa, leaving from the Red Sea and returning to Egypt via Gibraltar after three years of navigation. He also undertook the construction of a canal in the isthmus of Suez to join the Red Sea to the Mediterranean.

PSAMTIK II

Led an expedition into Nubia against the King of Kush to reconquer the gold mines.

APRIES

Apries opened Egypt to the Jews who were fleeing after the sack of Jerusalem by Nebuchadnezzar. He sent an army to put down a Libyan uprising against the Greeks of Cyrene but it was defeated and the resulting revolt led to the election of General Amosis as sovereign.

AMOSIS

The city of Naucratis was founded during his enlightened and reforming reign.

PSAMTIK III

He clashed with Cambyses, king of the Persians, who defeated the Egyptian army at Pelusium. The pharaoh was captured and, after a last vain attempt at resistence, committed suicide. Egypt was then annexed to Persia.

27th DYNASTY
(FIRST PERSIAN OCCUPATION)

From 525 to 404 BC Egypt was under Persian domination: the kings on the throne were, in succession, Cambyses, Darius I, Xerxes, Artaxerxes, and Darius II.

28th DYNASTY - 404-399 BC

AMYRTAEUS

After a long revolt, Amyrtaeus took control of

the national Egyptian party, freed Egypt from Persian domination, and regained much of the country's power.

29th DYNASTY (MENDESIAN)

NEPHERITES I

As commander of the army, he seized power. He came from Mendes, one of the large Delta cities, from which the 29th Dynasty takes its name.

ACHORIS

Reconstituted the naval fleet and made alliances with Athens and Cyprus against Persia and Sparta.

NEPHERITIS II

Reigned for only a few months.

30th DYNASTY (SEBENNITE)
380-343 BC

NECTANEBO I

From the city of Sebennito, from which the 30th Dynasty takes its name.

TEOS

Son of Nectanebo I, he mobilized all the economic resources of the country and obtained great military victories, rapidly conquering Palestine, but a coup d'état removed him from the throne.

NECTANEBO II

In 350 he succeeded in driving back Artaxerxes III, but in 343 the Persians definitively conquered the land and the sovereign was forced to flee south. He was the last pharaoh in Egypt's millenary history.

SECOND PERSIAN OCCUPATION ·
341-333 BC

Artaxerxes II Ochus, Arses, and Darius III Codoman were the Persian sovereigns who succeed one other on the throne. In 332 BC Egypt was conquered by Alexander the Great. He was welcomed as a liberator and the legitimate successor of the pharaohs; he was received as the son of Ra by the oracle of Luxor. Alexandria, which he founded in 331, became the ideal capital and the economic and cultural centre of the entire ancient world. Alexander was succeeded by his half-brother Philip Arrhidaeus. When Philip was assassinated, Alexander Aegos, thought to be the son of Alexander and Rossana, ascended the throne.

LAGIDA OR PTOLEMAIC DYNASTY

With the return of absolute power, various members of the Ptolemaic dynasty rose to the throne as pharaohs, including Ptolemy I Soter, Ptolemy II Philadelphus, Ptolemy III Evergetes, Ptolemy IV Philopator, Ptolemy V Epiphanes, Ptolemy VI Philometer, Ptolemy VII Neos Philopator, Ptolemy VIII (Evergetes II), Ptolemy IX Soter II, and Ptolemy XI Neos Dionysos, as well as various queens named Cleopatra - including Cleopatra VII, the last queen of Egypt. At her death, when she committed suicide with Antony, Egypt became a Roman province.

1-AKHENATON
2-TUTHMOSIS IV
3-RAMESSES II
4 - KHUFU
5-TUTANKHAMEN
6-AMENHOTEP II
7-SESOSTRIS I
8-AMENHOTEP III
9-MENKAURE
10-DJOSER
11-SESOSTRIS III
12-SESOSTRIS I
13-TUTHMOSIS III

"The Valley of the Tombs of the Kings," wrote Howard Carter in the book in which he recounted the discovery of Tutankhamen's tomb, "the very name is full of romance, and of all Egypt's wonders there is none, I suppose, that makes a more instant appeal to the imagination. Here, in this lonely valley-head, remote from every sound of life, with the "Horn", the highest peak in the Theban hills, standing sentinel like a natural pyramid above them, lay thirty or more kings, among them the greatest Egypt ever knew."

The pyramid-shaped mountain dominating the Valley of the Kings is called al-Qurn ("the Horn") and is dedicated to the goddess Merseger, whose name means "she who loves the silence".

Left, the Valley of the Kings photographed in 1921: in the foreground on the right is the tomb of Tutankhamen, below the tomb of Ramesses VI.

The valley of Biban el-Muluk, the **Gate of the Kings**: in this celebrated ravine, dominated by a pyramid-shaped mountain often called the "Crown of Thebes," is the necropolis of the great Egyptian sovereigns of the 18th to the 20th Dynasty.

The story of the Valley of the Kings begins with the sudden and unexpected decision of Tuthmosis I to separate his tomb from his mortuary temple - and moreover to bury his body not in a showy monument but in a secret, inaccessible place. His resolution brusquely interrupted a tradition that had lasted all of 1700 years! His chief architect, Ineni, excavated a shaft tomb in a lonely ravine, cut a steep stairway into the rock, and at its bottom built the sepulchre; this plan was followed by all the later pharaohs. Ineni himself has provided us with documentation of the utmost secrecy of the undertaking, in a phrase he had carved into the wall of the mortuary chapel: "I alone oversaw the construction of the rupestral tomb of His Majesty. No one saw anything; no one heard." Actually this last statement is not particularly credible and it is probable that the few workers were quite capable of keeping the secret.

But the repose of Tuthmosis I, like that of most of the pharaohs, was of short duration for even during the period of the pharaohs, despite surveillance by teams of guards by day and night, systematic plundering of the tombs occurred, removing the precious tomb furnishings. One of the objects most coveted was the so-called "heart scarab," the amulet placed on the mummy over the heart to permit the deceased to save himself on the day of judgement, when his actions were weighed.

By a curious twist of fate, these powerful kings were des-

THE VALLEY OF THE KINGS

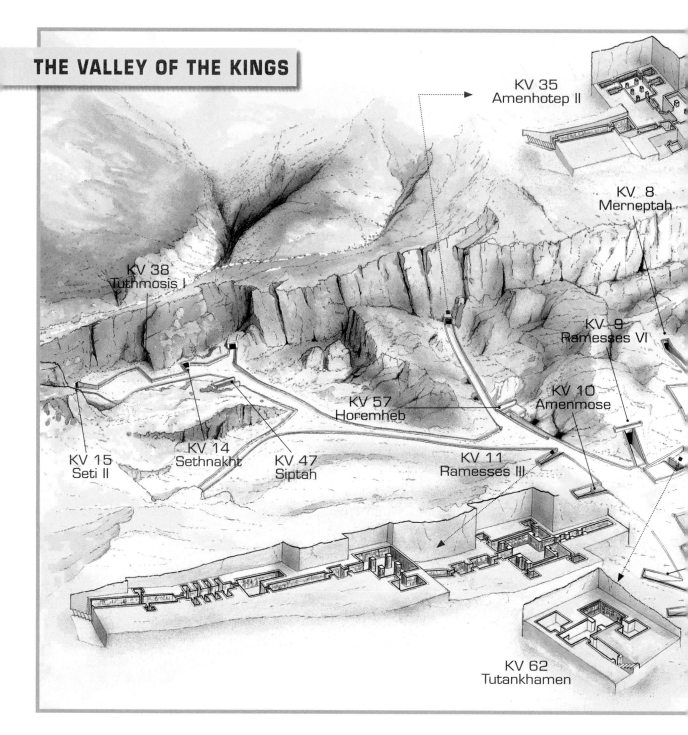

KV 35
Amenhotep II

KV 8
Merneptah

KV 38
Tuthmosis I

KV 9
Ramesses VI

KV 57
Horemheb

KV 10
Amenmose

KV 15
Seti II

KV 14
Sethnakht

KV 47
Siptah

KV 11
Ramesses III

KV 62
Tutankhamen

tined not to find peace even after death. During the weak reign of the Ramessides, the priests of Amun, once so powerful, lost all their authority. They nevertheless remained devoted to their deceased kings, and in order to ensure them an undisturbed afterlife and to avoid profanation of the tombs, began surreptitiously transporting the royal mummies from one burial site to another. These transferrals were so frequent that Ramesses III was buried all of three times! Finally, they decided to prepare a practically inaccessible secret hiding place: in the mountain of Deir el-Bahri, they had a shaft dug to a depth of about twelve metres. A long corridor led off from the bottom of the shaft into a spacious room. At night and in great secret,

with only a few torches to provide light, as stealthily as the tomb raiders themselves, the priests took the pharaohs from their sarcophagi in the Valley and laid them all to rest in this cave in the mountain, each with a name shield around the neck for identification.

Now, the greatest sovereigns in history lay all together, in no particular order, one beside another. Ahmose, the founder of the 18th Dynasty, lay beside the conqueror Tuthmosis III; the great Ramesses II close by his father Seti I. All in all, the bodies of the pharaohs which were to remain hidden in this anonymous tomb in the heart of the mountain for three thousand years numbered forty.

A young tomb robber named Ahmed Abd el-Rasul, from

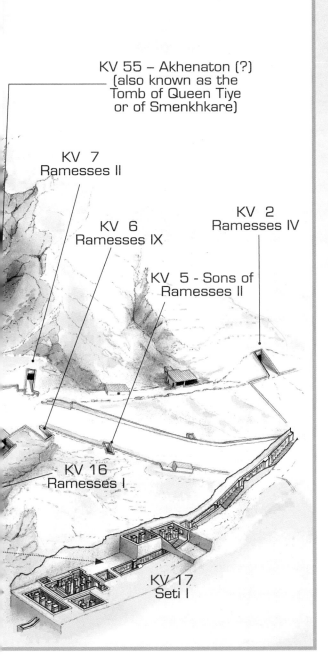

KV 55 – Akhenaton (?)
(also known as the
Tomb of Queen Tiye
or of Smenkhkare)

KV 7
Ramesses II

KV 6
Ramesses IX

KV 2
Ramesses IV

KV 5 - Sons of
Ramesses II

KV 16
Ramesses I

KV 17
Seti I

THE NUMBERING OF THE TOMBS

It is to John Gardner Wilkinson, one of the founders of Egyptology, that we owe the numbering of the tombs in the Valley of the Kings and the chronological cataloguing of the pharaohs who are buried there. In 1827, Wilkinson set out to number the tombs according to a simple but highly efficacious system: armed with a bucket of paint and a brush, he assigned a progressive number to each tomb by painting it on the entrance or on nearby rock. He began numbering with the tomb lowest down in the Valley (that of Ramesses VII, No. 1) and proceeded along the main path, numbering as he went on both the left and the right. By the time he reached the top of the Valley he had numbered 15 tombs.

He then descended again and began numbering those in the adjacent ravines. The known and numbered tombs are today 62, all bearing the abbreviation KV for King's Valley. But a great deal of the Valley has yet to be excavated.

the village of Qurna, discovered this hiding place by pure chance one day in 1875: for six years he and his brothers succeeded in keeping the secret, and became rich from trade in the objects they gradually stole from the royal mummies. Then the secret came out and on 5 July 1881, after lengthy questioning, the young Arab led Emil Brugsch, at the time deputy director of the Egyptian Museum of Cairo, to the entrance of the shaft. It is hard to imagine what the scholar must have felt when the flickering light of the torches illuminated the mortal remains of forty sovereigns of the ancient world! A few days later, the mummies were packed and carried down into the valley, where a ship was waiting

to take them to Cairo. What happened then was both strange and moving: on hearing that the pharaohs were leaving their centuries-old tomb, the peasants of the valley and their wives crowded along the banks of the Nile, and as the ship slowly passed they rendered homage to their ancient kings, the men firing guns in the air and the women keening laments and scattering dust on their heads and breasts.

The tombs are just as fascinating as ever: the countless graffiti on the walls mark the passage of travellers and pilgrims from Greek and Roman through modern times. One of these was the Englishman Dean Stanley, who in 1856 wrote a fine report of his journeys, remarking how seeing the tombs of the Kings was in his opinion tantamount to having seen all of Egyptian religion revealed as it appeared to the powerful of Egypt in the most salient moments of their lives.

The tombs are all more or less alike; each has an entrance cut into the rock wall, a sloping corridor about a hundred metres long opening onto niches and various rooms, the ceilings of which are supported by pillars, and the sarcophagus room at the end.

Today, the Valley of the Kings is served by a good road that, for much of its length, follows the route that the funeral procession must have taken.

THE DISCOVERY OF THE TOMB

At the time of Carter's excavations, the Valley of the Kings had already been searched from end to end. In the opinion of Theodore Davis, there were no further tombs to be found in the Valley of the Kings. But Carter did not agree and since 1917 he had examined the valley with a specific purpose: to find the tomb of Tutankhamen. Years passed, however, and the results of his research were discouraging: by 1922 Lord Carnarvon had already invested some £50,000 and he decided that this was to be the last expedition to Egypt. Carter was determined to excavate in a triangle of land that lay between the tombs of Ramesses II, Merneptah and Ramesses VI, convinced that there he would find the tomb of Tutankhamen. On the morning of 4 November 1922, almost at the base of the tomb of Ramesses VI a stone step came to light; it led to a second and then a third until altogether 12 were revealed and stopped before a plastered and sealed doorway. The seals were those of the royal necropolis, a hyena crouching over nine prisoners. Carter re-covered the steps and hurried to send a telegram announcing the discovery to Carnarvon: "At last have made wonderful discovery in valley; a magnificent tomb with seals intact; re-covered same for your arrival; congratulations." Carnarvon arrived in Luxor on 23 November with his daughter Evelyn and the next afternoon the excavations again started to completely free the access to the tomb. Carter experienced the greatest day of his life on the 26th of that month. As he wrote in his diary, "it was the most wonderful day of my life, indeed I will never live another like it." When he found a second door which had the seals of Tutankhamen still intact, he made a small hole in it and, on introducing an iron bar through this, it encountered only a void beyond. Carter then tested the air with a candle and found no presence of gases. Finally he put his head through the hole, and as his eyes gradually became used to the darkness, the flickering light of his candle revealed "...strange animals, statues and gold, everywhere the glitter of gold . . .".

"Wonderful things," Carter exclaimed, his voice full of emotion, in reply to the impatient Carnarvon behind who asked what he could see. The wonderful things were the magnificent mortuary furnishings, now considered one of the greatest treasures of antiquity found intact and today housed in the Egyptian museum of Cairo.

Portraits of Howard Carter (above left) and Lord Carnarvon, respectively discoverer of Tutankhamen's tomb and financier of this operation that involved much of the local population. Left, Tutankhamen's famous gold mask, found in the tomb.

The tomb of Tutankhamen was thus discovered on November 4 1922. Of all the precious items found in the sovereign's tomb the one that caused the greatest excitement was the great **sarcophagus**: a single enormous block of quartzite enclosed in four chests of gilded wood that fit one into the next. On 12 February 1924 a complex crane lifted the one and a half tons of granite that formed the cover. Inside was the first anthropoid sarcophagus, 2.25 metres in length, made of wood covered in gold leaf, inlaid with glass and semiprecious stones, showing the pharaoh as Osiris. This first

sarcophagus was opened a year later, on 25 January 1925: inside were more linen wrappings and garlands of flowers. Below the linen cloths was the second inner sarcophagus, again covered with gold leaf and decorated with glass paste inlay work and semiprecious stones. The third sarcophagus was a solid block of gold weighing 110.4 kilos. The king is figured wearing the headdress with the cobra and the vulture, a false beard, and a heavy necklace of gold and majolica beads, while in his hands he held the flagellum and the sceptre, symbols of the two Egyptian kingdoms. It is not difficult

to imagine the emotions of fear and reverence with which Carter must have approached the contents of this last coffin for he knew he would find intact the mummy of Tutankhamen. And the mummy appeared – completely covered with jewels and gold. Once more the delicate, serene features of the 19 year-old king were visible in the splendid gold funeral **mask**, inlaid with semi-precious stones, that covered the sovereign right down to the shoulders. Extremely elegant, the heavy blue-and-gold striped *nemes* with the royal symbols on the forehead is inlaid with lapis lazuli, turquoise, and cornelian.

Reconstruction of the tomb of Tutankhamen as it appeared to the early 20th-century discoverers; its magnificence almost entirely intact, it contained an incredible wealth of objects, many glistening with gold, some simply piled up in heaps, some still in the place where they were originally located when the tomb was closed.

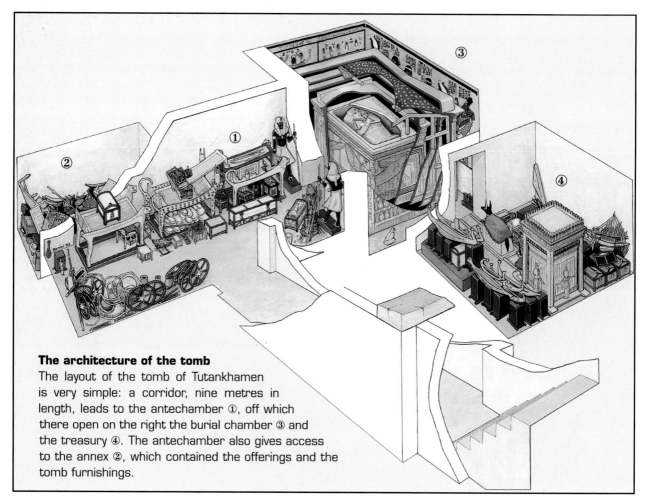

The architecture of the tomb
The layout of the tomb of Tutankhamen is very simple: a corridor, nine metres in length, leads to the antechamber ①, off which there open on the right the burial chamber ③ and the treasury ④. The antechamber also gives access to the annex ②, which contained the offerings and the tomb furnishings.

antechamber

The annex

The burial chamber

The Treasury

The Tomb of Ramesses VI

Known in antiquity as the Tomb of Memnon and also as La Tombe de la Métempsychose (Napoleonic expedition, 1798), the tomb of Ramesses VI was discovered by the Englishman James Burton. Like the other great Ramesside tombs, its entrance is set high, about 400 metres above the valley floor, exactly the contrary of the deeply-dug shaft tombs of the 18th Dynasty.

The front part is the oldest and was begun at the time of Ramesses V. The final, enlarged plan is quite linear, with a corridor leading to an antechamber, a pillared hall, a second corridor, and a second antechamber which precedes the *burial chamber*, where the ceiling is entirely decorated with astronomical scenes and the creation of the sun. A gigantic sky goddess Nut, portrayed twice, enfolds the western sphere. The tomb, in which many remains of workers' tools were found, was known and visited from oldest times as is evident from the many Greek and Coptic graffiti on the walls.

The burial chamber of Ramesses VI: the heavenly gods in the decoration of the astronomical ceiling and the god Thoth portrayed on a pilaster with the head of an ibis and crescent moon.

The Tomb of Ramesses IX

This unfortunately quite damaged tomb belongs to one of the last Ramessides of the 20th dynasty, whose reigns were marked by a long series of domestic disorders and by famine.

When it was opened, the tomb was found to contain an enormous pair of skids from the sledge on which the pharaoh's sacred boat was transported. Another interesting find consisted of several hundred shards on which the tomb labourers had recorded the number of tools, the hours of work,

Tomb of Ramesses IX: the pharaoh is shown twice, once with the crown of Upper Egypt and once with the crown of Lower Egypt.

the list of provisions, and so on. The tomb consists of a long staircase leading to a corridor that opens onto two rooms, one of which has four pillars, and a second smaller corridor that ends at the sarcophagus chamber.

Tomb of Ramesses IX: symbolic scenes with the scared scarab and the sun god Ra.

The Tomb of Ramesses III

Ramesses III was the second sovereign of the 20th Dynasty and was also the last great pharaoh of the Middle Kingdom. After him came a confusing period of internecine wars and disorders, and Egypt precipitated into chaos. Ramesses III initiated important administrative and social reforms. In the eighth year of his reign, he inflicted a heavy defeat on a coalition of the "Sea Peoples" and Libyan tribes; the great battle on the Delta is illustrated in the relief sculptures on the walls of the Temple of Medinet Habu, where Peleset prisoners, who later settled in Palestine and called themselves Philistines, are shown. In the 29th year of his reign, Ramesses III fell victim to a palace conspiracy, as we learn from a scroll known as the *Judicial Papyrus*, now in the Egyptian Museum of Turin, that documents the capture and judging of the guilty parties. The tomb is also known as "Bruce's Tomb," from the name of its discoverer, and as the "Harpists' Tomb," from the frescoes which show several men playing the harp in honour of the gods - a quite unusual subject in Egyptian art. The pharaoh's sarcophagus, a splendid block of pink granite, was removed from the tomb by the Paduan archaeologist Giovanni Battista Belzoni and later sold to the king of France, who exhibited it in the Louvre. The tomb measures 125 metres in length but lies only 10 metres below the level of the valley. Its present layout was inserted into the earlier tomb of Sethnakhte, Ramesses III's father, whose cartouches are still visible in the first corridor.

Tomb of Ramesses III: images of two Syrians with the characteristic pointed beard and a band around their hair.

149

The Tomb of Ramesses IV

The first tomb along the approach to the centre of the Valley is small (66 metres long), and contains the sarcophagus of Ramesses IV, sovereign of the 20th Dynasty and son of Ramesses III. The plan of the tomb appears on a papyrus in the Egyptian Museum of Turin. As early as the 5th century, it was used as a church by a small Christian community in the Valley. The plan of the tomb appears on a papyrus in the Egyptian Museum of Turin. The splendid decorations of the tomb are predominately texts, with scenes from the *Book of the Dead (Am-Tuat)*, the *Book of the Gates*, and the *Book of the Caverns*.

Left, the passage leading to the sarcophagus chamber in the tomb of Ramesses IV.

Below, the tomb of Horemheb: Ptah, the god of the Afterworld, shown as a mummy with the head enclosed in a cap.

The Tomb of Horemheb

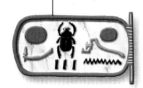

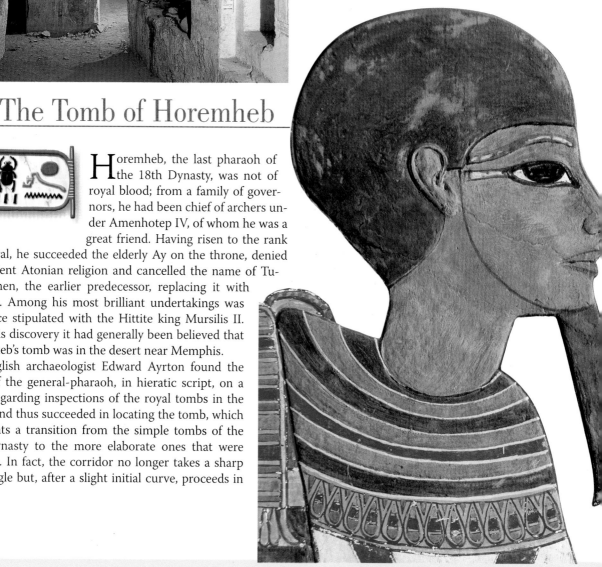

Horemheb, the last pharaoh of the 18th Dynasty, was not of royal blood; from a family of governors, he had been chief of archers under Amenhotep IV, of whom he was a great friend. Having risen to the rank of general, he succeeded the elderly Ay on the throne, denied the ancient Atonian religion and cancelled the name of Tutankhamen, the earlier predecessor, replacing it with his own. Among his most brilliant undertakings was the peace stipulated with the Hittite king Mursilis II. Until this discovery it had generally been believed that Horemheb's tomb was in the desert near Memphis.

The English archaeologist Edward Ayrton found the name of the general-pharaoh, in hieratic script, on a tablet regarding inspections of the royal tombs in the Valley, and thus succeeded in locating the tomb, which represents a transition from the simple tombs of the 18th Dynasty to the more elaborate ones that were to come. In fact, the corridor no longer takes a sharp right-angle but, after a slight initial curve, proceeds in

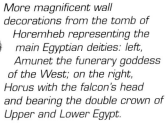

a practically straight line to the burial chamber. On discovery, the archaeologists found the *bas-reliefs* depicting the usual funeral repertory to be as brilliantly coloured and as perfect, fresh, and luminous as if they had just been painted.

More magnificent wall decorations from the tomb of Horemheb representing the main Egyptian deities: left, Amunet the funerary goddess of the West; on the right, Horus with the falcon's head and bearing the double crown of Upper and Lower Egypt.

The Tomb of Amenhotep II

This tomb, discovered by Victor Loret in 1898, is one of the most interesting in the Valley in terms of both architecture and decoration.

The burial chamber contains the great quartzite *sarcophagus*, which, when it was discovered, still contained the pharaoh's mummy, with a garland of mimosa flowers encircling

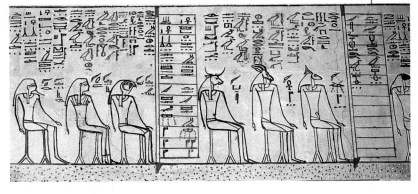

the neck. In an annex off the burial chamber, Loret found nine more sarcophagi, containing the mummies of the pharaohs Amenhotep III, Tuthmosis IV, Merneptah, Siptah, Seti II, Setnakht, Ramesses IV, Ramesses V, and Ramesses VI.

Above, a detail of the tomb decoration; left, the quartzite sarcophagus in which the mummy of the king was found.

AMENHOTEP II, THE ATHLETE-PHARAOH

Amenhotep II, born in Memphis, was the son of Tuthmosis III, the "Napoleon of Antiquity." Equaling the glory and power of such an illustrious father was no easy task, and in fact Amenhotep II is not famous for his great military exploits but rather for his qualities as a sportsman. The Great Stele of the Sphinx of Amenhotep II transmits a picture of him as a ruler "of triumphal vigour," unbeatable in archery with a bow that "no one could bend," an able horse-tamer, a fast runner, and a powerful oarsman, capable of manoeuvring an oar almost nine metres long at a speed greatly superior to that attained by any normal crew.

He also had a chance to prove his capabilities as a soldier when he was forced to quell revolts in a number of Asian cities. He was severe to the limits of cruelty, as we read in an inscription on a stele at Karnak that reports how Amenhotep II single-handedly broke the heads of seven princes with a mace during the Retenu revolt: the bodies of six were hung on the walls of the Temple of Karnak, while the seventh was carried as far as Napata in Nubia to discourage any thought of rebellion in that region.

According to the chronicles, Amenhotep II died at about 50 years of age.

The tomb of Ramesses I

The founder of the 19th Dynasty was a regular army officer, a general, and the vizier of Horemheb. His reign was very brief, barely two years, but in this period - as witnessed by the bas-reliefs in the hypostyle hall of Karnak - he advanced into Hittite territory "as far as the land of Kadesh." He immediately took his son Seti I as co-regent and chose Tanis as capital of the empire.

The structure of his tomb, discovered by Belzoni, is rather spare, since evidently the elderly pharaoh died suddenly while work was still in progress.

Below, Ramesses I between Horus on the left, and Anubis on the right. The cartouches of the pharaoh contain the last two names of his title: Ra-mes-su Men-pehety-ra.

The Tomb of Seti I

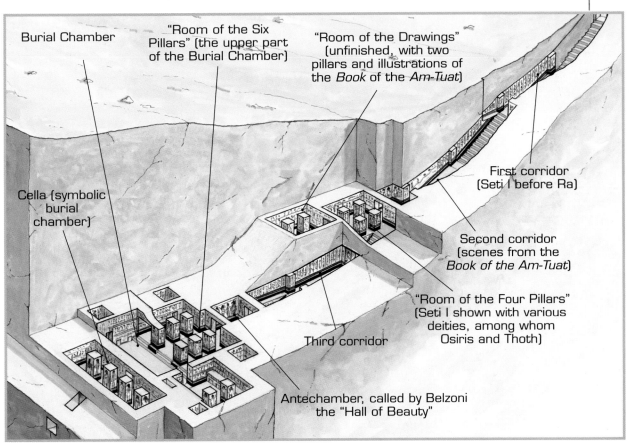

- Burial Chamber
- "Room of the Six Pillars" (the upper part of the Burial Chamber)
- "Room of the Drawings" (unfinished, with two pillars and illustrations of the *Book* of the *Am-Tuat*)
- First corridor (Seti I before Ra)
- Cella (symbolic burial chamber)
- Second corridor (scenes from the *Book of the Am-Tuat*)
- "Room of the Four Pillars" (Seti I shown with various deities, among whom Osiris and Thoth)
- Third corridor
- Antechamber, called by Belzoni the "Hall of Beauty"

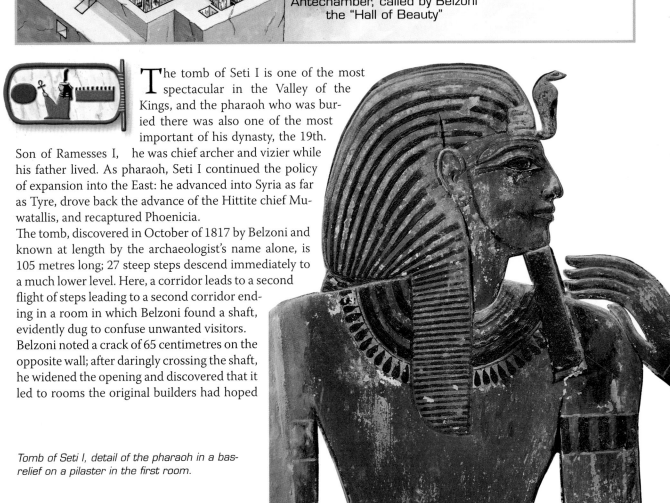

The tomb of Seti I is one of the most spectacular in the Valley of the Kings, and the pharaoh who was buried there was also one of the most important of his dynasty, the 19th. Son of Ramesses I, he was chief archer and vizier while his father lived. As pharaoh, Seti I continued the policy of expansion into the East: he advanced into Syria as far as Tyre, drove back the advance of the Hittite chief Muwatallis, and recaptured Phoenicia.

The tomb, discovered in October of 1817 by Belzoni and known at length by the archaeologist's name alone, is 105 metres long; 27 steep steps descend immediately to a much lower level. Here, a corridor leads to a second flight of steps leading to a second corridor ending in a room in which Belzoni found a shaft, evidently dug to confuse unwanted visitors. Belzoni noted a crack of 65 centimetres on the opposite wall; after daringly crossing the shaft, he widened the opening and discovered that it led to rooms the original builders had hoped

Tomb of Seti I, detail of the pharaoh in a bas-relief on a pilaster in the first room.

to keep hidden. Even so, none of these contained the sarcophagus: as it turned out, Belzoni was only halfway there. More corridors, more staircases, and more rooms finally led him to the sarcophagus chamber - but not the mummy, which was discovered only seventy years later, in Deir el-Bahri, while the lovely sarcophagus is today part of the Soane Collection in London. Apparently, however, the tomb was supposed to go even deeper into the heart of the earth. Belzoni began exploring a mysterious gallery that starts under the sarcophagus, but after about ninety metres the lack of air and the friability of the rock forced him to stop. Belzoni thought this was the finest tomb ever discovered in Egypt; the walls, columns, and ceilings are in fact literally covered with painted and bas-relief decoration full of meaning and symbolism.

Tomb of Seti I: above left, an image of the gods in the lake of fire; in the centre and below, two details of the decoration showing the procession of sacred boats: the serpent surrounds and protects the tabernacle on the boat carrying the god Ra with the head of a ram.

The Tomb of Tuthmosis III

About 10 metres above the valley floor, a steep metal stairway leads us to the tomb of the pharaoh rightly known as the "Napoleon of Antiquity". Illegitimate son of Tuthmosis II, on the death of his father he became pharaoh at a very early age but was deposed by his aunt and step-mother, Hatshepsut, wife of the deceased pharaoh, who proclaimed herself regent. Tuthmosis III only succeeded in regaining the throne on the death of his aunt, and indulged in his own belated vendetta by erasing the name, the cartouches, and the images of the hated queen from all the monuments in Egypt and replacing it with his own and his father's names. Under his rule the country enjoyed one of its most glorious moments: with seventeen military campaigns in Asia, Egypt reached the height of its power. During the eighth campaign, Tuthmosis

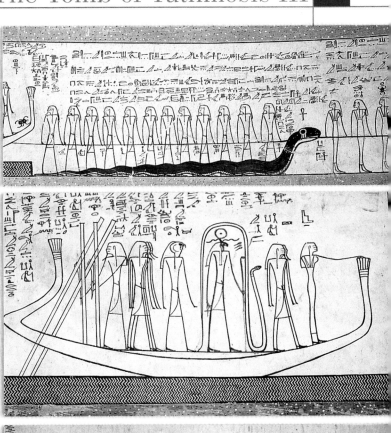

Right, three drawings of the texts engraved on the walls of the room, illustrating scenes from the Book of Am-Duat, *the journey of the Sun through the Afterworld. In the centre, note in particular the boat of the god Khnum carrying the spirits of earlier kings, who protect the pharaoh on his journey in the Afterworld.*

set out by sea to reach Phoenicia and then crossed Syria carrying the boats he had made in Byblos over the desert. His victories have remained famous: Kadesh, Megiddo, (where he defeated 330 Syrian princes), Karkhemish where he crossed the Euphrates and defeated the Mitanni on their own territory. At this time the Egyptian empire also included the "islands of the great circle", Crete, Cyprus and the Ciclades. About 1450, just before the end of his reign, Tuthmosis III pushed as far as the fourth cataract of the Nile, thus extending the borders of Egypt from the Euphrates to Napata in Nubia, now known as Gebel Barkal.

His tomb, excavated at the bottom of a mountain ravine at the southern end of the valley, has a simple structure and its most interesting feature is the *decoration* illustrating scenes of the journey of the sun through the world of the dead, executed in an almost surrealistic graphic style.

The Tomb of Ay

Beyond Deir el-Bahri, at the most western end of the Valley of the Kings, is the tomb of Ay. It is known that there are four tombs in this area, but only two of these are accessible. Ay's tomb has remained unfinished, but the *decorations* of the *burial chamber* are particularly fine.

The interior of the tomb of Ay with the sarcophagus (below) and details of the wall paintings illustrating scenes from the Book of Am-Duat (above) and the pharaoh shown with the gods (centre).

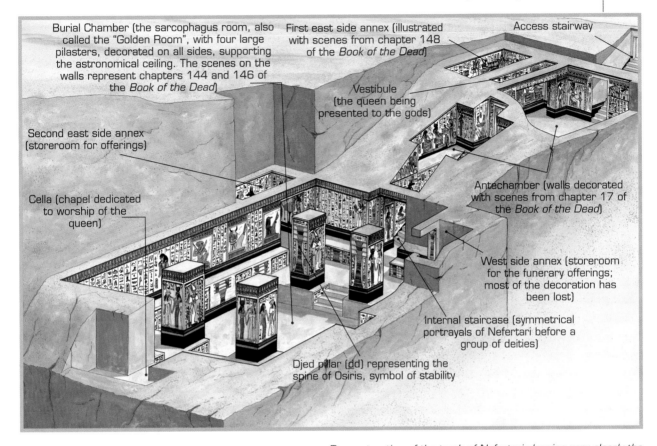

Burial Chamber (the sarcophagus room, also called the "Golden Room", with four large pilasters, decorated on all sides, supporting the astronomical ceiling. The scenes on the walls represent chapters 144 and 146 of the *Book of the Dead*)

First east side annex (illustrated with scenes from chapter 148 of the *Book of the Dead*)

Access stairway

Vestibule (the queen being presented to the gods)

Second east side annex (storeroom for offerings)

Antechamber (walls decorated with scenes from chapter 17 of the *Book of the Dead*)

Cella (chapel dedicated to worship of the queen)

West side annex (storeroom for the funerary offerings; most of the decoration has been lost)

Internal staircase (symmetrical portrayals of Nefertari before a group of deities)

Djed pillar (dd) representing the spine of Osiris, symbol of stability

Reconstruction of the tomb of Nefertari showing very clearly the structure and the magnificence of the decorations. Below, the serpent with a red crown, representing the goddess Wadjet.

This tomb, discovered in 1904 by the Italian Archaeological Expedition lead by Ernesto Schiaparelli, Director of the Egyptian Museum of Turin, was dug into the west flank of the valley for Nefertari, Meri-en-Mut, wife of Ramesses II and without doubt the best-loved of the many wives of this great pharaoh, who built the architectural jewel of the Small Temple of Abu Simbel for her.

The tomb is 27.5 metres long and lies about eight metres below ground level: since the layer of rock into which it is dug is particularly friable, the walls were bonded with such a thick layer of plaster that their pictorial decoration seems to be in relief. When the tomb was discovered, it was immediately apparent that it had been violated from early times: all the tomb furnishings had disappeared and the mummy of the woman who had been one of the most famous queens of Egypt was nothing but miserable remains. Only the splendid **paintings** survived to bear witness to the fact that this tomb was in its time the most important and loveliest of the entire Valley of the Queens. These depictions have provided us with much information about the complex religious world and the spiritual beliefs of the New Kingdom Egyptians.

In 1986, an agreement between the Egyptian Antiquities Service and the Getty Conservation Institute launched a project for systematic recovery of the tomb. An international team began studying the various problem areas, and it was discovered that rock salt, the major component of which is sodium chloride, was the agent mainly responsible for the damage to the tomb.

Restoration work began in 1988. The first step was to apply Japanese paper to stabilize the fragments of detached plaster and prevent them from falling; then and only then was it possible to remove the dust (using dentist's tools), reinforce the plaster and inject a special compound to fill the cracks, and finally smooth over the points of conjunction with fresh plaster. After cleaning with another special product applied with cotton swabs, the colours regained their original brilliance - so perfect were they that there was found to be no need for any retouching. Work was concluded in April 1992, but for the following three years the tomb was kept under observation by experts, until approval was given for reopening to the public in November 1995.

Tomb of Nefertari: right, Nefertari and Isis portrayed on the first pilaster of the sarcophagus room; further right, three details of the decorations showing, from above, the gods Ra-Harakti and Hathor seated; Ra with the ram's head between Isis and Nephthys, and below, the goddess Selket. Below, the winged goddess Maat. Opposite page, the beautiful face of Queen Nefertari.

The Tomb of Amen-hir-Khopshef

This tomb was originally built to contain the remains of another prince and son of Ramesses III, and only later became that of Amen-hir-Khopshef. Extremely simple in structure - a staircase leads to a square room and a corridor, which in turn leads to the *burial chamber* - the tomb is characterized by *decoration* in lively, intense colours; an unusual shade of turquoise predominates throughout.

The decoration of the *first room* shows the pharaoh presenting his young son to various divinities: Thoth, Ptah, and the four sons of Horus (Hapi, Imset, Duamuttef and Qebesenuf). The quartet, after having participated with Anubis in the mummification rites of Osiris, became the protectors of the canopic jars.

Tomb of Amen-hir-Khopshef: right, a detail of the god Horus, with a falcon's head; below, Ramesses III is embraced by Isis and prince Amen-hir-Khopshef is shown with a shaved head and a plait tied on one side only of the head as were all young Egyptian males.

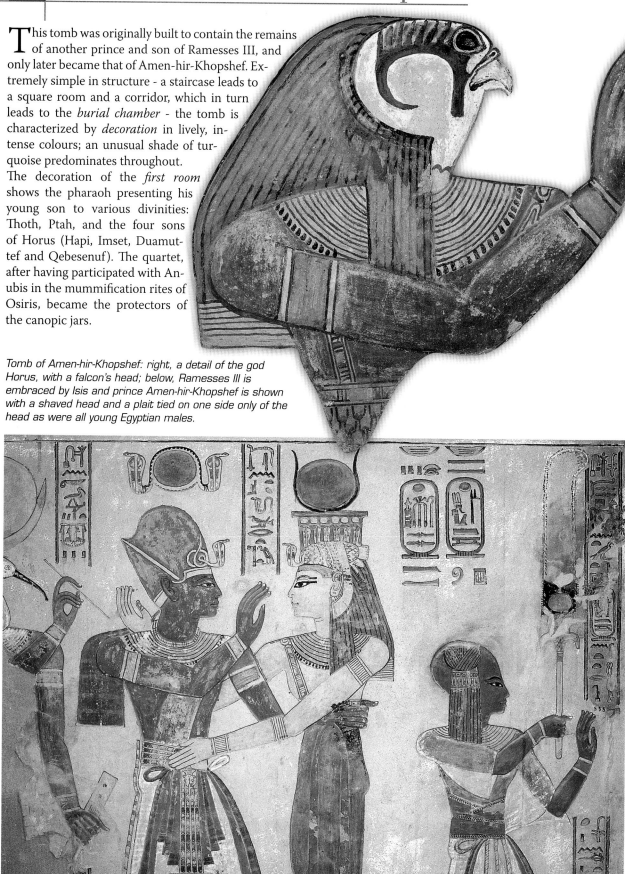

The Tomb of Queen Tyti

Tyti was the wife of one of the numerous Ramesses of the 20th Dynasty, perhaps Ramesses IV. Her long-abandoned tomb, which had even been used as a stable for donkeys, is, however, in quite good condition and is distinguished by its interesting limestone *relief decoration* dominated by a light rose colour.

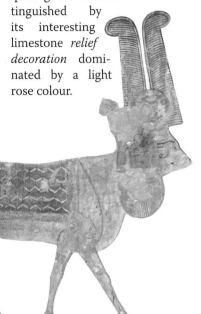

Tomb of queen Tyti: left, the goddess Hathor represented as a cow and, above, the tomb with partially ruined walls.

The Tomb of Prince Para'hirwenemef

Para'hirwenemef was another of the sons of Ramesses III, who died very young and who, like his brothers, was buried in this valley. The decoration of this tomb is quite similar to that of the others of its kind and here too the deceased prince is shown being presented to the various gods by his father. The predominant colours here, however, are yellow ochre and pink.

Tomb of Para'hirwenemef: some of the guardians who, according to the Book of the Dead, watched over the doors of Am-Duat. One is seen full-face, another, known as Sobek, has the head of a crocodile, while a third is shown as a vulture.

The Tomb of Kha'emweset

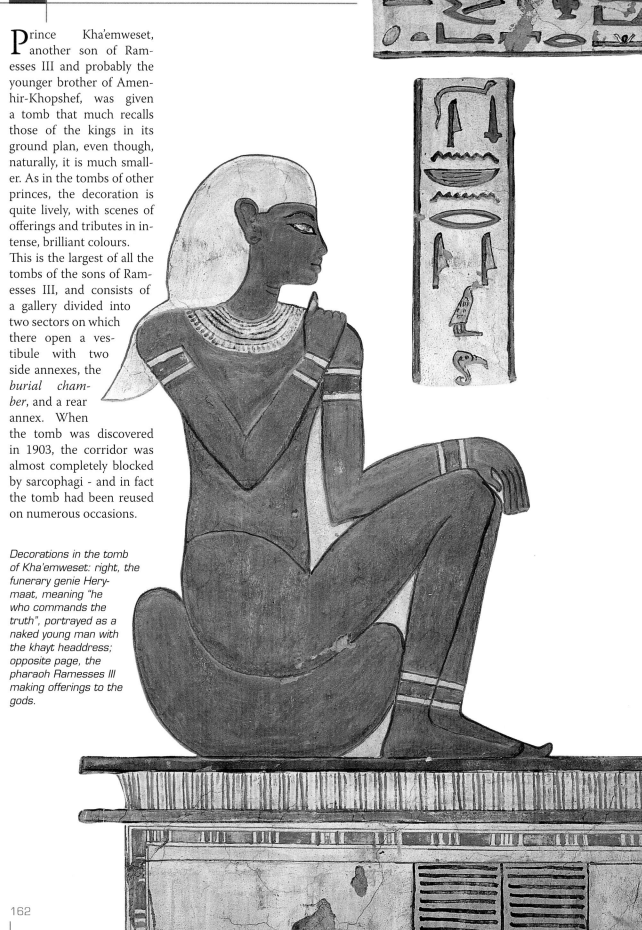

Prince Kha'emweset, another son of Ramesses III and probably the younger brother of Amenhir-Khopshef, was given a tomb that much recalls those of the kings in its ground plan, even though, naturally, it is much smaller. As in the tombs of other princes, the decoration is quite lively, with scenes of offerings and tributes in intense, brilliant colours. This is the largest of all the tombs of the sons of Ramesses III, and consists of a gallery divided into two sectors on which there open a vestibule with two side annexes, the *burial chamber*, and a rear annex. When the tomb was discovered in 1903, the corridor was almost completely blocked by sarcophagi - and in fact the tomb had been reused on numerous occasions.

Decorations in the tomb of Kha'emweset: right, the funerary genie Herymaat, meaning "he who commands the truth", portrayed as a naked young man with the khayt headdress; opposite page, the pharaoh Ramesses III making offerings to the gods.

Medinet Habu

For a long time, Medinet Habu was considered nothing more than a rich quarry where large ready-dressed stones could be found. In Christian times, a village rose and occupied most of the temple area - which the Copts called the *Mound of Djeme* - and, for once, this new use actually helped to preserve many remains which otherwise would have been lost.

Excavations have brought to light the traces of an entire city around the pharaoh's palace, but only one home has been found: that of an overseer of the necropolis.

The monumental complex of Medinet Habu includes the *Temple of Ramesses III*, preceded by the *shrine of Tuthmosis I* and the *chapels* of the adoring divinities of Amun. Formidable, almost military in appearance, is the fine *Southern Gate*, set between two towers, known as the Royal Pavilion above

Above, the façade of the temple with its impressive pylon; right, an internal wall of the pylon.
Opposite page, below, the Guards' Gate and the impressive High Gate or Royal Pavilion, with battle scenes and prisoners offered to the gods. The monumental architecture of the temple entrance was inspired by Syrian fortified towns.

The temple of Medinet Habu from the *Histoire de l'Art dans l'Antiquité* by Perrot and Chipiez, 1882. Paris, Bibliothèque des Arts Décoratifs.

Granite statues inside the temple of Ramesses III portraying the pharaoh with the god Thoth.

which open two rows of longitudinal windows. The martial aspect of this construction is further emphasized by the bas-reliefs on the walls of the towers: exemplary massacres of prisoners, the pharaoh leading captured enemies to the god Amon, and so on.

From the point of view of style, the **Temple of Ramesses III** is one of the most perfect buildings in all Egyptian art. A *pylon* 63 metres wide, decorated with scenes of war, leads to a *first court* with a gallery of Osiris pillars on the east side. Other pylons and other courts lead to the *last hypostyle hall*, dominated by a *statuary group* of Ramesses III with the god Thoth. But not all the decorations in the temple of Medinet Habu are military in character: in an architrave, for example, the goddess Nekhbet is shown as a vulture protecting Upper Egypt and, symbolically, the grandiose temple complex.

North Gate

Sanctuary

Hypostyle hall

Osiris Suite

Ramesses III Court

Second pylon

First pylon

High Gate
(Royal Pavilion)

Crenulated
enclosure
walls

Outer
enclosure
walls

Guard rooms

The Valley of the Artisans
The workmen's village

Arial view of the Workmen's Village. The necropolis lay on the hill to the west of the houses. Pa-demi, meaning "the town", was the name given to the village used by the Egyptians.

A few kilometres south of Sheikh Abd al-Qurna, on the west bank of the Nile and still within the area of the Thebes necropolis opposite the city of Luxor, is the valley now known as Deir el-Medina ("the Monastery of the Town" in Arabic), after a monastery that stood here during the Coptic period.

Located here are the remains of a *village* that developed at the time of Amenhotep I where the workers who built and decorated the royal tombs of Thebes lived. This activity existed in the valley for five centuries from 1550 to 1000 BC, and the craftsmen who lived here were stone cutters, masons, painters, and sculptors, who every morning travelled the steep path over the harsh hills around Deir el-Bahri to the royal necropolis. The children and the women instead stayed at the village, where they cultivated wheat and barley. The workers laboured at the royal necropolis eight hours a day for nine consecutive days, and on the tenth - the day of rest - they decorated their own tombs. The teams of artisans (called Servants of the Place of Truth) were directed by several overseers and were divided into two groups: those who worked on the right walls and those who worked on the left. As adepts of the royal tombs, these workers were considered "holders of secrets" and therefore subject to live in a village surrounded by walls.

The houses were small and very simple: built one next to the other, in mud brick, whitewashed inside. Generally, they consisted of a tiny entrance, a reception room, a second room, and the kitchen.

The house was entered from the street and, sometimes passing through a small chamber, the first room, lower than street level, contained the closed bed made of mud brick and beaten earth, where the man of the house slept on a mat wrapped in a linen sheet.

Next was the women's room where the wife and oth women of the family worked and rested on simple ma The wife probably slept on the divan.

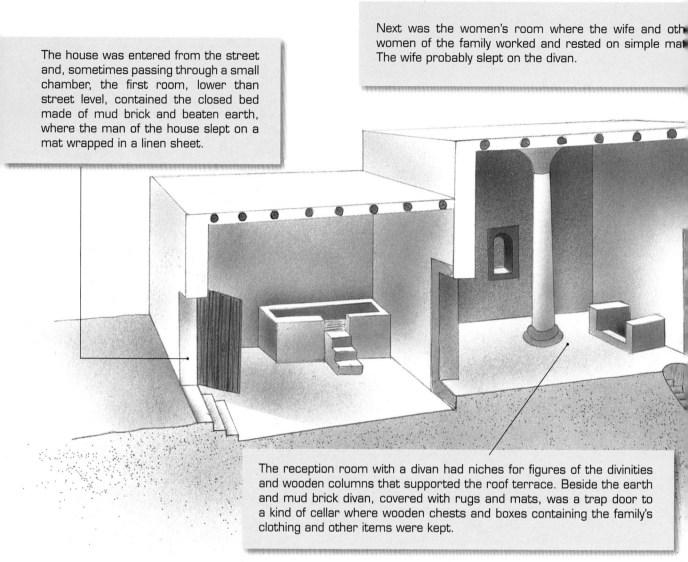

The reception room with a divan had niches for figures of the divinities and wooden columns that supported the roof terrace. Beside the earth and mud brick divan, covered with rugs and mats, was a trap door to a kind of cellar where wooden chests and boxes containing the family's clothing and other items were kept.

A TYPICAL WORKER'S HOUSE

The workers' village of Deir el-Medina provides an excellent opportunity to appreciate the daily life of its inhabitants during the New Kingdom, a rather rare event due to the infrequent and difficult identification of towns and villages in ancient Egypt. One of the features of this village, inhabited for over four centuries by some 700 people (from an initial group of 250 inhabitants) is that the structure of each house was preserved intact from one generation to another and the ground level remained unchanged. The 68 houses rested on a solid base without any foundations and were built of rough stone to a height of about 2.5 metres and then mud bricks up to the roof. The roofs were always flat serving the double function of a covering as well as a terrace for those who sought cool air on the hot summer nights. The floors of the rooms were beaten earth and only a few were plastered and perhaps painted red or white. Stone steps lead to the cellar and the terrace; there were no toilets, but portable wooden seats and bowls were used instead. The houses are all almost completely identical in size, layout and number of rooms: the first room, whitewashed and with a wooden entrance door, lead to the second, situated on the opposite side. This room, slightly below the level of the street, usually had a bed, made of mud bricks and filled with sand and silt from the Nile, in the corner with steps in front. This was followed by a larger reception room, also whitewashed and with a divan. There was often a cellar beneath this room for clothing and household items. A small room where the women of the family worked and rested, sleeping on simple mattresses, came next. There was also a kitchen and sometimes a small room where food and bread were prepared. The ceiling was made of tree branches or palms to facilitate ventilation and there was a series of store rooms or corridors while stairs lead to the terrace and cellar which was used to store food and sometimes contained a square bin for the grain.

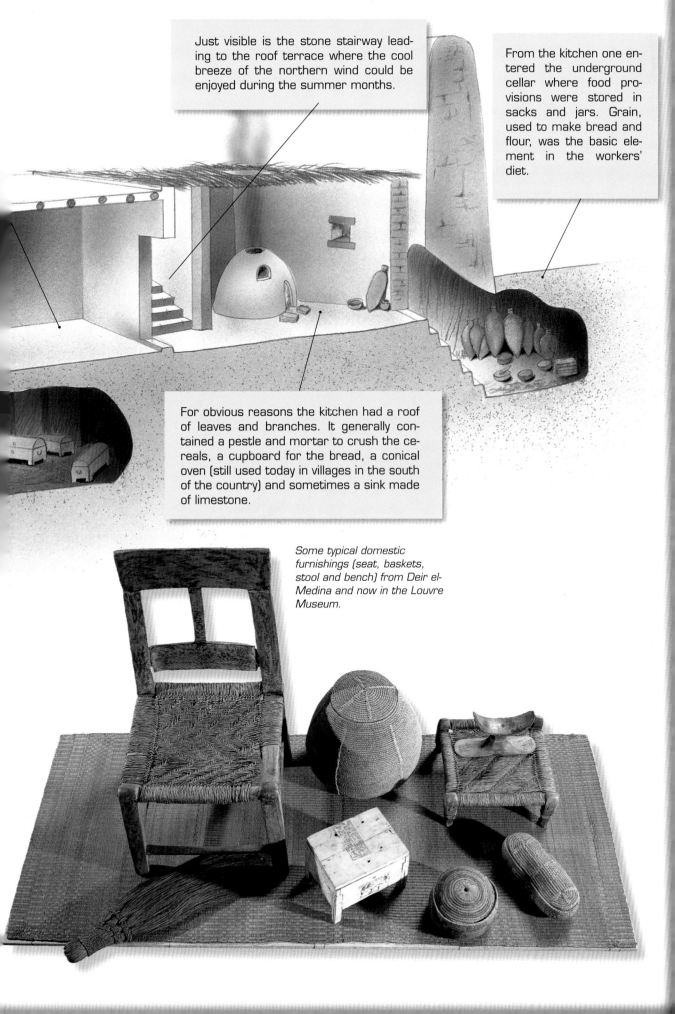

Just visible is the stone stairway leading to the roof terrace where the cool breeze of the northern wind could be enjoyed during the summer months.

From the kitchen one entered the underground cellar where food provisions were stored in sacks and jars. Grain, used to make bread and flour, was the basic element in the workers' diet.

For obvious reasons the kitchen had a roof of leaves and branches. It generally contained a pestle and mortar to crush the cereals, a cupboard for the bread, a conical oven (still used today in villages in the south of the country) and sometimes a sink made of limestone.

Some typical domestic furnishings (seat, baskets, stool and bench) from Deir el-Medina and now in the Louvre Museum.

The Tomb of Peshedu

This tomb, from the Ramesside era, is located high up in the central sector of the necropolis. A steep staircase leads to the subterranean apartment, in which an unadorned antechamber precedes the *burial chamber*, with its mudbrick walls covered with stucco and painted with tempera. Peshedu is shown with his wife Nediem-behedet and his sons, and is referred to as a Servant of the Place of Truth; that is, a simple construction worker at the royal necropolis. As an older man, Peshedu was perhaps promoted to the level of foreman.

Only recently opened to visitors, the tomb is of interest not only for the lively, brilliant colours of its wall *decorations*, but also for the spiritual and religious significance of the verses of the *Book of the Dead (Am-Tuat)* they contain.

Tomb of Peshedu: below, the parents of Peshedu, Menna and Huy, followed by Nefersekheru a colleague and probably a friend of Peshedu; right, a detail of the north wall with Nubnofre, a daughter of Peshedu, portrayed naked and with the characteristic children's hairstyle, standing at her father's feet in adoration. Opposite page, Peshedu kneeling beneath a dum palm tree and drinking the water of the Nile. The hieroglyphic text behind him is chapter 62 of the Book of the Dead *with the formula for drinking water in the Afterworld.*

The Tomb of Sennedjem

In the vivacity and freshness of its decoration, the tomb of Sennedjem, Servant of the Place of Truth and an official of the necropolis in the 19th Dynasty, is perhaps the finest to be found here. All that remains of it is the main burial chamber though this is almost perfectly intact; the furnishings that it held are now on exhibit in the Egyptian Museum of Cairo.

Detail of the painting showing Lyneferti, wife of Sennedjem. On her head is a cone of solid perfume made from fragrant creams that melted in the heat releasing a pleasant perfume that also imbued the hair and clothes.
The lotus flower in the hair of Sennedjem's wife was another widespread custom much used for banquets and ceremonial occasions.

Under Ramesses III and Ramesses IV, Anherkhe held the office of Chief of the Team of the Lord of the Two Lands in the Place of Truth; he was, in other words, a foreman, entrusted with coordinating the work of the labourers under his direction. He had two tombs built for himself, but only the one lower down the slope, closer to the village, has lively, imaginative decoration.

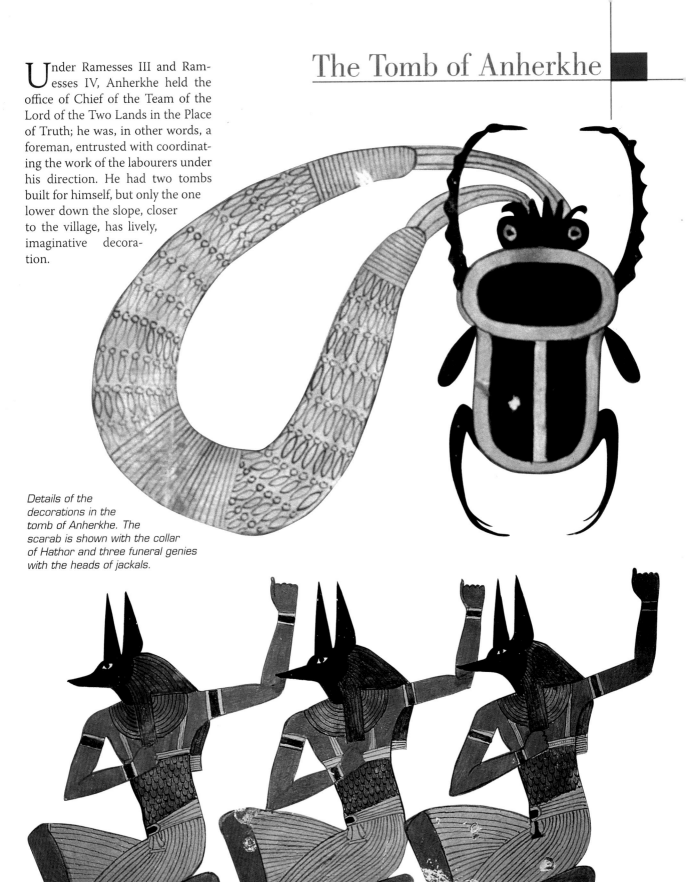

Details of the decorations in the tomb of Anherkhe. The scarab is shown with the collar of Hathor and three funeral genies with the heads of jackals.

The Tomb of Ipy

Ipy, a sculptor under Ramesses II, had his tomb decorated with unusual and curious scenes: even if the style is rather sketchy, the wealth of detail (for example, the oculist putting drops into the eyes of a patient) is such as to make this one of the best-known tombs in the necropolis.

A painting on a pilaster in the tomb of Ipy shows a fishing scene with a net cast from a light papyrus boat.

The Temple of Deir el-Medina

The Small Temple at Deir el-Medina, dedicated to the deities of the necropolis, Hathor and Ma'at, was begun by Ptolemy IV Philopator and completed under Euergetes II. Later occupied by Christian monks, the temple has survived complete with its enclosing walls and storehouses. On the rear wall, decorated near the top with seven masks of Hathor, are three chapels with beautiful ornamental reliefs.

The plain façade of the Ptolomaic temple and (opposite page, below) the temple in a drawing by David Roberts.

DEIR EL-MEDINA
AND HISTORY'S FIRST STRIKE

What we might call the first workers' strike in history occurred during the twenty-ninth year of the reign of Ramesses III. The craftsmen of Deir el-Medina involved in the construction and decoration of the tombs in the Valley of the Kings received salaries that consisted of sacks of grain (for bread) and of barley (for beer), though they also occasionally received fish, vegetables, oils and clothes. When, however, they had received no payment for a long time, they quite simply lay down their tools and went to the Temple of Tuthmosis III, where they complained to the Vizier, "We have come here driven by hunger and thirst. We have no clothes; we have neither oil nor fish nor grain …". The Vizier offered his guarantee that the pharaoh's promises would be fulfilled and convinced the labourers to take up work again. Not long afterwards, payments were again suspended.

The workers went out on strike again, but this time they occupied the Mortuary Temple of Ramesses III where they prevented the rituals taking place until their rations were provided.

Above, the "papyrus of the strike", Turin, Egyptian Museum.

The Valley of the Nobles
The Tomb of Sennufer

Compared with the tombs of the pharaohs, those of the high dignitaries of the Middle Kingdom dynasties are architecturally extremely simple and all have the same layout. They are preceded by an open-air terrace, followed by a vestibule with painted walls illustrating the terrestrial occupations of the owner. A corridor leads to a niche where a statue of the deceased, sometimes together with those of his wife or relatives, is often found. The paintings in these tombs are characterized by freshness and vivacity and an unusual realism, and bear witness to the life at court in ancient Egypt. The most frequent subjects are funeral banquets with music and dancing, work in the fields, crafts activities, and scenes of daily life in general.

A flight of 43 steps cut into the rock takes us into the lovely tomb of Sennufer, prince of the Southern City (Thebes) and Superintendent of the Granaries and Livestock of Amun under Amenhotep II.
The anonymous painter of this tomb decorated the ceiling with a marvellous pergola of purple grapes.

Two details of the tomb where Sennufer appears with his wife Senetnefer, a "royal wet-nurse", and their daughter Mutahi who is portrayed in miniature, as is normal, between the legs of her father during a banquet.

The Tomb of Rekhmire

This tomb, which structurally could be taken as an example of a Theban civilian tomb of the 18th Dynasty, belonged to Rekhmire, Viceroy and Governor of Thebes and vizier under Tuthmosis III and Amenhotep II. Both the vestibule and the chapel are decorated and the paintings are of immense historical interest since they provide many invaluable illustrations, in a great number of scenes, of Egypt's relations with other countries at the time. The liveliest depictions are those in which representatives of foreign countries bring their offerings: the emissaries of the land of Punt (probably Somalia), carrying ebony, ivory, and ostrich feathers, are clearly identifiable; likewise those of the land of Kefti (perhaps Crete) with their curly hair and long braids on their breasts. Then there are the black Africans of Kush, dressed in panther skins, who bring a jaguar, a giraffe, and monkeys, and the ambassadors of the land of Retenu (Syrians and Assyrians), who lead two horses, a bear, and an elephant.

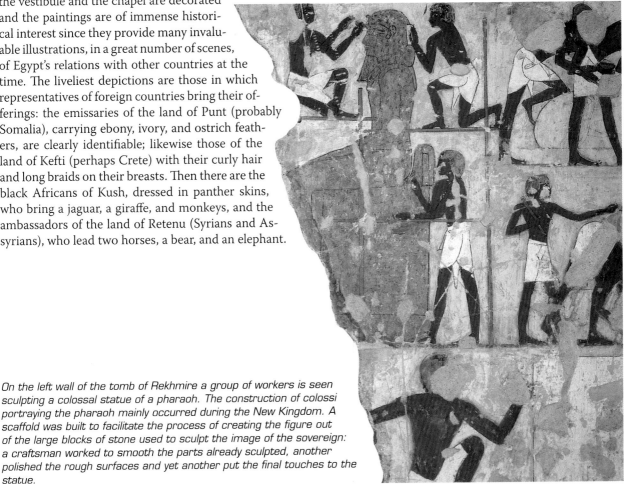

On the left wall of the tomb of Rekhmire a group of workers is seen sculpting a colossal statue of a pharaoh. The construction of colossi portraying the pharaoh mainly occurred during the New Kingdom. A scaffold was built to facilitate the process of creating the figure out of the large blocks of stone used to sculpt the image of the sovereign: a craftsman worked to smooth the parts already sculpted, another polished the rough surfaces and yet another put the final touches to the statue.

The Tomb of Userhat

Userhat, a royal scribe under Amenhotep II, had his tomb built and decorated with *paintings* which are still extraordinarily well preserved today. The unusual scene of a barber shaving his customer in a garden is famous.

THE BARBER

"The barber shaves until night-time ... he goes from street to street looking for someone to shave..."
A most popular figure, the barber worked in the street. His tools were a small stool on which the customer sat and a container with the razor, a simple blade of flint with a wooden handle which in time developed until it was made in bronze.
The wealthy and the nobility had their own private barbers who had a wide range of razors, blades and scissors.
From the earliest of times Egyptian men shaved and cut their hair, while foreigners had beards as indeed had the pharaoh, of course, though his beard was false.

The Tomb of Khaemhet

Khaemhet, also known as Mahu, was a royal scribe and inspector of the granaries of Upper and Lower Egypt under Amenhotep III. His tomb, decorated with fine bas-reliefs, is at the end of a court surrounded by other tombs of the same period. In the niche of the burial chamber, dug deep into the rock, are statues of the deceased and his relations, divided into three groups.

Rather poorly preserved, these statues of Khaemhet and his relation Imhotep, a royal scribe, are located in a niche in the first large room of the tomb.

The Tomb of Neferhabef

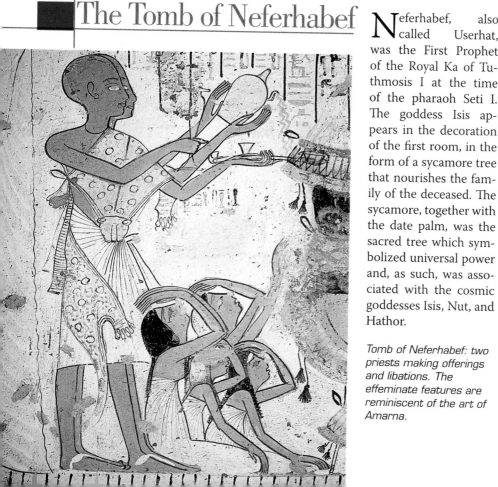

Neferhabef, also called Userhat, was the First Prophet of the Royal Ka of Tuthmosis I at the time of the pharaoh Seti I. The goddess Isis appears in the decoration of the first room, in the form of a sycamore tree that nourishes the family of the deceased. The sycamore, together with the date palm, was the sacred tree which symbolized universal power and, as such, was associated with the cosmic goddesses Isis, Nut, and Hathor.

Tomb of Neferhabef: two priests making offerings and libations. The effeminate features are reminiscent of the art of Amarna.

THE SCRIBE

If we are today in a position to know, at least partly, many aspects of the Egyptians and their world we should be grateful for the skill and learning of generations of scribes who wrote texts on numerous papyruses, tombs or monuments telling us who these people were, how they were organised, how they lived and what they believed in.

The unusual Egyptian way of thinking gave enormous importance to words and it was believed necessary to write the word on any kind of material so that it would become reality and the object or concept represented by it would come to exist in the fullest sense. The simple fact that being able to read the text gave life to the words; thus if it were a threat, it would be carried out, if a prayer, it would be answered, if it were the story of the life of the deceased the text would perpetuate his name and actions for eternity and help ensure his survival in the afterlife. Given such beliefs, it was therefore inevitable that the scribes enjoyed a special status and had a foremost position in Egyptian society as they controlled reading and writing. Moreover, the bureaucratic organization of the Egyptian state of necessity depended on the professionalism of the scribes who recorded on papyrus the administrative documents necessary for the efficient running of the country.

The tomb of Ramose, Governor of Thebes and vizier under Amenhotep III and later Akhenaton, is a splendid example of the delicate moment of transition in Egyptian art toward the new Amarna style.

The tomb was never finished, since during its construction the capital was moved from Thebes to Amarna, but the *decoration* that has remained - mostly bas-relief - is nevertheless sufficient to illustrate the refined lifestyle of Ramose and his wife.

One of the most striking works is the scene of the newlyweds at table, dressed in light linen tunics and wearing heavy wigs arranged in ringlets. Like other everyday objects, the wig also evolved through history: from simple and straight in the Old Kingdom, it became more elaborate and voluminous with time.

The Tomb of Ramose

The hypostyle hall is the only decorated room in the tomb. The famous scene of Ramose's funeral procession is on the south side and provides a perfect description of the grandeur and fine details of the ceremony. Particularly dramatic is the group of professional mourners, their hair loose in a sign of mourning and the arms raised as they weep and wail in grief for the death of Ramose. Always present at funeral ceremonies, the professional weepers were paid with various gifts and food to lament the deceased.

HAIRDRESSERS AND WIGS

The Egyptians paid great attention to their physical appearance and both men and women completed their toilette with hair styles and wigs that helped to emphasise their clothes and jewels. Numerous images painted on tombs and papyrus and full relief statues have provided us with a wide range permitting the classification of fashions and trends of the various historic periods. The Egyptians of the Old Kingdom did not always wear wigs; many had completely shaven heads while others had short hair. Before entering the temple, priests had to shave their heads and entire body as part of the purification process. Wigs of various styles and shapes were widely, if not universally, used during the Middle and New Kingdoms.

The Tomb of Nakht

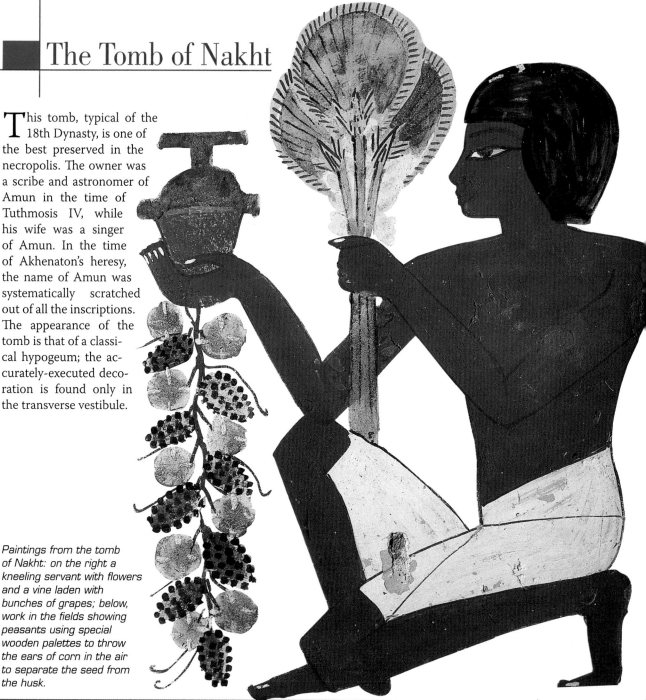

This tomb, typical of the 18th Dynasty, is one of the best preserved in the necropolis. The owner was a scribe and astronomer of Amun in the time of Tuthmosis IV, while his wife was a singer of Amun. In the time of Akhenaton's heresy, the name of Amun was systematically scratched out of all the inscriptions. The appearance of the tomb is that of a classical hypogeum; the accurately-executed decoration is found only in the transverse vestibule.

Paintings from the tomb of Nakht: on the right a kneeling servant with flowers and a vine laden with bunches of grapes; below, work in the fields showing peasants using special wooden palettes to throw the ears of corn in the air to separate the seed from the husk.

FARMING

Farming was the basis of the ancient Egyptian economy and the basis of farming was the annual flooding of the river Nile which for centuries determined its rhythms. As the river ebbed back, it left behind a thick layer of mud which enabled the Egyptians to have two harvests a year. The sovereign owned large extensions of land which were measured and controlled by the scribes and land-surveyors, while the peasants had small gardens and plots. The peasant was entitled to part of the harvest and used this to make bread and beer. A quantity was also stored as reserve in case of famine and as seed for the next year.

PLOUGHING

When the flood waters of the Nile

The owner of this tomb was Menna, scribe of the Land Registry under Tuthmosis IV. To create it, he requisitioned - and enlarged - an earlier tomb. The brilliant paintings that embellish its walls with detailed, lively scenes are generally considered to be among the most elegant in the whole necropolis and depict scenes of hunting and farming.

The Tomb of Menna

Tomb of Menna: two young girls dressed in light linen tunics. The first carries a jar of perfume and a bunch of flowers.

Below, Menna hunting in the marshes, shown with his daughter seated between his legs.

withdrew the land began to be prepared. The peasant used a plough to work the ground, manually driven by the poor or drawn by a pair of cows or oxen yoked together. The ploughshare consisted of a simple wooden blade to break up the soil, but if the surface was particularly hard, the peasant would have to use a hoe made from a piece of wood bound by cord to a longer shaft.

SOWING

Once the ground had been prepared, sowing could take place. The person who sowed could be in front of or beside the oxen. Sometimes flocks of sheep or goats were used to press the soil back down, burying the seed, though sometimes the peasants themselves used tools to ensure it was covered.

HARVEST

At last harvest time arrived and the entire family participated happily and joyously entertained by songs specifically composed and performed to celebrate such an important moment in the life and economy of ancient Egypt. The entire process of harvesting was carefully watched and checked by the royal scribes.

The Tomb of Nebamun and Ipuky

This tomb was prepared for two sculptors, both active under Amenhotep III and Amenhotep IV. Nebamun was Chief Sculptor of the Master of the Two Lands; Ipuky was Sculptor of the Master of the Two Lands. Known also as the tomb of the engravers, its interesting decoration shows much about how the artisans of ancient Egypt worked.

Tomb of Nebamun and Ipuky: the deceased were purified before being entombed; standing before the mummies of the two men is the widow Henutnofret who had married both the sculptors.

The Tomb of Kiki

The tomb of Kiki, "Superintendent of the Animals in the Temple of Amun", was long abandoned and even used as stables.

Its decoration is brilliant and lively in both subject matter and execution. An entire wall is dedicated to scenes of the journey of the dead to Abydos.

All Egyptians were required to make a pilgrimage to the temple of this sacred city, dedicated entirely to the worship of Osiris, at least once in their lifetimes. Traditionally, Abydos was the sanctuary where the head of Osiris was preserved, and the greatest wish of all religious Egyptians was to have a mortuary chapel there - or at the very least a commemorative stele.

Tomb of Kiki: detail of the boat and canopy with the mummy of the deceased.

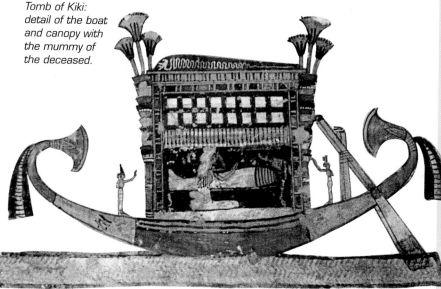

FUNERALS

Although events of great pain and sadness, the funerals of ancient Egypt were also quite dramatic as family members wailed and gesticulated without embarrassment during the entire funeral procession. Beginning in the New Kingdom, papyrus containing collections of funerary rites have been found deposited in tombs and often in the sarcophagus. These were precise rituals named the *Book of the Dead* by the scholar Richard Lepsius in 1842, while the Egyptian title was "Formulae for going out to the day", meaning for being born again in the life beyond earth. The sarcophagus was first placed on a boat drawn by oxen and was then covered by a catafalque from which hung curtains of embroidered cloth. The procession was accompanied by hired mourners, their faces stained with mud and dust. Their cries and wailing were intended to drive off forces hostile to the deceased. They were followed by numerous priests whose task was to keep at bay evil influences. Next was the cart with the chest (often decorated with the hyena figure Anubis) containing the four canopic vases that held the entrails of the deceased and the casket with the funerary statues called "*ushabti*" or "*shuebeti*".

The Tomb of Kheruef Sena'a

Kheruef Sena'a was the "Superintendent of the Great Royal Bride"; who was named Tiye, a Syrian princess famous for her beauty, the beloved wife of Amenhotep III and mother of Akhenaton, the heretic pharaoh.

The tomb the intendant had built is vast but unfinished. The western part of the court, with its depiction of Amenhotep III's Jubilee celebration (*Heb Sed*), is a true masterpiece.

MUSIC AND DANCE

Music in ancient Egypt had extremely ancient roots; Bes was the god of music and dance and Thoth was the inventor of music as well as the writer of songs dedicated to the gods. Music did not accompany only religious ceremonies, but also feasts, popular festivals, and special events such as births and funerals, as well as work, for music was played during the harvests and grape pressing. Until the New Kingdom, music probably took the form of voices accompanied by percussion although it is known that the Egyptians also had instruments such as the sistrum, tambourines, flutes and harps. During the 18th Dynasty musicians discovered more instruments such as cithara, lyres and pipes and groups of female musicians replaced male players. Music was played at the court of the pharaoh too, and both singers and musicians had a privileged position. Dance was just as much appreciated as music by the Egyptians and dancing took place at feasts, but also during religious ceremonies, processions and funeral banquets. Dancing was in groups or pairs, though always of the same sex and usually women.

The exquisite bas-reliefs in the tomb of Kheruef Sena'a illustrate young women conversing and dancing. It is interesting to see the characteristic costume of the dancers, consisting of a short skirt with braces crossed and tied in front, permitting the greatest freedom of movement. The dance shown in this tomb was performed to celebrate the jubilee of Amenhotep III.

Deir el-Bahri
The valley of the Goddess Hathor

A view of the monuments of Deir el-Bahri. The cult of the goddess Hathor was practiced in this temple as is evident from the Hathor capitals (left), portraying the head of the goddess with the ears of a cow, surmounted by a sistrum. The style of the column is also called after Hathor and the sistrum.

One thousand two hundred years after Imhotep, another architect, Senmut, appeared on the scene of Egyptian history and created another architectural masterpiece. Queen Hatshepsut, more a patron of the arts than a military leader, ordered a funerary monument for her father Tuthmosis I and for herself and chose an impervious valley already consecrated to the goddess Hathor who, in the form of a heifer, received the deceased in the Afterworld. Queen Hatshepsut's monument was in later times abandoned; at one point in history it became a Christian convent called the Convent of the North, and this fact not only gave the area its present name of Deir el-Bahri but also protected the Pharaonic temple from further destruction.

The famous architect and minister Senmut brilliantly exploited the dramatic fan of ochre-coloured rock that stretches out behind the monument, which was built according to a new and revolutionary concept.

The east-facing **Temple of Hatshepsut**, called in antiquity *Djeser-djeseru*, "more splendid than splendid," is unique in Egyptian architecture. It consisted of a series of vast *terraces* which, via ramps, led up to the sanctuary. An avenue of sphinxes and obelisks led up to the *first terrace*, closed at the back by a portico of 22 pillars and flanked by two Osiris pillars, from which another ramp led to the *second terrace*, also equipped with a portico of two rows of square pillars. On one of the walls, beautiful *bas-reliefs* narrate the stories of the queen's birth and childhood and of the expedition sent by her to the mysterious land of Punt, most probably today's Somalia, to judge from the giraffes, monkeys, panther skins, and ivory objects that are shown.

On the last wall, 18 niches, large and small, must have held just as many statues of the queen in standing and seated poses. Also located in the temple is the *16-faceted pillar* so admired for its elegance by Champollion that he called it "proto-Doric."

Although the **tomb of Senmut** is about 15 metres from the east corner of the first terrace, he was not buried here but at Sheikh Abd el-Qurna.

187

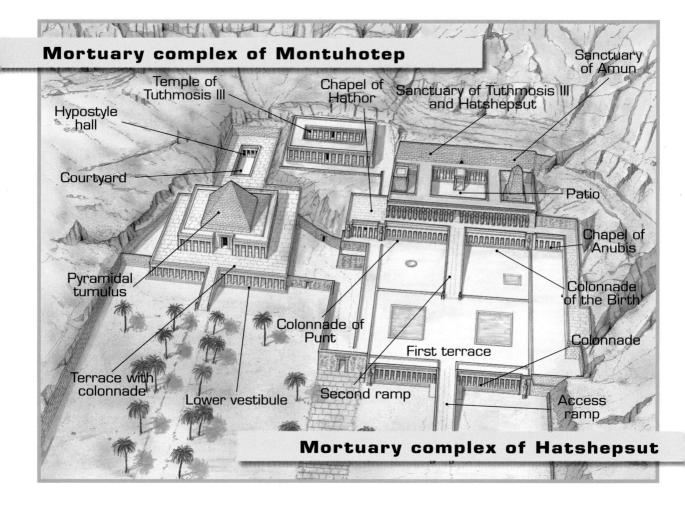

Mortuary complex of Montuhotep

Sanctuary of Amun

Temple of Tuthmosis III

Chapel of Hathor

Sanctuary of Tuthmosis III and Hatshepsut

Hypostyle hall

Courtyard

Patio

Chapel of Anubis

Pyramidal tumulus

Colonnade 'of the Birth'

Colonnade of Punt

First terrace

Colonnade

Terrace with colonnade

Lower vestibule

Second ramp

Access ramp

Mortuary complex of Hatshepsut

The entire left side of the valley was occupied by the gigantic **mortuary Temple of Montuhotep I** built five hundred years before Hatshepsut decided to install hers in the same place. In the main, the tomb reflects the architectural canons typical of the Middle Kingdom, but in many respects also heralds New Kingdom tomb structure. The monumental complex consists of a gigantic *tomb* with a *pyramidal tumulus*, at the centre of which was the king's sepulchre.

The **Temple of Tuthmosis III**, now completely in ruins, later stood between this and the top terrace of Hatshepsut's temple.

Left, a view of the temple showing the characteristic sixteen-sided pillars, also known as early Doric.
Right, a detail of an Osiris pilaster in which Hatshepsut is portrayed with a beard, a traditional masculine attribute of regal dignity.

Hatshepsut, she who would be King

At the time of Tuthmosis I's death, the issue regarding the succession at court was quite complex. Since the two eldest sons had died, the legitimate heir to the throne was the third son, Tuthmosis II, who was made to marry his half-sister Hatshepsut, the eldest daughter of Tuthmosis I and Queen Ahmose-Nofretari. The couple reigned jointly for a few years. Tuthmosis II died prematurely, leaving as heir an illegitimate son by a concubine, also named Tuthmosis and nominated legitimate heir by his father, who certainly guessed at the ambitious designs of his half-sister and wife. The future Tuthmosis III was still a child when Hatshepsut, his step-mother and aunt, assumed the post of regent. Hatshepsut was an intelligent woman of uncommon ability, with a keen political sense. She was also attractive, and ambitious: she wanted to be king, not a mere queen, and thus desired divine legitimation. Accordingly, she appealed to Theban religion and clergy and orchestrated a public statement of legitimacy: the god Amun, in the likeness of the pharaoh Tuthmosis I, would have lain with Queen Ahmose and fathered Hatshepsut, who was therefore by divine right the "daughter of the king, sister of the king, wife of the god, and the Great Royal Wife". At this point Hatshepsut began to assume masculine characteristics: she adopted royal protocol, wore men's clothing and the postiche beard, and suppressed the feminine endings of her names. "Pharaoh Hatshepsut" also began dedicating her time to architecture and to an expanding commercial policy, which culminated in the expedition to the Land of Punt.

Montuhotep II and the Courtier Meket-Ra

The 11th Dynasty, of which Montuhotep was the fourth ruler, brought to an end the long and tormented First Intermediate Period, which was marked by power struggles and social strife. During his fifty-year reign, Montuhotep II, partly thanks to the support of the Egyptian bourgeoisie, re-established control over Lower Egypt, freeing the land of the dangerous local governors or nomarchs who had drained power during the preceding period. Montuhotep, whose name means Montu is Satisfied, (Montu was the Theban god of war), conducted a considerable amount of military activity, at least in the first years of his reign. Meket-Ra was the pharaoh's Grand Superintendent and Governor of the Six Great Tribunals; it was his wish that when he died he be entombed not with golden objects but with twenty-four wooden models representing that which he had possessed during his life: the carpenter's workshop, the weavers' shop, the bakery, the beer factory, the scene of the livestock count, in which Meket-Ra himself is shown sitting under a portico with four scribes beside him. As the end of his reign drew near, Montuhotep had his mortuary temple built on the same plain at Deir el-Bahri that many years later was to also be chosen by Hatshepsut. The magnificent painted grey sandstone statue of the seated Montuhotep (above), wearing the Red Crown and the short white tunic of the Jubilee, was found here. The pharaoh's face, hands, and legs are coloured black in order that he might resemble Osiris more closely.

The Ramesseum

The name *Ramesseum* was given in the 19th century to the temple complex which Ramesses II had built by the architect Penre between the desert and the village of Qurna. Diodorus Siculus was highly impressed by its complexity and the architectural grandeur of the monument. Today, sadly, it is only a few ruins: the pillars with the *statues* of the pharaoh in the semblance of Osiris (and therefore known as Osiris pillars) on the façade of the *hypostyle hall* and, like a toppled giant, what is left of the syenite statue of the seated Ramesses II enthroned. It is calculated that it must have been 17 metres tall and weighed more than 1,000 tons.

The decorations of the temple once more repeat the pharaoh's exploits in stopping the Hittite advance. But there are also scenes of the festivals held the first month of summer in honour of Min, the prehistoric god of fertility, to whom the pharaoh sacrificed a white bull.

Above, a view of the Ramesseum with the four Osiris columns of the vestibule on the façade of the hypostyle hall. Only the columns of the central rows in the hall still remain, altogether twenty-nine of the original forty-eight. Part of the ceiling decorated with gold stars on a blue background still also exists. Right, the head of the colossal figure of Ramesses II.

To build his "temple of a million years" Ramesses II quite happily removed stones and decorative elements from the temple of Hatshepsut at Deir el-Bahri. On the other hand, years later, Ramesses III took useful building material from the Ramesseum to build his own temple at Medinet Habu.

When David Roberts painted the Ramesseum the statue of Ramesses lay broken on the ground. François Champollion said of this temple that it was "perhaps the most noble and pure of all found at Thebes".

In the traditional dedicatory engraving of the temple, Ramesses II affirmed that he had built "...this grand hall with great columns like flowers...". The hypostyle hall of the Ramesseum was similar in form to that of Karnak, with higher columns in the central aisle that those of the side aisles.

The Ramesseum was not only the "temple of a million years" of Ramesses II, it was also the administrative centre of the sovereign's lands and an active cultural point of reference for theologians and scholars alike.

Another interesting and unusual decoration is on one wall of the hypostyle hall: the sons and daughters of Ramesses, in a double row, are lined up in order of succession and of birth. Merneptah, who was to succeed Ramesses II on the Egyptian throne, is in thirteenth place.

Painted in the 19th century by a fascinated Hector Horeau, this romantic view of the Ramesseum shows its extraordinary and sophisticated magnificence.

193

The mortuary temple of Seti

Consecrated to the god Amun, the temple was begun by Seti I and completed by Seti's son Ramesses II, who was also responsible for the sumptuous decoration. Although, unfortunately, the temple has been partially destroyed, the beauty of its bas-reliefs is on a par with Abydos.

The vestibule still contains nine of the ten original bundled papyrus *columns* with closed capitals. In the *hypostyle hall* instead there remain six, with bas-reliefs of the two pharaohs bearing offerings to Amun. The *chapels* on the far side of the hall are decorated with *bas-reliefs* of Seti and his ka, Thoth, and Osiris; the *sanctuary* that housed the sacred boat is likewise beautifully decorated.

Although this ancient temple is now sadly much ruined, it is still possible to imagine its past splendour and how fascinating and majestic its beauty must have been from the exquisite decoration and sophisticated detail that amaze visitors today just as much as those of the 19th century, such as Karl Lepsius who made the charming drawing reproduced above of the temple of Seti I in November 1844. Between 1842 and 1845 this German scholar, an enthusiast of Egypt and its history, was the leader of a large expedition encouraged and supported by the king of Prussia. Like Champollion, who published the *Monuments d'Egypte et de Nubie,* when Lepsius returned from this mission he published the twelve-volume *Denkmäler aus Aegypten und Aethiopien.*

Below, engravings decorating one of the walls of the internal court with a sun altar in the centre. Below, left, detail of the temple vestibule (opposite page, below, general view of the façade), showing a bundled papyrus column with a closed capital, and on the right, fine engravings on pilasters in the temple with ritual scenes of veneration and offerings to the gods.

The colossi of Memnon

The **southern colossus** is considerably damaged but is in slightly better shape than the other and legend recounts how in 27 BC a terrible earthquake seriously damaged almost all the monuments of Thebes also opening an enormous crack on the colossus from the top halfway to the ground before it toppled over. It was subsequently noted that every morning, at sunrise, the statue emitted a prolonged, indistinct sound, which to some travellers seemed like a sad but harmonious song. Great historians such as Strabo, Pausanias, Tacitus, Lucian, and Philostratus corroborated the fact - and the Greek poets soon turned it into a fine legend.

The "singing stone," they said, was Memnon, the mythical son of Aurora and Tithonus. Sent by his father to aid Troy, besieged by the Greek army, Memnon covered himself with glory, killing Antilochus, son of Nestor, in battle, but in turn he fell under the vengeful hand of Achilles. Aurora appealed in tears to Jupiter to have her son resuscitated at least once a day. Thus, every morning, as Aurora caresses her son with her rays, he answers his inconsolable mother with protracted lamentations.

Despite the legend, the phenomenon can be scientifically explained. The sounds were caused by vibrations produced on the broken surfaces by the brusque passage from the cold of the night to the warmth of the first rays of the sun.

Over the course of the centuries, the legs of the colossus have accumulated engraved epigrams and other, sometimes quite curious, inscriptions.

Seated colossi of the pharaoh

Access pylon to the mortuary Temple of Amenhotep III

Statue of Mutemuya, mother of the pharaoh

Royal symbols

In the vast plain that stretches between the Nile and the Valley of the Kings, are the remains of the monumental road which led to the mortuary Temple of Amenhotep III. The temple, unfortunately, has disappeared - what remains is commonly known as the Colossi of Memnon.

These two gigantic statues (20 metres high, their feet alone measuring two metres in length and 1 metre thick), cut in monolithic blocks of sandstone, represent the pharaoh seated on a throne, with his hands resting on his knees.

The amazing majesty of the colossi of Memnon in views that illustrate how they appear today and how David Roberts saw them surrounded by the flood waters of the Nile.

One of the spectacular composite capitals in the hypostyle hall of the temple of Esna.

The area between Luxor and Aswan is known as the Valley of the Upper Nile. The last evidence of the ancient Egyptian culture, dating to the Ptolemaic period and gradually blending with the Greek, Roman, and Coptic civilizations, is found in these 200 kilometres. Not only the architecture, represented by the three temples of Esna, Edfu, and Kom Omb, is of interest however. The landscape too is quite striking as the broad loops of the ever-present Nile wind through the desert and an undulating green ribbon comprised of flourishing vegetation and farmlands extends on either side. Crafts and trade flourished here, particularly at Esna, which 19th-century travellers already defined as offering "more luxury and a more refined industry than any other city in Upper Egypt".

Echoes of its prosperous past are still to be found in Esna which is situated about 64 km. south of Luxor, on the left bank of the Nile where farmlands jut out into the surrounding desert. Capital of the 3rd *nome* of Upper Egypt, the Greeks called it *Latopolis* for this was where the sacred fish Lato was worshipped, with a special cult of its own and of which many mummified examples have been found. Esna lay at the end of the caravan route from the Sudan: after a 40-day trip the camels arrived here, bearing precious elephant tusks, brightly coloured ostrich feathers, the famous gum arabic, from Sennar to Egypt. For a long time the resulting trade in exotic goods was a source of income for Esna. But the town's real prosperity lay in the so-called "white gold", cotton, with the entire population of the neighbouring villages participating in the harvest between October and November.

Esna is still an agricultural and rural town: travellers landing here from one of the many cruise crafts that ply the Nile are struck first of all by the peace and quiet that reign on the boulevard that flanks the river, lined with eucalyptus trees and sycamores. The market is a stone's throw away - all one has to do is follow the continuous low hum to its source. The products for sale are those found elsewhere in the region: cotton, painted baskets made of woven palm fronds, terracotta. The way to the **temple of Esna** leads through the streets where the market is held. Dedicated to Khnum, the ram-headed god who modelled human beings on his potter's wheel

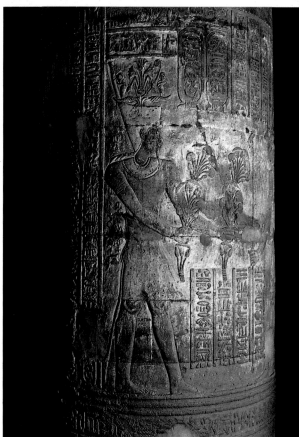

Top, an overall view of the theatrical hypostyle hall of the temple at Esna dedicated to the god Khnum and, above, a detail of one of the gigantic columns.

(and is therefore the patron of potters), this Ptolemaic temple was built in the second century BC by Ptolemy VI Philometor and by Euergetes II on the remains of an earlier 18th-Dynasty sanctuary. Originally it must have been similar in structure to the temples of Edfu and Dendera with a precinct wall around the sanctuary, the sacred lake, and the secondary chapels. All that remains today is the *hypostyle hall*, a forest of 24 columns, over thirteen metres high, with composite tetralobe capitals, all different, and low decorated screen walls between the first six columns. This hall (33m. x 16.5m.) was built in the 1st century AD by the Roman emperors Tiberius, Claudius and Vespasian, and now constitutes the façade of the temple. The *decoration of the ceiling* is particularly interesting, with the signs of the zodiac and astronomical scenes. The columns, on the other hand, present the *calendar of the three most important festivals* celebrated at Esna. These numerous well-preserved texts have permitted scholars to reconstruct the religious life and magic rites which were held in Esna before the advent of Christianity: on the north wall, for example, the magical ritual by which the pharaoh and the gods captured the enemies of Egypt in their nets, together with fish and birds is shown. Another unusual feature of this temple is that one must go below street level to reach it, for the hypostyle hall stands in a dip some nine metres below ground level. The explanation lies in the fact that with its flourishing market, Esna was continuously inhabited, first by the Egyptians, followed by the Copts and then the Arabs. When the houses that crowded around the temple fell into ruin, they were rebuilt directly on the remains of the previous structures until the level of the dwellings was higher than that of the temple. There was so much rubble in the court that Napoleon's soldiers could easily scratch their names on the tops of the columns. The temple was thereafter transformed into a granary and then a warehouse for cotton: some of the 19th century travellers noted that it had been closed in the traditional Egyptian way by stretching a canvas across the sealed door.

It was not until modern times that the temple was restored and could once more be appreciated: the harmony of the proportions, the imagination evident in the twenty-four individual capitals which imitate the shapes of flowers and plants, the mysterious play of light and shade inside the hall, together with the fact that it is in almost perfect condition, make it one of the most highly admired temples in the Valley of the Upper Nile.

The Ptolemaic temple of Esna, now well below ground level due to many progressive layers of debris, is still striking with its impressive vestibule and 24 enormous columns topped with elaborate composite capitals. David Roberts, who journeyed so enthusiastically throughout Egypt, was also amazed by them in 1838.

Below, another view of the hypostyle hall in the temple of Khnum.

Elkab

An important cult and funerary centre in the southern region of Upper Egypt, Elkab stands on the eastern bank of the river, south of Thebes and was dedicated to the goddess Nekhbet. The city was surrounded by massive brick walls, while inside many small temples were dotted around the **Great Temple** which also had a sacred lake. The necropolis, dating from the predynastic era, was opposite the twin town of *Hieraconpolis* (*Nekhen*) on the opposite bank of the Nile. Tombs of the Middle and New Kingdoms lay beyond the city walls. Known in ancient times as *Nekheb el-Kab* and later by the Greek name *Eileithyiapolis*, Elkab still conserves impor-

Two views of the ruins of the temple of Nekhbet which, despite their fragmentary nature, allow us to imagine the majestic appearance of the original building.

tant ruins of the large temple built around 2700 BC and which included a temple dedicated to the god Thoth and a Roman fortification. Thus Elkab boasts ruins relating to the many and various periods of Egyptian civilization.

Edfu

The present-day city of Edfu owes its fame to the fact that it contains the best pre-served **temple** in Egypt, situated in the centre of the inhabited area and dedicated to the falcon-headed Horus. When Apollo was identified with Horus, the Greeks called the ancient capital of the 2nd *nome* of Upper Egypt *Apollinopolis Magna*. In referring to Esna, much has been said about the town, its market and trade, but in Edfu attention centres entirely on the temple, a masterpiece of harmoni-ous architectural principles. It is exceptionally well preserved, thanks to the fact that for a long time it was almost completely covered with sand up to the capi-tals. In 1860 when Mariette decided to free it, the state of abandon was such that almost a hundred *fellah* hovels leaning up against the temple on all sides had to be demolished. When the enormous mass of sand was removed, the monument turned out to be practically intact. Not even the temple of Karnak, the only one larger than Edfu, is so well preserved. Some 137 metres long and with a pylon measuring 79 metres at the front and 36 metres high, the plan is extremely homogeneous. With its flight of progressively smaller and darker rooms leading to the privacy of the sanctuary, the *"sancta sanctorum"*, it can be considered the archetype of the Egyptian temple.
Before arriving at the temple, a visit to the **mammisi** or Birth House on the left is of interest. Built under Ptolemy IX Soter II, it must initially have been part of the temple of Horus, later becoming an independent shrine. A peristyle surrounds the vestibule flanked by two small rooms and a sanctuary: the pilaster *capitals* are unique with their heads of Bes, a birth divinity. The term mammisi derives from the Coptic and means Place of Birth. Every year the mystery of the birth of Horus was renewed here, making it a sacred place for all women about to give birth.

In the most spectacular and pure Ptolemaic style, the numerous inscriptions and extremely detailed bas-reliefs narrate the story of the temple almost in its entirety. The first stone was laid on the seventh day of the month of Epiphi, in the tenth year of the reign of Ptolemy III Euergetes, this being 23 August, 237 BC. The bas-reliefs also tell us when the temple was terminated: on 5 December, 57 BC. It took almost two centuries to complete this enormous sanctuary, built on a shrine that already existed in the time of Tuthmosis III. According to an inscription on the naos, the project was the brainchild of Imhotep, son of Ptah. Imhotep, however, was a vizier of Djoser, the builder of the step pyramid of Saqqara, who lived twenty-three centuries earlier. The explanation may lie in the fact that the priest architects of this temple considered Imhotep an ideal to which they aspired, a sort of mythical forerunner, who ensured the perfection of their work. Attributing the temple of Edfu to him, in other words, gave them the assurance of perfection.

Here, too, as in Dendera and Kalabshah, a sandstone precinct wall surrounds the temple and a sort of guard walk was installed between the two. The façade of the temple rises up in all its majesty with the magnificent *pylon* consisting of two massive towers on either side of the entrance. The long grooves in which the standards were fixed are still visible on the pylon, which is divided internally into four floors of rooms and is decorated externally with scenes showing Ptolemy XII sacrificing prisoners to Horus and Hathor. On either side of the entrance is a black granite *statue* of Horus. Next comes the *court*, called the "Court of Offerings", with columns on three sides. Each *capital* differs from the others but corresponds to the one opposite.

At the back of the court, almost as if he were guarding the pronaos, is the beautiful, majestic *statue* in black granite of the falcon Horus, wearing the double crown of Upper and Lower Egypt. The *hypostyle hall* that follows has eighteen columns, set in two rows of six each,

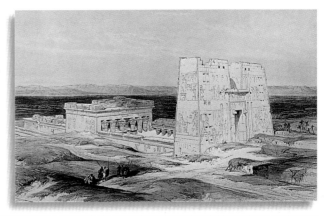

The majestic pylon of the temple of Horus, almost completely covered with engraving, as it is today (below) and how it appeared in the 19th century to David Roberts who described this religious complex as "the most beautiful temple in Egypt".

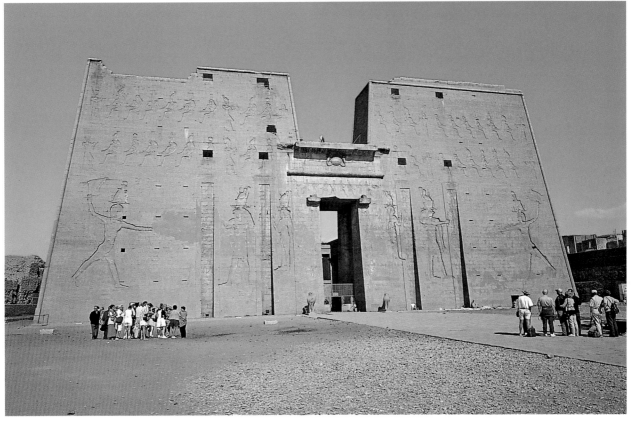

preceded by the other six which are connected halfway up by screen walls. In these, on either side of the entrance, are openings that lead into two small **chambers**: the one on the left - the "morning house" - served to purify the priests before the ritual, and all the material which was used by them during their sacred offices was kept there. The room on the right was the liturgical library and the catalogue of the papyruses kept there was engraved on the walls.

Next is the *second hypostyle hall*, smaller, with three rows of four columns, and communicating with the chambers from which the "dry and wet offerings" were brought in. Another room served as a workshop in which the offerings were prepared. On the walls is to be found a list of the ingredients used in the ritual. Adjacent to this room is the *offering chamber*, which then leads to the terrace above, via two flights of stairs. Crossing yet another room, the *central* or *intermediate hall*, with the entrance to the *chapel of the god Min* on the left, a series of symbolic and evocative rooms that became gradually narrower and darker, led to the *sacrarium*, in which the image of the god was housed. The last chamber still has its *naos*, a superb monolithic tabernacle in grey granite four metres high, erected in 360 BC

at the time of Nectanebo II, and part, therefore, of the older temple. The *corridor of the mysteries* runs around the sanctuary and ten rooms open off it, each with its specific attributes and each dedicated to the divinities associated with the cult of Horus, such as Osiris, Sokar, Khonsu, etc. The rich *decoration* of the interior also continues on the external walls of the large

Above, a view of the impressive façade of the pronaos in the temple of Horus at Edfu and, left, a detail of the beautiful statue of the god at the entrance. Below, the interior of the temple in another attractive 19th-century drawing by David Roberts.

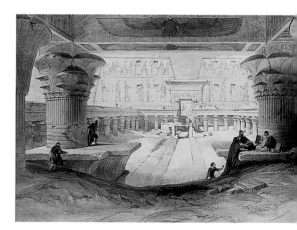

corridor: the scenes, all religious in nature, are of great interest. They depict the laying of the first stone of the temple, the hymn to Mut, the birth and the cult of Horus, his victory over the enemies of his father Osiris, and other religious events. There are a great number of liturgical scenes: three particularly important festivals took place in the temple of Edfu: New Year, the annual marriage of Horus with Hathor of Dendera, the celebration of the triumph of Horus over Seth. Just as noteworthy was the crowning of a live falcon which took place in the large court. The temple custodians had an aviary where they raised falcons and every year one of these birds became the living symbol of Horus for twelve months. No trace remains of this aviary, known as the "temple of the falcon", but the image of the god is omnipresent, magically petrified in the large granite statues, immobile sentinels guarding their temple.

The massive walls surrounding the temple of Horus, entirely decorated with a series of interesting bas-reliefs (below, a fine detail).

Kom Ombo

Shortly after Edfu the landscape changes once again: the Arabian mountains lie behind us as we move on into a fertile plain, called the "New Nubia". Formerly it was desert sand - today, thanks to irrigation, sugar cane plantations stretch out over about 12,000 hectares. The stimulus of agriculture also led to the development of industries and the establishment of important sugar refineries: every village has been transformed into an industrial centre, with schools, hospitals and administrative centres. When the High Dam was built and the problem of the Nubians whose villages would be submerged arose, the Wadi Kom Ombo and its valley seemed most suited for their resettlement. At least 100,000 Nubians were thus installed in this new location, increasing the manpower required for work in the fields. The new villages that sprang up to receive them took the names of those that had been abandoned and were now submerged: Kalabshah, Amadah, Abu Simbel.

This gentle evocative landscape is the perfect background for the **temple** that stands on a small hill overlooking the Nile (the Arab word *kom* in fact means "small mountain"), almost a sort of Greek acropolis.

Perhaps because it was covered with sand for so long, the stone differs from that of all the other temples, yet the outstanding feature is the unusual, even unique, ground plan, which resulted from the unification of two adjacent temples, each dedicated to a distinct divinity: the crocodile-headed Sobek, god of fertility and creator of the world, and Haroeris or the ancient falcon-headed Horus, the solar war god. Consequently the temple was called both "House of the Crocodile" and "Castle of the Falcon". An imaginary line divides the temple longitudinally into two parts, each with its entrance, hypostyle halls, chapels, etc. The right part of the temple was consecrated to Sobek, the left to Haroeris, whose winged disk that protects from all evil is depicted over all the entrance portals. This temple, too, was the work of the Ptolemies, who built it

Above, the ruins of the courtyard of the temple of Kom Ombo and the sixteen columns around the sides which, at the time of David Roberts, were still partially buried by the sand as is clearly shown in his evocative reproduction.

on the site of a much older and smaller sanctuary of which little remains.

All that is left of the great entrance *pylon* is the right hand part, where the Roman emperor Domitian can be seen with various gods rendering homage to the triad of Sobek, Hathor and Khonsu, together with a long text of 52 lines in hieroglyphics. The *court* that follows must originally have been quite lovely, with its sixteen painted columns on three sides. Now only the base and lower part are left, with, at the centre, the remains of the altar on which the sacred boat was placed during processions. The bas-reliefs on the columns show the emperor Tiberius, whose name is cut into the cartouches that accompany the figures, as he makes offerings to the gods. The north part of the court is closed by the exterior wall of the pronaos, or first hypostyle hall. The two entrances that correspond to the temples of Haroeris and Sobek open in this wall. On either side of the doors, Ptolemy XII Neos Dionysos is shown purified by Horus, Thoth, and Haroeris (in the part on the left) and by Horus, Thoth and Sobek on the right.

The *first hypostyle hall* has three transversal rows each of five sheath columns with a bell capital. Some of them are lotus-shaped, others papyrus, and one is even palm-shaped. The ceiling is decorated with astronomical scenes, with the vulture, the symbol of Nekhbet. The column shafts are all carved with reliefs: at the top, beneath the capitals, is a band of hieroglyphs with the symbol of life (*ankh*), and below the pharaoh is seen rendering homage to the various gods. The same offering scenes are repeated on the walls of the hall: the pharaohs depicted are all of the Ptolemaic period, and include Cleopatra VI. The central row of columns ideally indicates the division of the two sanctuaries. From here two distinctly separate entrances lead to the smaller *second hypostyle hall*, or "hall of offerings". Here too the central row of columns acts as a division. Both the architecture and the decoration are the same as in the first hall, and even the same scenes and subjects are repeated, though the figures depicted this time are Ptolemy VIII Euergetes II, his wife Cleopatra and Ptolemy XII Neos Dionysos.

After this hall come *three vestibules* arranged transversally, the last of which leads to the sanctuary, or more precisely, the two *sanctuaries of Haroeris and Sobek*. These three chambers were built by Ptolemy VI Philometor and he is shown in the reliefs on the walls. In one of these on the internal wall of the last vestibule, the pharaoh is seen wearing his Macedonian mantle, before the triad of Haroeris, Sobek, and Khonsu, who writes the number of the jubilees of the king on a palm trunk. Unfortunately not much is left of the *sanctuaries* dedicated to the two divinities: unlike the rest of the temple in which the right and left hand parts merged, the sanctuaries were clearly separated by an intermediate wall. A fragment in the sanctuary of Haroeris provides an idea of how rich the decoration must have been. The long dedica-

Views of the splendid columns of the ancient temple, which still preserve clear traces of painting in the relief engravings.

tory inscription with the name of Cleopatra on the left door is still intact.

A double *corridor* surrounds the entire temple: seven small rooms open off the interior corridor behind the shrines. We are still not sure what they were used for. A staircase leads from the central room to the terrace above, with a breathtaking view over the entire temple.

Views of the structures and wall decorations of the temple of Kom Ombo. Particularly interesting, below, is the architrave, still brightly coloured, portraying a row of vultures, symbols of the goddess Nekhbet.

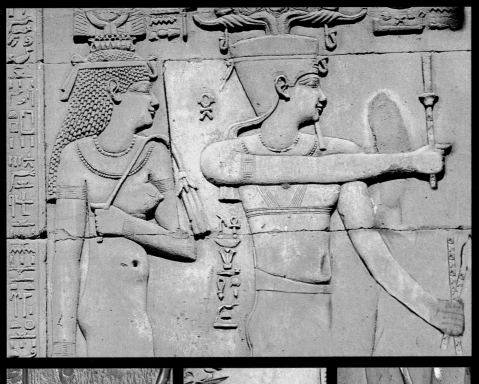

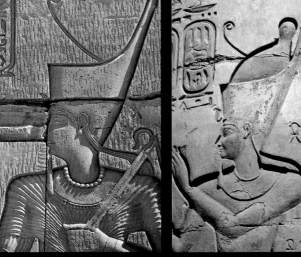

These chapels were also decorated, though the bas-reliefs often remained unfinished. Luckily the relief on the internal façade of the second wall has survived. It depicts a whole series of surgeon's instruments: scalpels, forceps, pincers, etc., confirming once again the high degree of skill achieved by the Egyptians in the field of medicine.

The "Birth House" or **mammisi** and the **Hathor chapel** also belonged to the temple complex of Kom Ombo. The former, on the left in front of the entrance to the temple, was built by Ptolemy VIII Euergetes II and has now in great part been swallowed by the Nile. The Hathor Chapel is in better condition. Situated to the right of the temple, it was built by Domitian in honour of Hathor whom the Greeks identified with Aphrodite. Many mummies and crocodile sarcophagi from the excavations of a neighbouring necropolis can now be seen in this chapel, which was donated by a wealthy Roman matron.

A range of details highlighting the extreme elegance and wealth of the decorative elements that enhance the entire complex of the temple of Kom Ombo, with images of divinities, sovereigns and intense colours here and there where the ancients assertively surface.

Aswan

Aswan (Assuan), the ancient Syene, lies on the right bank of the Nile, 886 kilometres from Cairo. This is where the Valley of the Nile with its typically gentle landscape ends. This is where Egypt ends and Nubia begins. Gone are the farmlands which accompany the bends of the river, replaced now by endless kilometres of desert sands and the majestic still waters of Lake Nasser. The Nile too is transformed and the smooth tranquil waters give way to the sudden troubled waters leaping and eddying around the rocks of the First Cataract.

Trade and barter went on here as early as the third millennium. Nubia, whose ancient name nub (nbw) means "gold", has always been a land of conquest and exploitation. The doorway to black Africa, the only communications route between the sea and the heart of the black continent, Nubia provided the pharaohs with their best soldiers, highly prized woods, precious ivory, perfumed spices, the finest ostrich feathers – as well as gold. Syenite – that pink granite so widely used in Egyptian religious architecture for building temples, and for sculpting colossi and obelisks – came from its many rich quarries. It was so abundant that the quarries were still in use in Roman times. Syene was also of fundamental importance in controlling both the river traffic and that of the desert caravans. The pharaohs maintained an armed garrison there and made Syene the capital of the first nome of Upper Egypt.

In medieval times the city was subject first to the incursions of the Blemi, from Ethiopia, then fell victim to a violent outbreak of the plague. It was gradually abandoned and only began to revive after the Turkish conquest of Egypt. Its modern name derives from the old Egyptian swenet meaning "trade", transformed into the Coptic suan and then into Aswan.

Nowadays, in addition to its purely historical and archaeological interest, the mildness of its climate has made Aswan an ideal winter resort, with excellent and stylish hotels.

Characteristic views of Aswan: left, felucca on the Nile and, above, a rock carved with inscriptions much eroded by the waters of the river.

Elephantine Island

While the rich granite quarries were in ancient Syene, most of the trade took place on Elephantine Island. It was here that the governor of the province had his residence, and it was also the centre of the cult of the ram-headed god Khnum. Originally the island was named *Yebu*, which means "elephant" in Egyptian. The Greeks translated it into Elephantine, probably because this was where ivory from Africa was traded. The island is 1500 metres long and 500 metres wide. It now incorporates two typical Nubian villages and the large "Hotel Assuan Oberoi" as well as the **Museum of Aswan** and the **archaeological zone of Yebu**. To land on the island one passes below enormous rocks covered with graffiti and inscriptions dating principally to the 18th (Tuthmosis III and Amenhotep III) and the 26th Dynasties (Psamtik II), docking at the tiny pier constructed of material that was taken from buildings dating to the New Kingdom.

THE BAZAAR

For atmosphere and charm the bazaar of Aswan in is second only to that of Cairo.

Parallel to the *Corniche* – the avenue which runs along the Nile, shaded by tall hibiscus trees laden with red flowers – it winds through the narrow streets of the old city. There is a real feel of Africa in the air of this *souk*: the tall wicker baskets set on the ground are full of exotic spices and enticing brightly coloured powders, from *karkade* to *henne*, from saffron pistils to curry, from red pepper to the dark-leafed mint tea. Objects in braided straw, in ebony, in ivory abound. Everywhere a teeming of dark-skinned peoples (the Nubians are thinner and darker than the rest of the Egyptian population) and a fluttering of long white robes.

The Aswan Museum

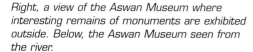

Since 1912 this small museum has been located in the villa that belonged to William Wellicocks, the English engineer who designed the Old Dam of Aswan. In fact it has all the appearance of a charming inviting colonial house, with a veranda opening out onto the garden, flowers and plants growing all around. The archaeological finds in the museum all come from excavations undertaken in Aswan and other sites in Lower

Right, a view of the Aswan Museum where interesting remains of monuments are exhibited outside. Below, the Aswan Museum seen from the river.

Nubia. Of particular interest is *the mummy of the sacred ram* in a gilded sarcophagus. It dates to 330-305 BC and was found in a tomb just behind the museum building. Khnum was considered the creator of mankind and since he was said to have modelled the first man from the clay of a vase, he was worshipped as the patron of potters. At Aswan he was associated in a triad with Anukis, goddess of the island of Seheil and with Satis, goddess of Elephantine Island. The ancients also believed that Khnum lived in a cave nearby and that this was where he hid the flood which periodically overran the island. Also to be noted is the *cosmetic palette in slate* kept in a showcase in the first room, unusual as it is in the shape of a rhinoceros - an animal which was unknown in Egypt at the time.

A series of images that illustrate well the wealth of the collections exhibited in the Aswan Museum.

NILOMETER

"... there are marks which measure the height of the water for irrigation. They are used by the farmers to measure the flow of the water, while the state officials use it to establish the amount of taxes. In fact, the higher the water the higher the taxes". This is what Strabo once wrote about the Nilometer, a staircase of 90 steps which descended into the waters of the Nile and made it possible to know in advance the date of the flood and the amount of water, thanks to a graduated scale engraved on its walls. The inscriptions are in Greek (a scale with Arab measurements was added later) and record some of the famous floods, from Augustus up to Septimius Severus.

The Nilometer showing the steps that lead directly to the river and the measurements engraved on the inner walls. As the water rose over the steps, it was possible to measure the volume and thus foresee the extent of the flood.

Ancient Abu

Further on, beyond the Nilometer, is what remains of the ancient city of Abu. The main building was the **temple dedicated to Khnum**, begun in the 30th Dynasty under Nectanebo II and continued under the Ptolemies and the Romans. It consisted of a court behind which was the *hypostyle hall* and the *sanctuary*. We can still see a large portal in granite with cartouches of Alexander Aegos and a naos, also of grey granite, with the pharaoh Nectanebo II worshipping Khnum. In the vicinity, the small **temple of Heka-ib** also came to light. Heka-ib was a nomarch at the end of the Old Kingdom to whom his successors dedicated this small temple that consists of a court surrounded by *naos-chapels*, each of which contained a statue of Heka-ib.

Even further towards the southernmost tip of the island stands another *chapel* of the Ptolemaic period rebuilt by using material found in Kalabsha when the temple there was dismantled.

The perfect colonial style of the "Old Cataract Hotel" in Aswan, where some scenes of "Murder on the Nile" were filmed.

Kitchener Island

North of Elephantine is the Island of Trees, better known as Kitchener Island. Lord Horatio Kitchener was an English general who had fought valiantly in the Sudan in 1898, defeating the army of the Mahadi. Consul General in Egypt, he fell in love with this island set in the middle of the Nile, where he could fully indulge his passion for exotic flowers and plants. This splendid *botanical garden* contains the rarest examples from Africa and Asia: a symphony of colours and fragrances accompanies us on our leisurely wanderings along shady avenues. Bougainvilleas and poinsettias, hibiscus and clematis, mangoes and sycamores. fragrances that are pungent or subtle, shades of colour ranging from brilliant reds to delicate pinks. Birds also love this enchanted garden and live here undisturbed among the bushes and the undergrowth. In the southern part of the island, a tiny bay populated by white ducks has been created under a lovely terrace.

Nubian Villages

Immersed in the green of the palm groves on Elephantine Island, three Nubian villages appear quite suddenly transporting us into a different world. Here the inhabitants are extremely courteous and are always ready to offer the visitor a cup of perfumed mint tea. The houses are brightly coloured in green, blue and yellow. Often the black cube of Mecca, the sacred *Kaaba*, is painted on the exterior, a sign that the owner of the house had journeyed on a pilgrimage to the holy city of Mecca. Sometimes the means of transportation is also painted – a plane, a ship, a car...

Right, luxuriant vegetation on Kitchener Island.
Below, a typical village of Nubia.

Mausolaum of the Aga Khan

In 1957 the Aga Khan III Mohammed Shah, spiritual head of the Ismailian Muslims, died. This community, whose centre is in India, has about four million followers, scattered throughout the world.

Extremely rich, he used to spend part of the winter in this villa on the left bank of the Nile. As stated in his will, two years after his death the Aga Khan was buried here, in the mausoleum called the Begum built above the white house, which he left to his wife. The mausoleum was built in pink limestone, on the model of the Cairo mosque of El-Guyushi, in the unadorned Fatimid style. Inside, the tomb is of white Carrara marble, with inscriptions from the Koran round the walls, so beautifully engraved they look like embroidery. A fresh red rose has been laid on his tomb every day since his burial.

Monastery of St Simeon

Once, cultivated fields covered this small valley right up to the Nile. Today the imposing ruins of this monastery, a genuine fortress, are set against the savage beauty of the desert.

The *Deir Amba Samaan* (as it is called in Arab) is one of the largest and best preserved Coptic monasteries in all of Egypt. Following the death of bishop Hadra, it was built between the 6th and 8th centuries. It could house up to 300 monks and offer shelter to many hundreds of pilgrims. After existing for almost five hundred years, it was destroyed by the Arabs in 1321, when many of the monks were killed and the survivors were driven out. The surrounding wall of stone and unbaked brick flanked by towers ten metres high lend it a majestic and solemn air which induces respect and awe. Inside, the convent was designed like a real city in miniature. On the first level is the tripartite **church** with an apse with three chapels. Traces of frescoes depicting *Christ Pantokrator* and *twenty-four seated saints* are still visible. Above each saint a

letter of the Coptic alphabet is painted. A staircase leads to the second floor, where the real monastery is, with a long corridor onto which the monks' *cells* face, and the service rooms for the community, such as kitchen, bakery, cellar, are situated. If we climb to the top of the walls, the desert stretches before us in all its majesty. All around is sand, with camels slowly crossing it to bring visitors here. At the end of the valley we are struck by the stunning contrast of Aswan overlooking the blue waters of the Nile and the white feluccas lazily waiting, half hidden in the green of the palm groves. It is particularly lovely to approach the monastery at sunset, when the ruins take on a rosy hue that blends with the sand from which they seem to emerge as if by magic.

Opposite page, two views of the Aga Khan's mausoleum which stands out from the rocks and gardens below with its pale pink sandstone.
This page, above, a general view of the Monastery of St Simeon. Right: the central chapel in the apse of the church with traces of frescoes where it is possible to make out the figure of Christ Pantocrator.

Necropolis of the Princes

The left bank of the Nile is dominated by the hill called *Qubett el Hawa* (the "summit of the winds") with a small ruined temple offering an unforgettable spectacle of Aswan, the mass of rocks which form the First Cataract

and the desert all around. Immediately below, are about forty tombs that go to make up the interesting necropolis of the princes of Elephantine. Contemporaries of the last pharaohs of the Old Kingdom, these dignitaries had their tombs dug into the rock. Entrance was via a steep ramp which served to haul up the sarcophagus. The layout of the tomb is generally very schematic: a rectangular chamber with pillars, the chapel and the sarcophagus room. The decoration is also extremely simple and consists only of paintings, as the limestone in which the tomb was cut was not suitable for relief sculpture.

Tomb of Heka-ib

Discovered in 1947, this tomb belonged to Heka-ib, a dignitary about whom we know only that he was governor of Elephantine at the end of the Old Kingdom, during the 6th Dynasty. Though he seems to have been popular, his success was posthumous as, for a reason that is unknown to us, he was deified and the small temple already seen on Elephantine Island near the temple of Khnum was erected in his honour. His tomb is not large nor does it have any outstanding decoration. When it was discovered, however, about sixty *steles* dedicated to him were found in the court.

Above, the "Summit of the Winds" where about forty tomb chapels of the princes of Elephantine are excavated.
Left: the steep stairway leading to the tombs.

Tombs of Mehu and Sabni

These two tombs at the southernmost end of the necropolis are intercommunicating for their owners were father and son. Mehu, "hereditary prince" and "only friend" during the 6th Dynasty, had travelled as far south as the Second Cataract and during the journey encountered death. His son Sabni, as can be read on the sides of the entrance to the second tomb, organized an expedition to go in search of his father's body and bring it back home where solemn funeral rites were celebrated, with expert embalmers called in to mummify him.

Mehu's tomb has a vast hall with three rows of six columns each. At the centre between two pillars is a block of granite which served as an offering table: to be noted are the symbols for bread and the drainage canals for the ritual libations. Sabni's tomb is divided by twelve pillars arranged in two rows and is decorated with scenes of hunting and fishing.

Tomb of Sirenput I

Very little remains of this tomb, in which the son of Satet-hotep, a 12th-Dynasty prince at the time of Amenemhet II was buried, to indicate that it was the

Above and centre left, the exterior of the tomb of Heqa-ib and the decorations showing scenes of hunting and fishing. Below and centre right, the exterior of the tombs of Mehu and Sabni with a detail of offering scenes in the frescoes that decorate the interior.

largest and most richly endowed tomb in the entire necropolis. Even so, part of the enclosure and the entrance portal in limestone still exist, with fine bas-reliefs depicting the deceased prince, the "Superior of the prophets of Satis". The façade of the tomb had a portico with six piers. The interior consisted of a chamber with four pilasters which must originally have been richly decorated with paintings though now in very poor condition: the scenes referred to daily life on land and sea.

Tomb of Sirenput II

The tomb, one of the best preserved, belonged to the "Superior of the prophets of Khnum" during the 12th Dynasty. It consisted of a first chamber with six pillars, a gallery flanked by six niches each of which contained the mummy-like statue of the deceased prince, and a second square chamber with four pillars, each of which was decorated with a lovely image of Sirenput. This is followed by the back chapel which is painted: the prince is shown with his small son rendering him homage before a table set with bread, sweets, fruit, even a duck and bunches of grapes. The adjacent wall is decorated with the figure of the wife of the prince, who was a priestess of Hathor, also shown seated before a prepared table.

Above, the tomb of Sirenput I; left, decorations in the tomb of Sirenput II showing the prince portrayed with his son.

THE UNFINISHED OBELISK

If this obelisk had been finished it would have been a candidate for the *Guinness Book of Records*. It would in fact have been over 41 metres high with a base of four metres and consequently a weight of 1,267 tons! But a crack in the granite, perhaps the result of a tremor, or the poor quality of the stone, brought the work to a halt and the obelisk remained as we see it now, abandoned on the ground near those granite quarries which reveal much about how the ancient Egyptians cut stone. Once the ancient quarries of Aswan stretched for more than six kilometres from the Nile. This was the stone the Egyptians favoured for the facing of their pyramids, and since it was near the river, the stone could easily be loaded onto boats and carried upstream.

The incisions cut regularly into the rock provide indications of how the blocks of stone were quarried. Wooden wedges or quoins were inserted into these grooves, which indicated the surface to be extracted and these were then soaked with water. As the wood expanded, the quoins burst, splitting off the rock in the desired direction, with surfaces that were relatively smooth and ready for polishing.

The High Dam

About five kilometres south of the city the course of the Nile is crossed by the Old Dam of Aswan (*Es Saad*, the dam), built by the English between 1898 and 1902 with an initial height of 30.5 metres and a capacity of a billion cubic metres of water. Before long this proved insufficient and in two stages (from 1907 to 1912 and from 1929 to 1934) the dam was enlarged to its present size: 41.5 metres high and with a capacity of five billion cubic metres of water. Still this was not enough to meet the requirements of the Egyptian territory. The drama of Egypt is to be found in two numbers: 900,000 square kilometres of land of which only 38,000, not much more than 4%, can be cultivated. A new dam would not only increase the amount of farmland, but irrigation would become a reality and the annual production of electricity would be increased. It was thus decided to embark upon the construction of a new barrier, called the "barrier against hunger", a new dam which, as Nasser said, "would set Egypt on the road to modernity".

The High Dam (*Saad el Aali*) is about eight kilometres upstream from the Old Dam. The Soviet Union was entrusted with the study of the project. Construction began in January 1960; on May 14, 1964 the waters of the Nile were deviated into a branch canal and in 1972 the work – of vast dimensions – could be considered finished. The body of water thus formed, Lake Nasser,

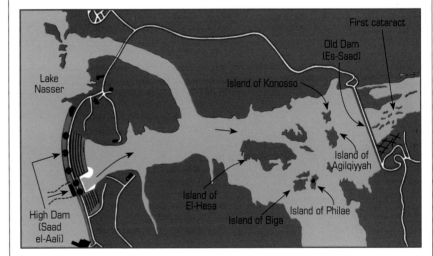

MAP OF THE TWO ASWAN DAMS

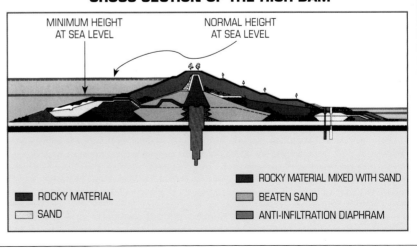

CROSS SECTION OF THE HIGH DAM

is 500 kilometres long (150 of which are in Sudanese territory) and has a capacity of 157 billion cubic metres of water: second only to the dam of Kariba on the Zambesi River.

The creation of this artificial basin obviously brought about radical modifications in the landscape and in the environment. First of all, the numerous Nubian villages in the area involved had to be evacuated. Then attention was centred on the dramatic situation of the many important archaeological sites in Nubia which would inevitably have been submerged. When it was realized that the economic improvement of Egypt meant the irreparable destruction of its archaeological inheritance, UNESCO reacted to the call for aid launched by the Egyptian and Sudanese governments and set in motion a gigantic campaign to raise the funds needed to save the threatened temples. Not one of the fourteen temples involved has been preserved on its original site: once

dismantled, they have been faithfully reconstructed elsewhere.

Among these, the temple of **Kalabsha**, clearly visible from the High Dam, is one of the finest and best preserved.

Above, the modern monument in the shape of a stylised lotus flower erected as a reminder of the immense undertaking and commitment of those who built the High Dam (seen below).

THE DESTINY OF THE TEMPLES

When the governments of Egypt and Sudan made their dramatic appeal to UNESCO for help, it was impossible to estimate the scope of the task, just as it was impossible to estimate the heritage to be saved from destruction and preserved for humanity. Their own contribution was, however, just as great. In return for such an immense operation, Egypt would donate half of the material excavated and four of the temples saved. Thus, of all the monuments threatened by flooding none was preserved in its original location. Only the temple of Gerf Hussein could not be saved due to the extreme brittleness of the rock. The other fourteen were all dismantled and faithfully reconstructed, ten located near their original sites (Kalabsha, Qertas, Beit el-Wali, Wadi al-Sabu, Dakkah, Maharraqah, Amada, Derr, Abu Simbel and Abu Oda) and four were donated to the countries that had done most to rescue them: El-Lesiya to Italy, Taffeh to the Netherlands, Dendur to the United States and Dabod to Spain.

Kalabasha

Kalabsha was the ancient *Talmis*, the most important city of the Dodecaschenum ("Land of the twelve miles"), and was situated about forty kilometres south of its present site. The god Mandulis was worshipped there – his head surmounted by a complicated diadem – identified with Horus by the Egyptians. In importance and size, the **sanctuary** dedicated to this local god was second only to Abu Simbel. Seventy-one metres long and thirty-five wide, it was defined by the English writer Amelia Edwards as the "Karnak of Nubia". Of the "inner sanctuary" type, the temple was built on an earlier one from the time of Amenophis II. The plan includes a pylon, a court, a pronaos and a naos formed by three successive chambers. The pylon is 41 metres high and it is possible to climb to the top to admire the beautiful panorama of the High Dam and Lake Nasser. The *pylon* leads to the paved *court* 20 metres long, where worshippers had access during the great festivals. It is surrounded on three sides by a porch and columns which collapsed when an earthquake struck but which were partially reconstructed when the temple was recomposed. Then comes the *pronaos* which had twelve columns with bell capitals. The façade is decorated with numerous inscriptions. One, in Greek, narrates how Silco, king of Ethiopia in the middle of the 6th century AD, had come to destroy Talmis, inhabited by his enemies. Another inscription, also in Greek, notes the decree issued by the governor Aurelio Besarione who, around the year 250, ordered on religious grounds that all the swineherds and their pigs had to leave the temple within fifteen days. The interior of the pronaos is also decorated with figures of Mandulis, Thoth, Horus, etc. Until the late 19th century, the decorations still had their original colours. Nowadays, unfortunately, all trace has been lost and we must trust in the descriptions and drawings of travellers in the past who were lucky enough to see and copy them. After the *pronaos* come the three chambers which formed the *naos*, each one lower than the one before, and with columns supporting the ceiling. In the *cell* which contained the statue of Mandulis, interesting decorations, characterized by a certain freshness of execution, have survived.

Only the first of the original encircling walls of the temple still exists. A sort of spacious sentry cor-

Above, two views of the hypostyle hall and, below the mighty pylon of the temple of Kalabsha.

Above, an attractive view of the little temple of Kertassi, and on the left, a detail of the two pillars with their unusual Hathor capitals. Below, the courtyard that precedes the rock temple of Beit el-Wali with, on the right wall, the celebratory representation of Ramasses II's victory over the Syrians and Lybians.

ridor, which also contains a Nilometer, is set between the stone wall and that of the temple. To the west, on the external wall, is an enormous relief sculpture of Mandulis: he is shown twice, on the right in his human aspect and on the left in his divine aspect.

At the time of the great rescue of the Nubian temples, technicians of the German Federal Republic were responsible for Kalabsha and, after dismantling it into 13,000 blocks they rebuilt it on this promontory, a stone sentinel for the endless expanse of Lake Nasser.

Kertassi

Erected on high ground above the Nile, the **small temple** of Kertassi was dedicated to Isis and originally was in the town of Tzitzis. It closely recalls Trajan's Kiosk at Philae, of rectangular form with columns and composite capitals joined by screen walls and with two large Hathor pillars at the portal. Only one of the architraves which once supported the roof – which no longer exists – remains now and it is covered with numerous inscriptions.

Beit el-Wali

The **rock-cut temple** of Beit et Wali is not far from the large temple of Kalabsha. The name means "House of the Governor" and it was built by the viceroy of Kush (Upper

Nubia) for Ramesses II. It is a *speos* cut into the mountain and consists of only two chambers, a long hall and the *sanctuary*, both preceded by an open court, the walls of which are decorated in relief with military scenes that commemorate the victorious campaigns of Ramesses II: over Syria and Libya on the right wall and over Ethiopia on the left. The vestibule, which was transformed into a church in the 6th century, has two proto-Doric columns supporting the ceiling: here the bas-reliefs of religious scenes still have their original colours fairly well preserved. Ramesses II is shown before the hawk-headed Horus and Selkis, and the pharaoh is also seen making offerings to the holy triad of Khnum, Satis and Anukis.

This page, some of the almost two hundred inscriptions that are found on the rocks of the Island of Seheil.

Island of Seheil

Upstream, a few kilometres from Aswan, is the First Cataract of the Nile, a vast zone of turbulent waters and whirlpools with innumerable rocks and islets. Seen from above, the cataract really looks like primordial chaos. River traffic was interrupted here: the boats unloaded their camels which went round the rocks carrying the goods, and then sailed on greatly lightened, thus passing with ease through the narrow passages formed by the islets. The pharaoh Sesostris III, in the 12th Dynasty, had a canal dug parallel to the river to allow the ships to continue their journey towards the farthest parts of Nubia.

Travellers, soldiers, merchants: all left traces of their journey in dozens and dozens of graffiti which cover the black granite on Seheil. The island was sacred to Anukis, represented in female form and with plumes on her head, and to whom a *temple* that is no longer exists was dedicated. All that is left are the remains of two other small **temples**, one from the time of Amenophis II (18th dynasty) and the other from the time of Ptolemy XIV Philopator. There are about two hundred inscriptions on the island, and they range from the 6th Dynasty to the Ptolemaic period. The most interesting is no. 81, known also as the "*famine stele*" of the Ptolemaic period. It refers to the terrible famine which had smitten Egypt for seven years and how the pharaoh Djoser thanked Khnum with the erection of a temple because the god had finally sent a flood of the Nile plain. The text of this stele made it possible to identify Djoser as the pharaoh who had the step pyramid in Saqqara built.

In the midst of a fascinating landscape of granite rocks, the sacred island, domain of the goddess Isis, raises its columns and pillars towards the cloudless sky, giving one the impression of being in a purely imaginary place. The **temple of Philae** is one of the three best preserved Ptolemaic temples, the other two being those of Edfu and Dendera.

Philae was the largest of the three islands at the south end of the group of rocks that comprise the First Cataract, and is 400 metres long and 135 metres wide. The name itself reveals its unique geographic position: *Pilak* in fact, as it was called in the ancient texts, meant "the corner island" or "the end island". For originally Philae was on the east bank of the Nile, in the corner of a small bay, and also at the southernmost tip of the First Cataract. Of the other two islets, **Bigah** (today partially submerged) was particularly sacred for it was Osiris' place of eternal sleep and therefore out of bounds to all human beings. Only priests who came by boat from Philae were allowed there to celebrate their sacred rites on the 360 offering tables which indicated where Osiris was buried. The temples on Philae were dedicated to his bride Isis who with the force of her love had recomposed his scattered limbs and resuscitated him. The cult of the goddess on this island dates to extremely ancient times and it was a tradition that at least once a year Egyptians should go on pilgrimage to the sacred island. It was not until AD 535, under the reign of Justinian, that the priests dedicated to the cult were removed.

The third islet is **Agilqiyyah**: and this is where we can now admire the temple complex which was originally on Philae, barely 500 metres away.

Views that illustrate perfectly the amazing majesty of the temple of Isis on the island of Agilqiyyah, with its two impressive pylons and a wonderful pattern of engravings and decorations (right, a detail).

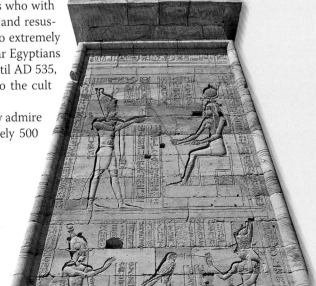

Further images of the temple of Isis with a view from above of the second pylon and the massive colonnade of the dromos (left). On the right, also at Philae, a detail of one of the Hathor capitals on the papyrus columns in the elegant temple of Nectanebo I.

The sacred island, in fact, was above water throughout the year until 1898. With the construction of the Old Dam, it remained submerged by the artificial lake most of the year. Only in August and September when the lock-gates of the dam were opened to alleviate the pressure of the flood waters, did the island emerge so it could be visited. The construction of the High Dam put Philae in a critical situation: the sacred island would have found itself in a closed basin in which the waters, no longer twenty metres high as before but only four, would have created a continual ebb and flow that, with the passing of the years, would have inevitably eroded the foundations of the temples which sooner or later would have collapsed.

Thus, between 1972 and 1980, they were dismantled and rebuilt on this islet (where the topography of Philae was recreated) in a position that was higher above the waters of the lake. The temple complex includes the **pavilion of Nectanebo**, the monumental **temple of Isis** with its annexes, the charming **pavilion of Trajan** and the small **Hathor temple**.

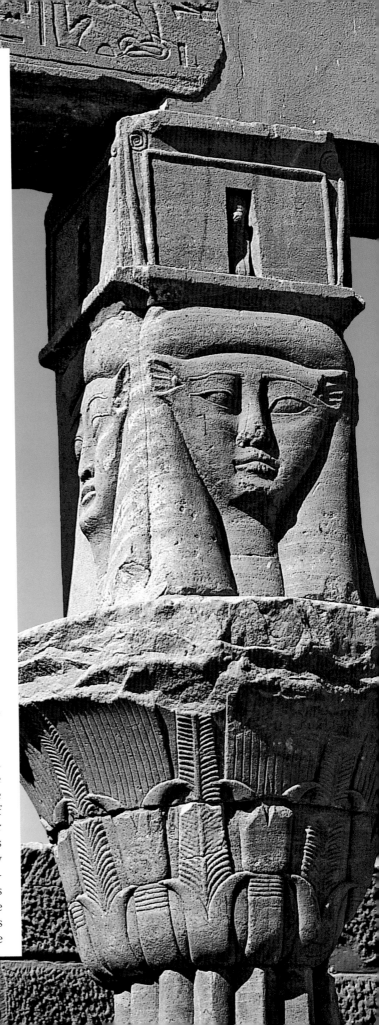

Pavilion of Nectanebo I

The landing-stage for the boats that bring tourists to visit the complex of Philae lies at the southwest tip of the island.

The first building to be encountered is the **pavilion of Nectanebo I**, a rectangular portico with fourteen bell columns and Hathor capitals: here the broad face of the goddess also has the ears of a cow (fairly common in all later capitals) so that it also represents the form of a sistrum, the favourite musical instrument of Isis, and also a symbol of Ihi, Hathor's young son. The pavilion dates to the 4th century B.C. and is therefore considered the oldest temple in the complex. In front is the large *dromos*, with porticoes on either side. The one on the right was never finished; the one on the left has 32 columns with traces of decoration on the ceiling and offering scenes on the columns and the back wall. The plant-shaped capitals differ one from the other.

Temple of Isis

The **temple of Isis** stands majestically with its monumental *first pylon*: it is 18 metres high and 45.5 metres wide and consists of two massive towers which flank the portal. On the tower the pharaoh Ptolomy XI Neos Dionysos grasps, in customary pose, his prisoners by the hair and prepares to sacrifice them to the gods Isis, Horus and Hathor. In the left tower, the reliefs which show the pharaoh armed with a staff and about to kill the enemy prisoners are in poorer condition. Passing between the two pylons, under the portal built by Nectanebo I whose cartouches can be seen, we find on the right a relief commemorating the French victory over the Mamelukes in the "an VII de la République" (1799). We are now in the temple *court* with the back wall formed by the second pylon and the right by a porticoed building with various annexes used by the priests. The elegant **mammisi** temple on the left side is a peripteral building (surrounded on four sides by columns with capitals terminating in Hathor sistrums), with three rooms preceded by a pronaos. Isis and her son Horus, whose birth, childhood and education are narrated in the fine decorations, were worshipped in the mammisi. Also to be noted above on the outer façade, the reproduction of the text of the Rosetta stone which made it possible to decipher Egyptian hieroglyphics. The *second pylon* (22 metres high and 32 wide) is higher than but not exactly parallel to the first. On the façade it also has the customary scene of Pharaoh Ptolemy XI Neos Dionysos massacring the prisoners before the gods. On the right, an enormous block of granite commemorates a donation of lands that Ptolemy VI made to the

Bastion of Hadrian

While most of the decorations at Philae regard sacred rites and tributes to the gods, there is one that stands out for its originality and the quite atypical subject represented. This is the gate or bastion of Hadrian, an aedicule that dates to Antonine times and that is situated in the western wing of the temple of Isis, on a level with the second pylon. Inside the gate, on the north wall, a *relief* sculpture illustrates the Egyptian concept of the source of the Nile. In fact Hapy, the deification of the Upper and Lower Nile, is shown in an anthropomorphic and hermaphroditic form. The god is shown in a cave surrounded by a serpent and he holds two vases from which water flows. In fact, the ancient Egyptians believed that the source of the Nile was in the neighbourhood of the First Cataract near a mountain called Mu Hapy (meaning "water of Hapy"). The annual rites in honour of the god were celebrated by the pharaoh himself and began in the middle of June when the star Sotis marked the beginning of the river flood.

Trajan's pavilion

On the other side - on the right side of the temple of Isis - is another jewel of this great Ptolemaic complex of Philae: Trajan's pavilion. Overlooking the river, extremely elegant and finely proportioned, it has in a sense become the symbol of the entire island. In olden times this was where the sacred

Above, a small hypostyle chamber that leads to the entrance gate of the temple of Isis as it was represented by David Roberts, still glowing with its brilliant decorations. Right, a view of Hadrian's Gate.

temple. A few steps lead to the *hypostyle hall*, with ten columns with polychrome floral capitals and traces of decoration on the ceiling: symbols of Upper and Lower Egypt, sun boats, astronomical symbols. In the 6th century at the time of the bishop Theodorus, the pronaos was transformed into a Christian church as witnessed by the many Coptic crosses engraved on the walls. From here access is gained to the *naos*, which consists of twelve rooms and a crypt, all decorated with liturgical scenes. After this came the sanctuary, containing the boat with the image of the goddess. A staircase leads to the terrace where a vestibule and a chamber comprise the *funerary chapel of Osiris*: the decoration narrates the Osiris cycle with the death, funeral and magical rites and the resurrection of the god.

barge with the statue of Isis landed during the magnificent processions on the river. Rebuilt by the emperor Trajan, the rectangular kiosk has fourteen columns with bell capitals and screen walls, two of which are decorated with scenes representing Trajan making offerings to Isis, Osiris and Horus.

Temple of Hathor

Beyond the kiosk is the **small temple of Hathor**, erected by Ptolemy VI Philometer and Euergetes II, but decorated later by Augustus. Some of the reliefs are rather amusing and show, among other things, a priest playing the double flute and some monkeys dancing while one plays the lute.
Philae represents a perfect synthesis of the Egyptian, Greek and Roman civilizations: here architecture and design are one. It should be remembered that once, before the waters of the Old Dam washed them clean, all the capitals were painted in brilliant colours – blue, red, yellow and green – as is seen in the paintings of those travellers who saw them before the temple was submerged in the artificial basin of Aswan. Despite the fact that all the original colour has disappeared, Philae remains that masterpiece of grace and enchantment, as Amelia Edwards wrote, a marvellous example of elegance and charm, which led Pierre Loti to call it the "pearl of Egypt".

The elegant Pavilion, or Kiosk, of Trajan that stands beside the temple on the island of Agilqiyyah, and, right, a detail of one of the elaborate capitals of its columns.

Lower Nubia

The colonization of Lower Nubia by the Egyptians - the region between Aswan, the first cataract of the Nile and the second, the rocks of Abusir to the south of the Halfa wadi, began during the Old Kingdom although the complete conquest dates from the Middle Kingdom. In addition to the temples of Abu Simbel, Ramesses II had five **sanctuaries** built along a narrow strip of land in Nubia, some of which were completely cut into the rock, while some were partially stone-built: Beit el-Wali, Gerf Hussein, Wadi al-Sabu, Derr, Aksha. However, some monuments did already exist at the time in Lower Nubia, especially *fortresses*. Later, during the New Kingdom, various kings, including Tuthmosis III, his son Amenhotep II and grandson Tuthmosis IV built other temples, such as Kalabsha, Amadah and the pillared vestibule opposite the Amadah temple, now lost to us. These sanctuaries were intended to represent the power of the Egyptian kings, who also wished to convert the local population to their religion, and were probably used to house the boat of the god Amun-Ra, which departed from Elephantine Island on its journeys along the river for Anibah and Abu Simbel, then returning into Egypt. But the temples had another purpose of a quite specific religious nature. The three main gods of the Egyptian pantheon – Amun, Ra and Ptah – found in all the temples of Nubia, had to provide a single, united religious image, and the fact that the sovereign appeared in the cell of these temples together with the three gods indicated that the king was himself another aspect of the divine power. It should also be remembered that Nubia was the country of gold and the sun. In fact, the Egyptians considered it to be the region closest to the rising sun and therefore an area particularly suited for the worship of Ra and the king, who was his incarnation. In 1963, as we have seen, in order to avoid destruction by the waters of Lake Nasser, some temples were dismantled or removed, transported to a safer location and rebuilt – though some were taken from their original site and entirely reconstructed in the countries that had assisted in their preservation. Thus it is that today,

Two views of the rock temple of Wadi al-Sabu with, at top, the majestic second pylon preceded by a row of sphinxes, and above, an impressive statue of Ramesses II.
Opposite page, the great pylon of the temple of Dakka, and a detail of the interesting relief decorations that enhance the temple.

in Turin we can visit the **temple of El-Lesiya**, dedicated to Horus and Satet, originally located 200 kilometres from Aswan; in Madrid we find the massive **temple of Dabod** dedicated to Isis, that once stood 15 kilometres from Philae; in the Netherlands, at Leiden is the **temple of Taffeh** dedicated to Amun and Isis, originally 40 kilometres from Philae, and in New York is the **temple of Dendur**, built at the time of Augustus 77 kilometres from Philae, dedicated to the brothers Peteese and Pihar who were deified. Other temples instead were relocated closer to their original site, thus remaining in Lower Nubia or in Egypt. The **temple of Gerf Hussein** was submerged however, though the statues were saved and its inscriptions were copied. Three great temples have been rebuilt on the banks of the vast Lake Nasser: **Wadi al-Sabu**, **Dakkah** and **Mahar-**

raqah. Other temples have been located 60 kilometres from here, such as **Amadah** and **Derr**, as well as the **tomb of Penniut**, governor of Uauat during the reign of Ramesses VI

Wadi al-Sabu

The **rock temple** dedicated to Amun-Ra and Ra Harakhte by Ramesses II is situated about 120 km. from Aswan on the east bank of the Nile at Wadi al-Sabu, meaning the "Valley of

the Lions", and named after the lion sphinxes. The sanctuary is now 2 km. north west of the original site and although the temple was cleaned and restored in 1905, the entire area was subsequently covered in sand. The temple is entered through a monumental doorway on both sides of which are a sphinx and a colossal statue. Through the doorway is a *first court-yard* with a short *dromos* or avenue flanked by two rows of three sphinxes. At the end was the first *pylon*, now destroyed, made of rough bricks with a stone portal, that lead to a *second courtyard* with four sphinxes (two on each side) with a lion's body and head of a falcon and a stairway to a terrace where a second sandstone *pylon* stands 24.5 metres wide and 20 high. Only one of the four statues representing the king that stood in front of the pylon now remains. The small figure beside the leg of Ramesses II is of the "royal daughter" and "royal bride" of Benetanat. From the pylon we reach the *third courtyard* where another stairway leads to a second terrace and to the wall of the temple cut into the mountain side. Double doors lead to a square room with a ceiling 6 metres high. A vestibule is reached from the entrance, followed by five chapels with a cruciform arrangement, where the central chapel forms the inner sanctum. The temple became a Christian church in the 6th century AD and there is still some evidence of this transformation as the Egyptian reliefs were covered with plaster and on the far wall is the image of St Peter with the key of paradise in his hand.

Dakkah

Dedicated to the god Thoth, the **temple** of Dakkah was built in the Ptolomaic and Roman periods. Facing rather unusually to the north, the building stood 40 km. to the north of its present site, about 1 km. to the north east of Ramesses II temple. On the west bank of the Nile, Dakkah is the precise location where a temple dedicated to Selqet, an ancient scorpion goddess, once stood. The lofty and regular structure that

we see today dates from the Ptolomaic period; the original nucleus consisted of a stone portal, *courtyard* and a *chapel* which had a vaulted ceiling, an atrium, two vestibules and a cell. The nucleus was created by Ptolemy IV Philopator and king Ergamenes, his subject. In 146 BC Ptolemy VI Philopator added a *second courtyard* while the Roman emperors built an impressive undecorated sandstone *pylon* around the portal, still well preserved, completed the decoration of the cell, possibly also enlarging it, and at the time of Augustus, added a chapel on the left. Only a few fragments remain of the granite *tabernacle* that was placed in the cell, though it was similar to the Ptolemaic or Roman one in the temple of Dabod now in Madrid. Beside the sanctuary, on the west bank of the Nile and in front of the Egyptian fortress of Quban, during the Ptolemaic period a city called *Pselchis* by the Greeks was founded and became an important military centre in Roman times. From the western bank it guarded the entrance to the Alagi wadi towards the east, where the gold mines already in use during the Middle Kingdom were located.

Maharraqah

The southern boundary of Roman Nubia passed through Maharraqah dividing it from the kingdom of Meroe where there was a large market for trade between Nubian and Egyptian products. Now known as the temple of *Ophedunia* a Roman **temple** dedicated to both Isis and Serapis, the patron of travellers, was located in Maharraqah. Built about 10 km. further south of the present site and heavily restored in 1905, the building now stands about 500 metres to the east of the temple of Dakkah and has an almost square plan of 12 metres by 15, with an entrance that opens to the east and an attractive internal colonnade, though the capitals of the columns were never completed. Inscriptions indicate that the temple was built before 37 AD and was subsequently turned into a church.

Amadah

Lying on the west bank of the river, the area of Amadah was already colonized by the Egyptians during the Middle Kingdom. Here, king Tuthmosis III dedicated a temple, later completed by his son Amenhotep II and enlarged by his grandson Tuthmosis IV, to the gods Amun-Ra and Ra Harakhte. The images of the god Amun were erased by order of Akhenaton who favoured the cult of the solar disc Aton, but were restored by Seti I. The **sanctuary** itself is quite small and well-preserved (23 metres by 10) and originally stood about 2.6 km. south of the present site. The temple was slowly moved in a single block 2600 metres over a gradient of 65 metres winching it along a device with three tracks of rollers. France provided the work force and capital for the operation and the small pronaos was dismantled and reconstructed by the Egyptian Antiquities Service. The original complex of Tuthmosis III had a *courtyard* with a portico in front, four grooved columns, a *vestibule* and three *shrines*, the most important of which is located at the back in two chapels. Tuthmosis IV made the courtyard into an atrium or *hypostyle hall* and Seti I restored the temple and built a kiosk nearby which no longer exists. The *solar boat* is in the central chapel or *cell* and carries Amun-Ra, Ra-Harakhte and king Amenhotep II who offers them jugs of wine. On the rear wall the twenty horizontal lines of the great *stele* of Amenhotep II describe the work that the pharaoh carried out in the temple during the third year of his reign and a rapid military campaign in Syria to repress a revolt.

Above, a fascinating view from behind of the Maharraqah temple. Below, the temple of Amadah.

One of the most unusual features of the Maharraqah temple is, without doubt, the spiral staircase, the only one of its kind found in the temples of Nubia. In ancient times it provided access to the terrace and, still intact today, provides evidence of the great architectural expertise of the builders.

Derr

Now entirely vanished, Derr, or El-Derr, was a large town in Nubia, once the seat of an autonomous governorate. The **rock temple** built by Ramesses II and dedicated to Ra-Harakhte is excavated 33 metres into the rock and has been called the "miniature Abu Simbel". It was situated on the eastern bank 11 kilometres south of its present site, which is now on the opposite bank, about 500 metres south of the temple of Amadah. The temple consists of an entrance *hall with columns* followed by a *hypostyle hall* with an unusual arrangement: three aisles are divided by six pillars and three chapels, the central of which is the *cell*. The decorations are of mili-

The temple of Derr in its rocky setting, and the profile of Ramesses II as he is portrayed in one of the rooms.

tary subjects: in the first room battles against the Nubians are represented, while in the second are scenes of the cult of Ra-Harakhte and of Ramesses II deified. At the back of the temple stand four statues of Ptah, Amun-Ra, the deified Ramesses II and Ra-Harakhte, the same statues that are also found in the great temple at Abu Simbel.

Anibah

Anibah (Miam) was an important stronghold and still remaining are part of the defensive walls, a fortress dating from the Middle Kingdom with a triple circle of walls and ramparts, the ruins of a temple, houses and stores of the 18th Dynasty during the reign of Tuthmosis III. The necropolis included a group of rock cut burial chambers, only one of which, created for an official of the 20th Dynasty and containing the most interesting decorations, was saved from the waters. The tomb of Penniut, whose name means "belonging to the city" was 40 kilometres from its present site and now stands a kilometre from the temple of Derr; Niut was Thebes, the greatest of cities. Penniut was the governor of Uauat during the reign of

Ramesses VI, about 1100 BC. After defeating Nubia the Egyptian kings of the 18th Dynasty divided the region into two provinces – Uauat in the north and Kush in the south. The capital of the Egyptians, Miam, developed on the west bank in the area of Anibah, and had many important buildings including a temple dedicated to Horus, houses and warehouses. It was already entirely in ruins before the waters of Lake Nasser flooded the area. Cut into the mountainside, the **tomb of Penniut**, is cruciform with an *atrium* and the *alcove for the cult*, a form frequently used during the New Kingdom. The walls of the atrium have scenes of the life of Penniut in this world and in the next, and of his funeral. On the south wall of the atrium, to the right of the entrance, engraved on the rock, is most of a text concerning the gift of a statue, or perhaps two, of king Ramesses VII that Penniut made to the temple of Derr. He also donated some properties located near to Anibah to the priests of the sanctuary as an endowment for the cult of the statue of the king. As thanks for the gift, Ramesses VI sent Penniut two silver vases. The burial shaft opened from the floor of the atrium and sculpted into the rock of the alcove are three unfinished statues of divinities.

The tomb of Penniut, cut into the mountain, with a detail of its decoration above.

235

For many centuries the two rock-cut temples of Abu Simbel on the banks of the Nile were seen not only as a memorial to the power and deification of Ramesses II, but as the achievement of an architectural and technical challenge – a challenge that two thousand years later faced engineers and technicians from around the world again. The danger that the temples would be submerged by the waters of Lake Nasser drew global attention and the temple became symbolic of the campaign to save all the monuments of Nubia. Abu Simbel was, without doubt, the most impressive temple, but it was also the most difficult to save due to its location, the material used in its construction and its architectural structure. Between 10-12 June 1963 the Egyptian government gave its final approval to a project that involved complete removal of the entire mass of rock by cutting the temple into blocks and subsequently rebuilding it on a higher site. The rescue operation was immensely complex and involved the organization of thousands of workmen and engineers. The task was also a furious race against time. Work began in April 1964 but already by the end of the summer the waters of the artificial lake had risen more rapidly than expected. Just some figures: 1,036 blocks with an average weight of 30 tons each were moved, while a further 1,112 were cut from the rock around the temples and 33 tons of resin were used to consolidate the rock structure - it was the most incredible project of dismantling and reconstruction that archaeologists had ever attempted. The two temples were rebuilt on ground 90 metres higher, exactly as before. It was

A reconstruction and views illustrating how the temples of Abu Simbel were dismantled bit by bit, taken from their original sites, now entirely submerged by the waters, and rebuilt perfectly identical in every way, in a safe and dry area.

realised however, that straightforward reconstruction was not possible as the weight of the artificial mountain covering the monument would have crushed it. Two enormous domes of reinforced concrete were therefore built to bear the pressure from the mountain above and so protect the temples like an enormous bell. The backfill was used to cover the domes and the sand itself would rapidly fill in the cracks. A great ceremony held on 22 September 1968 in the presence of the Minister of Culture Sarwat Okasha and René Maheu, Executive Director of

UNESCO, celebrated the conclusion of the work on the temples of Abu Simbel, and barely in time as the waters were already slowly flowing into the enormous, desolately empty caverns left below. The vast rock complex above was completed and, as punctually as ever, in 1969 the "miracle of the sun" occurred just as before. Once again, the rays of the sun illuminated the gods within the sanctuary as they had done for three thousand years. Despite everything, Ramesses II and his architectural masterpiece continue to survive.

© UNESCO/Nenadovic

Abu Simbel

A fascinating image of the waters lapping the arid rocky banks of the immense Lake Nasser where the two temples of Abu Simbel, skilfully reconstructed, once more appear in all their magnificent splendour.

The most beautiful and imposing construction of the greatest pharaoh in Egyptian history, Abu Simbel is situated in the heart of the Nubian territory, almost on the border with Sudan, 40 minutes by air from Aswan, but also within reach by river boat, bus or car (circa 280 kilometres in the western desert). In theory, the temple of Abu Simbel was dedicated to the triad Amon-Ra, Harmakis and Ptah, but in practice it was erected solely to glorify in the centuries its builder Ramesses II the Great. Abu Simbel is not only one of the finest temples in Egypt - certainly the most unusual and majestic - but is also the symbol of the vast enterprise undertaken to save all the Nubian temples threatened by Lake Nasser. Long forgotten, it was pure chance that *Ybsambul* - as it was called - once more saw the light of day. On May 22, 1813, the Swiss Johann Ludwig Burckhardt happened to see the upper part of four stone giants emerging, as if by magic, from the sand. On August 1, 1817 the Italian Giovanni Battista Belzoni liberated the upper part of a portal from the sand and found the entrance. After him, travellers, scholars, archaeologists, tourists arrived in their hundreds to admire the architectural masterpiece of Ramesses II, finally free. The danger of its disappear-

ing under the waters of Lake Nasser became an issue that echoed throughout the world. While Abu Simbel may be the most beautiful and imposing of the temples of Nubia, it was also the most difficult to save due to its particular characteristics. Despite the problems, however, sheer determination and the wonders of technology combined to achieve one of the most incredible feats of dismantling and reconstruction ever undertaken by archaeologists, thus saving the temple and perpetuating its memory throughout the centuries.

The **rock-cut temple** of Abu Simbel is an exact transferral of the architectural form of an Egyptian inner sanctuary temple cut deep inside the rock.

Sculpted into the mountain, the *façade* is 38 metres long and 31 high. This is framed by a convex 'torus' moulding, and is surmounted by a cornice with uraei (the sacred asp) above which is carved a row of 22 seated baboons, each two and a half metres high. Below the torus moulding is a cornice engraved with dedicatory hieroglyphics, and in a niche below this in the middle of the façade is a large high-relief statue representing Ra-Harakhti with a falcon's head, flanked by two bas-relief figures of Ramesses II.

The monumental façade of the rock-cut temple in Abu Simbel showing the statue of Re-Harakhte with the head of a sparrow-hawk, preceded by four splendid seated colossi, the features of which are similar to Ramesses II.

Four colossal *statues* of Ramesses II seated form the supporting columns of the façade. Even on this monumental scale they reproduce the true features of the monarch. They are 20 metres high and measure more than 4 m. from ear to ear, while the lips, measuring over a metre, express a soft, gentle smile. The pharaoh is represented with his hands resting in his lap, wearing the double crown and a headdress with deep folds on either side of his face. The second statue on the left is broken and part of the head and body lie on the ground.

Beside and between the legs of each colossus are other statues representing members of the royal family including a daughter (who was also his wife) Bentanat, his mother Tuya, his wife Nefertari, his son Amen-hir-khopshef, and another daughter and wife, Merytamun. On the base and along the sides of the seats are figures of African and Asiatic prisoners. A "multitude of workers imprisoned by his sword" worked on the monumental façade under the orders of Pyay, head of all the sculptors, as we read inside the temple. The work of the sculptors was followed by that of the painters for, at the time of Ram-

In his diary, Giovanni Battista Belzoni described the moment of entering the Great Temple of Abu Simbel: "The sand, heaped up against the rock that dominates the temple by the wind coming from the north, had gradually encroached across the façade and buried the entrance by three quarters. Thus the first time that I approached the temple I lost hope of freeing the entrance as it seemed quite impossible to reach the doorway. ... The sand was slipping across from one side to the other of the façade and consequently it was pointless to try to open a straight access towards the entrance; it was thus necessary to excavate in the opposite direction so that the sand fell beyond the façade. ... The morning of the first of August we went to the temple very early, excited by the idea of finally entering the underground chambers that we had uncovered. ... We stepped into the passage we had opened and had the pleasure of being the first to descend into the largest and most beautiful underground chamber in Nubia, and to examine a monument comparable to the most beautiful in all of Egypt. ... We were at first astonished by the immensity of the place; we found magnificent antiquities, paintings, sculptures and massive statues."

esses, the temple was most probably richly painted and decorated.

The *pronaos* is a vast rectangular hall 18 metres long and 16.70 wide. This is flanked by eight Osiris pillars ten metres tall arranged in two rows, representing Osiris with the features of Ramesses. The colossi on the left wear the white crown of Upper Egypt, while those on the right, the "pschent" or double crown. Their arms, crossed over their chests, hold the sceptre and flail. Decorating the roof of the central nave is the great vulture of the goddess Nekhbet, protrectress of Upper Egypt, while the aisles on either side are painted with stars.

The wall *decorations* celebrate the military victories of Ramesses II. The most interesting and famous is on the north wall where one can follow the various phases of the Battle of Kadesh which concluded the pharaoh's military campaign against the Hittites in the fifth year of his reign. A long epic poem written by Pentaur was engraved in hieroglyphics not only here in Abu Simbel but also on the walls of the temples of Luxor and Karnak.

The pronaos leads into the *hypostyle hall*, with four square pillars painted with images of the pharaoh before the various gods. The walls are also painted with liturgical scenes, including the transportation of the sacred boat. Finally, sixty-five metres from the entrance door, in the heart of the mountain, lies the *sanctuary*, the most intimate and secret part of the temple, a small room measuring four by seven metres. Here sits the statue of Ramesses II deified, together with the triad Ptah, Amon-Ra and Harmakis. Regarding these statues, as early as the nineteenth century scholars realized that the entire temple had been built according to a precise plan and some, first among whom François Champollion, had noted what was later defined as the *"miracle of the*

sun". Twice a year at dawn, coinciding with the solstices, the sun penetrates the entire length of the temple and its rays fall on the statues of Amon, Harmakis and the pharaoh; after about twenty minutes the light disappears and it is remarkable that Ptah is never struck by the rays of the sun for Ptah is the god of Darkness. Eight other smaller rooms open off at the sides: this was where the Nubian tributes were stored.

The **temple of Hathor**, which the pharaoh dedicated to Nefertari, his queen - not his only wife, but certainly the best loved - is on the left upon leaving the Great Temple. Never before in the Egypt of the pharaohs had the consort of a sovereign been depicted on the facade of a temple, as large as the statues of her husband. For her, for the Great Royal Bride, Nefertari-Mery-en-Mut ("beloved of Mut"), This extremely harmonious little temple was built by Ramesses. The six statues, ten metres tall, their left legs set slightly forward, seem to emerge from the rock and move towards the light. Nefertari is shown as Hathor with the horns of the sacred cow, the solar disk and two plumes.

The interior of the richly decorated Great Temple with the massive Osiris columns and, on the right, the statues in the Sanctuary where the "miracle of the sun" takes place.

HATHOR

The origins of the
goddess Hathor are
extremely ancient. The
name means 'The
House of Horus'.
Usually represented
in feminine form, the
head of the goddess is
surmounted with the horns
of a cow. Goddess of love,
she was also the patron
of music and dance.
She was one of the
most popular deities of
Egypt and was especially
venerated in
Dendera.

*The graceful façade of the temple of Hathor, with six large
statues rather unusually representing Nefertari the same
height as her husband, beside. Right, the simple interior,
elaborately decorated, and the characteristic Hathor pillars.*

The divine consecration of the queen is also celebrated
in the delightfully simple interior – an almost square
chamber with six pilasters in two rows, carved with images of Hathor. Engraved beneath the head of the goddess are stories of Nefertari and Ramesses. The walls
of this chamber too are decorated with the customary
scenes of sacrifice and the massacre of prisoners by the
warrior king. The hall leads to a vestibule and beyond to
the *sanctuary* where the pharaoh is represented honour-
ing Hathor, identified as his consort. Set between two
pillars, and portrayed in the likeness of the sacred cow,
the goddess truly seems to stand away from the rock with
particularly striking effect.

The **speos of Abu Oda** has not yet been restored. It
contains paintings of Horemheb and Egyptian divinities
but also St George and the dragon as well as Christ, since
it had been transformed into a Coptic church. And the
same holds for the **tomb of Paser**, governor of Ethiopia
under Ay, which has various ritual scenes.

Al-Fayyum

Views of Fayyum and its monuments, the waterways and characteristic wheels operated by the flow of canal water, and the pyramids (below, Hawarah).

Right, originally from Fayyum and now in the Egyptian Museum in Cairo, these two fascinating portraits are datable to the Greek period and provide evidence of a distant but noble past.

Lying along the Nile valley about one hundred kilometres from the south-west of Cairo, with one million residents this splendid oasis is the largest in Egypt and is fed from the river by the Bahr Yusuf canal. In ancient times, when the floods were more abundant, life in Al-Fayyum was regulated by flow of the river. This fact was not always positive, however, as during certain periods of the year the flood waters were particularly abundant and the oasis became rather like a swamp with lush vegetation providing attractive shelter for crocodiles. Thus the pharaohs of the 12th Dynasty and later the Ptolomies in particular, made irrigation systems and canals in an effort to make life more peaceful and pleasant, and encouraged settlement by veterans and the Greeks who introduced viticulture. Splendid temples and small towns also developed at this time and numerous and important ruins are now concentrated in five main sites: **Hauara** (with a famous pyramid), **Medinet el-Fayum** (with characteristic wheels), **Biyahmu**, **Medinet Madi** (with a *temple*) and **Kasr Karun**.

THE OASES

When we think of the desert, inevitably we think not only of sand scorched by an implacable blazing sun, but also of verdant oases, both large and small, that offer occasional opportunities of refreshment with luxuriant plants and abundant water. The western desert of Egypt also benefits from this tradition and is indeed famous for the many oases scattered throughout the area found travelling through the *New Valley Province*. The nearest to Cairo, for example, is the **Bahareya oasis**, its luxuriant woods of palm trees creating an unusual stretch of green framed by black hills. The most populous settlement is Bawiti while Ain al-Beshmo, a natural spring already known to the Romans for its therapeutic thermal waters, is one of the most popular attractions, and the *"Valley of the Mummies"* where the tombs are indeed full of mummies, and the Roman ruins here are some of the most interesting archaeological finds made recently. **Khargah** is instead the largest and most developed oasis in the New Valley Province, famous for the *temple of Hibis*, dating from the 6th century BC, built by Darius I (the largest existing Persian temple in Egypt) and dedicated to the triad of Thebes, it once represented the centre of the city of Hibis, the ancient capital of the oasis. Slightly further north the interesting *Christian necropolis of Al-Bagawat* begins, an ancient cemetery with hundreds of tombs made of mud bricks with images of biblical stories. Inhabited since prehistoric times, 189 kilometres to the west of Khargah is the **oasis of Dakhlah**, extremely well-endowed with water that flows from over 600 springs forming numerous natural small lakes. With a population of about 70,000 people, this area of orchards and characteristic mud-brick villages produces rice, mangoes, oranges, olives, dates and apricots. The **Farafrah oasis** is also noted for a surprising abundance of water – over a hundred wells and springs – and the *White Desert* surrounding it, an unusual region with blindingly white rock formations sculpted by wind erosion. Farafrah is inhabited mainly by Bedouins while the **Siwah oasis**, particularly fertile and luxuriant, is mainly Berber and the quite unique customs and traditions of these people are proudly preserved here. Almost on the border with Libya, 550 kilometres to the west of Cairo, this is one of the most picturesque areas in all of Egypt, standing on the ancient route for the date trade that leads to Memphis. The items still produced here by skilled craftsmen are the result of centuries of tradition, and in this same area are the *Baths of Cleopatra* where water flows into a large basin that the inhabitants still use to bathe in, as well as the ruins of the *temple of Amun*.

The second city of Egypt, Alexandria was built by Alexander the Great on the site of an old fishing village that had a port conveniently protected by the island of Pharos. Seeing the potential of the site, in 332 BC after having liberated Egypt from Persian occupation and crowned himself as pharaoh in the oasis of Siwah, he directed the architect Dinocrates to plan the city. At the time, in fact, there were no important outlets to the Mediterranean and the small ports of Naukratis, Tanis and Pelusium, situated on the delta, were not capable of competing with the Phoenician ports.

It was under his successors, the Ptolemies, however, that the city was made capital. Ptolemy I Soter linked the island of Pharos to the mainland with a road (the *Heptastadion*) thus creating two ports connected by passages beneath the two bridges of the *Heptastadion.* An entire district was reserved for the Jews and residents of the city were to include Demetrius Phaleres, founder of the famous *library* (created by the first Greek pharaoh of Egypt, Ptolemy I Soter, greatly favoured and much endowed by all the Ptolemaic dynasties), Euclid and Apelles, one of the greatest painters in antiquity. Under the rule of Ptolemy II Philadelphus the city was enhanced not only with one of the seven wonders of the world, the Great Lighthouse, Pharos, named for the island where it stood, but also with an Academy that was at-

Today, Alexandria is best known as an important port and popular seaside resort. Where once the mythical Beacon stood in times past, there are now beaches, quays and the fine Qayt-bay Fort (right and above, a view of the port shows once more the perfect reconstruction of the fortress, completed in 1982). Yet the splendours of the past are still recalled both in the impressive ruins such as (opposite page, above) Pompey's Pillar in the Serapeum, the main temple of the ancient city, and in the name of its famous founder (left, a bust of the young Alexander the Great in the Acropolis Museum, Athens).

THE REDISCOVERY OF THE BEACON

The beacon of Alexandria was built for Ptolemy I and Ptolemy II by the famous architect Sostrates and stood above the port some 140 metres high formed by three towers one above the other. The light produced by fires was reflected from the top using a system of mirrors so that the beacon signalling the entrance to the port of Alexandria was visible from great distances, even as far as 10 kilometres. It fell into disuse, however, and damaged by two earthquakes in the 11th and 14th centuries it eventually collapsed entirely. In 2005, after a decade of research carried out by marine archaeologists from the Centre d'Études Alexandrines, various remains and blocks weighing 60-70 tons believed to have been part of the Beacon were found and the enormous base of what was the seventh wonder of the world has emerged from the depths of the port, representing the first, fundamental step towards its reclamation with a demanding project to restore the remains that have been found to date.

The Alexandria Museum is a modern and worthy heir to the place once held sacred by the Muses where, at the time of Ptolemy II Philadelphus, artistic items, manuscripts and natural curiosities were housed. Exhibited here today are interesting masterpieces of Greek, Roman and Byzantine art, such as the bust of Serapis, a fine example of Hellenic art (left) and the Good Shepherd (below) a remarkable Byzantine work.

tended by the most famous intellectuals of the Greek civilization. During this period moreover, scholars assembled here to translate the *Old Testament* into Greek for the first time, producing the famous "version of the Seventy". Despite a series of internal rebellions and plots, Alexandria continued to maintain its role as cosmopolitan capital with a rich intellectual life and flourishing commerce. In 48 BC, during the reign of Cleopatra, the last queen of Egypt, Caesar besieged the city causing the fire that destroyed the library. Egypt became a Roman province and Alexandria, which was already a point of communication between East and West (the Red Sea and the Indies), assumed the role of second city of the Empire. The process of conversion to Christianity began in 40 AD (according to tradition, the apostle Mark founded the church of Alexandria) and the city rapidly became an important religious centre. During the second century, a school (the *Didascaleion*) run by famous theologians was founded but fierce controversies soon arose that subsequently developed into heresy. In addition uprisings by religious and racial minorities took place leading to repression and persecution. The first victims were the Christians (under Caracalla, Decius and Diocletian) and later the pagans following the edict of Theodosius (392).

In 642 the city was conquered by Amr Ibn el-As, a general

On 16 October 2002 Alexandria witnessed
the triumphal rebirth of a myth with the official
inauguration of the new library, (this and
following page) which opened to the public just
four days later. This event of extraordinary
historical and cultural importance was
completed under the auspices of UNESCO and
with the collaboration of some twenty countries,
signatories of the Aswan Declaration of 1990.
More than five hundred architects participated
in the international competition for the design
of the new library, which was won by the
Norwegian architect Christoph Kapellar of the
Snohetta Studio, Oslo. The building also houses
an institute for the restoration of antique books,
a children's library, a school of information
sciences, meeting and conference rooms. It will
house eight million books over eleven floors with
a total surface area of 85,000 square metres
and a reading room of 25,000 square metres
providing study space for about 2,500 scholars.

in the army of caliph Omar Ibn al-Quatab,
who defeated the Byzantines and took the
entire country. Cairo was chosen to be capital
and for Alexandria a period of continual and
steady decline set in.
A revival of the city only began with the arrival of Napoleon and of scholars who brought

with them modern ideas for improving the country, and in particular under Mohammed Ali and his successors who began to put them into practice. Thus, with the introduction of cotton production, followed by the opening of the Suez Canal, commercial trade was stimulated, industries developed, foreigners came to live in Alexandria and, with the construction of residential areas with hotels, tree-lined avenues, shops and casinos, the city took on an entirely Mediterranean aspect.

After the revolution of 1952 all that remained was the memory of this elegant and worldly society seen in the façades of buildings that belonged to foreigners and the summer residences of Cairo's bourgeoisie. The area of *Lake Maryut* has become an industrial area, the *port* has been extended and new docks have been built, yet Alexandria still maintains its special role as the country's foremost seaside resort.

The Suez Canal (*Qanâ al-Suweis*) is an artificial waterway 161 kilometres long cut through the isthmus that stretches between Port Said on the Mediterranean and Suez on the Red Sea thus providing a sea route between Europe and Asia without having to circumnavigate Africa. Built between 1859 and 1869 by the Compagnie Universelle du Canal Maritime de Suez, directed by Ferdinand de Lesseps and designed by an Austrian engineer, Alois Negrelli, the canal was officially opened on 17 September 1869. The property of the Egyptian government and France, its opening had an immediate effect on world trade as the Red Sea became one of the most strategic marine routes in the world and European access to Africa was facilitated. The creation of a navigable link between the Red Sea, with its routes towards Asia, and the Mediterranean, had for centuries been an important and coveted objective. Ramesses II, Nectanebo II, the Persian king, Darius I, as well as the Arabs had all made various attempts to build the waterway first known as the Pharaohs' Canal and later as the Canal of the Princes of the Faith joining the Red Sea and the Nile. For reasons of defence, however, in 842 the caliph Abu Giafar closed it completely, and thus the situation remained until the 19th century when the canal, eight metres deep and 22 wide, was built. With the passing of time and the increasing tonnage of vessels, work was continually required to widen and deepen the channel. Troubled by debts, in 1882 the Egyptian government sold its share in the company that managed the canal to the United Kingdom. But on 28 July 1956, Egypt reversed this decision and nationalised the canal, provoking reaction from France, the United Kingdom and Israel. This resulted in a conflict during which the canal was closed for several months until the United Nations ruled that it was the property of Egypt. Today, it can be travelled in 15 hours and ships with a draught of up to 15 metres can navigate it though this will increase to 22 by 2010 to permit the passage of super tankers. Currently its measurements are between 70 and 125 metres width at surface and from 45 to 100 on the canal bed. In 1951 an 11 metre stretch between El-Qantara and El-Firdan was doubled in width to facilitate the passage of traffic in both directions.

SNORKELLING

The area of the Red Sea is extremely well suited to exploring the depths by snorkelling with flippers, mask and mouthpiece. The seas are, in fact, characterised by reefs that appear on the surface or are semi-submerged, so that even those who only swim on the surface can tranquilly observe the entire underwater environment and its numerous, colourful inhabitants.

Indeed, most of the fish and animals that live in this sea can be found in the first few metres of the lively, brightly-coloured reef. Diving to even only a slight depth, it is possible to observe the creatures that live in the caves and on the sandy sea bed. And those who submerge to greater depths may be surprised by some truly exciting confrontations with large marine animals and predators such as barracuda and sharks, more easily approached by divers who do not use an aqualung and thus benefit from the silence.

The depths of the Red Sea host a wealth of living organisms, swarming around the coral reefs that constitute a vast ecosystem of their own and support an enormous quantity of animal and plant species. The main builders of the barriers are the madrepores, also known as reef builders. Entire shoals of multiform and multicoloured fish glide around them without any apparent aim or direction: elegant angel fish, the butterfly fish, the spectacular parrot fish and the surgeon fish. The warm waters of the Red Sea offer other surprising sights – Moray eels, for example, adroitly manoeuvring through the narrow cavities and gaps of the coral reef, or the magnificent coral bass, or the tireless cleaner fish intent on removing parasites and old scales from other fish, and the majestic Napoleon fish. However, while all sights and experiences below the Red Sea may be described as fascinating, not all can be considered peaceable. Never trust, for example, the trigger-fish – capable of attacking and biting if it feels threatened. And above all, watch out for the scorpion fish and the stone fish which have defensive venomous spines connected to poisonous glands and, if touched or trampled, can sting by injecting a nasty poison. Less dangerous, but just as unpleasant, is contact with the ordinary fire coral, jellyfish and even with some kinds of sea anemones that are capable of inflicting serious stings. The diadem sea urchins can also be painful to come across as well as the ray fish. But, roaming amongst the molluscs and crustaceans, the shellfish and starfish, it is not unusual to come across a harmless tortoise and, in particular, sharks that do not present an immediate danger as, at the first sign of an encounter, instinctively they are more inclined to escape than attack.

The Tiràn Strait

Just a few miles of sea, where the two islands of *Tiràn* and *Sanafir* are, separate the Egyptian Sinai coast from the coast of Saudi Arabia. The depths of this stretch of sea are among the most beautiful in the world with reefs covered by extraordinary colonies of soft coral (Alcyonarians) and magnificent, brilliantly-coloured Gorgonian sea fans, while the beaches provide a suitable environment for marine tortoises to reproduce. The numerous coral reefs just below the surface have, however, always been a danger for the ships that sail these waters and the numerous wrecks that are visible or that lie on the sea bed are evidence of this.

Ras Mohammed National Park

Ras Mohammed, the furthest point of the Sinai Peninsula, rightly classified as one of the ten best areas in the world for diving. In 1983 some 97 square kilometres were declared a protected area and this has increased to 480 today. The Park, flanked on the east by the Aqabah Gulf and on the west by Suez, has a series of obligatory routes, indicated by different colours, enabling the visitor to discover hidden inlets, isolated beaches, magnificent views or lovely and unusual corners. As well as one of the most beautiful coral reefs, there are desert wolves, hyenas, gazelles, osprey, swans and elegant grey herons to be seen resting in the shade of gigantic mangroves.

Golf in the desert

Sharm el Sheikh now offers a new and entertaining experience to visitors – a round of golf with the Sinai Mountains in the background. In 1998, located between Naama Bay and the airport, a well-equipped 18-hole golf course was opened – the *Jolie Ville Movenpick Golf Resort* where numerous competitions are organised every year. And where better to refresh yourself after a game than the luxurious *Club House*, a genuine source of national pride, chosen on various occasions to host important Middle East peace conferences.

The Red Sea Wrecks

"Louille", "Maria Schroeder", "Thistlegorm", "Dunraven", "Carnatic" – names that are now part of the eternal history of the sea.

Each name has its own history and its own adventure, some more exciting than others. And when a ship has become a wreck, corals and fish take possession. But none of these ships is really dead: they have become a great attraction for divers not only for discovering the flora and fauna of the depths, but also for their extraordinary value in providing a truly unique source of historic information.

Sharm el Sheikh

In Arabic, the word *Sharm* means 'a bay', so the name of the city translates as 'the bay of the sheik'.

In fact, the coast here consists of a series of splendid bays where hotels compete for the most modern architecture and the best range of sports facilities.

To the east is the *bay of Sharm el Maya*, with a port, followed by the high rocky spur of *Ras Umm Sidd* with its luxurious hotel complexes, then *Naama Bay*, the resort that has benefited from the tourist boom more than any other in this part of Sinai, and *Coral Bay* with a modern residential complex, and lastly beautiful little *Shark Bay*.

Hurghada

Just a few decades ago, Hurghada was no more than a small fishing village, barely visible on the map.

The explosion of tourism and the attraction of the area for divers have transformed it into one of the largest tourist centres on the Red Sea, greatly appreciated by enthusiasts of water sports of all kinds. Every year, thousands of tourists come to this rapidly growing town to enjoy the sun and the beautiful beaches as well as to have fun, for in the clubs and bars here, the day begins at midnight!

The biblical appearance of Sinai is an evocative mix of rugged rocks scoured and shaped by the wind, sands and lonely stretches of desert.

Without doubt, anyone travelling over the tracks and routes of the Sinai area today will enjoy one of the most beautiful and moving sights that nature has to offer. Through its long and troubled history the land here has remained unspoilt. Nature, not man, still rules supreme, sole witness to the passing of time where nothing has changed for centuries.

To enter the magical world of the Sinai is to enter a world of craggy rocks, the shifting scenery of sand dunes, constantly changing shape as quickly as the desert wind changes its direction. Here, the Bedouins live, maintaining their secret life, an ancient and unchanged existence with the same rhythms, customs and elements as 3000 years ago. One can journey through the dried-up bed of a wadi, entirely surrounded by rock and stone, suddenly discovering a plant stubbornly determined to grow. In addition to the spirituality that the visitor can find within the walls of **Saint Catherine's Monastery**, Sinai, exudes the rarified atmosphere of a world of rock, sand, solitude and silence. Perhaps this is one of the few places left in the world where man has the chance to find his inner self once more.

Above, the massive, fortified Monastery of Saint Catherine, with the rocky mass of the Sinai behind.
Left, the simple façade of the Church of the Transfiguration and the elegant bell tower.

The Monastery of St Catherine

The smallest diocese in the world is, at the same time, the oldest existing Christian monastery and also houses the richest collection of icons and rare manuscripts in existence. In 330 Elena, mother of the Emperor Constantine, requested that a small chapel dedicated to the Virgin should be built on the spot of the burning bush. In the years that followed, the increasing spread of Christianity brought great wealth to the Monastery as well, however, as a series of raids by nomadic desert tribes, until finally in 530 Emperor Justinian ordered that a much larger basilica should be built, known as the **Church of the Transfiguration**, with the appearance of a mighty fortress that is still so familiar today. After the Arab conquest in 640, it assumed the role of isolated bastion of Christianity entirely surrounded by the vast Islamic world. During the war to liberate the Holy Lands, many important personages stayed here, such as Henry II of Brunswick, Philip of Artois and Duke Albert of Austria. Over the following centuries many travellers, drawn by the fascination of biblical sites, visited the monastery and its treasures withstanding both the dangers and the discomfort of the journey to these lands. In the 19th century, however, tourism increasingly developed and took on a more peaceful aspect. Today, comfortable roads, hotels and even a small airport nearby have encouraged increasing numbers of tourists to come to St Catherine's. The monastery still belongs to the Greek Orthodox Church and most of the monks who live here are Greek, belonging to the rule of St Basil of Caesarea, a monk, theologian and bishop who lived between 329 and 379. To the south of the Monastery is *Jebel Musa*, or **Mount Moses,** 2285 metres high and traditionally identified as the biblical Mount Horeb where the God of Israel is said to have

Right, the interior of the Church of the Transfiguration, gleaming with gold and rare woods and enhanced with numerous candelabra and silver lamps. Below, the spot where traditionally Moses is said to have seen the burning bush, now protected by a low wall.

given Moses the Tablets with the Ten Commandments. Considered sacred by the three great monotheistic religions (Jewish, Christian and Islamic) it takes almost three hours to climb the mountain. However, at 2642 metres the highest mountain in the whole Sinai peninsula is *Jebel Katrin,* or **Mount St Catherine** which owes its name to the legend according to which angels brought the body of the martyred St Catherine here from Alexandria. It takes almost five hours walking to reach the summit. On the way is the **Monastery of the Forty Martyrs** (*Deir al-Arbain*), built in memory of the monks killed by the Blemmi tribe. At the top is a chapel dedicated to the saint, built by the monk Callistus.

Left, the Confessional Gate on Jebel Musa, where pilgrims came to confess their sins.
Below, the Chapel of the Holy Trinity, at the top of Mount Moses, where tourists and pilgrims can enjoy a splendid panorama over Sinai.

Index

HISTORICAL FACTS
AND INFORMATION

* * *

Printed in the European Union
Centro Stampa Editoriale Bonechi
Sesto Fiorentino – Florence – Italy

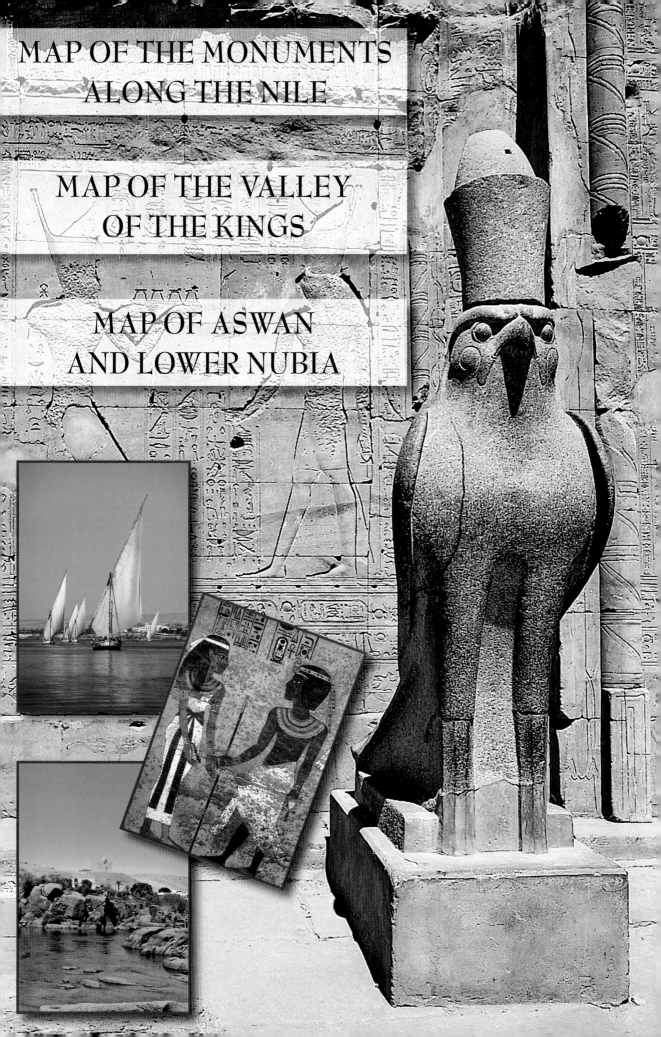

MAP OF THE MONUMENTS
ALONG THE NILE

MAP OF THE VALLEY
OF THE KINGS

MAP OF ASWAN
AND LOWER NUBIA

MAP OF THE MONUMENTS ALONG THE NILE

© All rights reserved. No part of this book may be reproduced without the written permission of the Publisher. Project and realization by Casa Editrice Bonechi. Under © protection.

MEDITERRANEAN SEA

The **Nile Delta** consists of that large triangle formed by the two branches of the river and the two principal routes, one leading from Cairo to Damietta, and the other which goes to Tanis. The Delta, with its cities of Tanis, Sais and Bubastis, was extremely important in Egyptian history. The landscape is still extraordinary, with its far flung stretches of rice and cotton. Then as now, numerous species of aquatic birds, such as egrets, flamingoes and pelicans gather on Lake Manzala.

The **Rosetta Stone**, which held the key to deciphering hieroglyphics, is a fragment of a black basalt stele. The original is now in the British Museum in London. The inscription consists of three scripts: 14 lines of hieroglyphs, 32 of demotic Egyptian and 54 in Greek. The Frenchman François Champollion was the man who succeeded in deciphering it in 1822.

Rosetta

Alexandria

Alexandria is the second largest city of Egypt, founded by Alexander the Great on the site of an ancient fishing village, and with a harbor that was protected by the island of Pharos. Only a few submerged fragments remain of the famous Lighthouse or Pharos, one of the Seven Wonders of the World, erected by Sostratus of Knidos: it was a terraced tower, 120 meters tall, and mirrors reflected the light of the fire of resinous wood burning at the top up to a hundred miles away.

EGYPT ALONG THE NILE

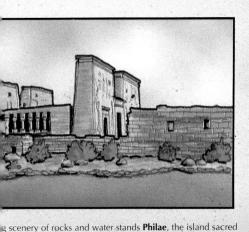

Lake Nasser, 500 kilometers long (150 of which are in Sudanese territory) was created when the High Dam of Aswan was built. It has a capacity of 157 billion cubic meters of water, second in the world after the Kariba on the Zambesi. The creation of this artificial basin meant not only a radical modification in the landscape and environment, but also the dismantling and subsequent re-erection of the 14 endangered Nubian temples, which were all faithfully reconstructed in a site that was higher than the waters of the lake.

g scenery of rocks and water stands **Philae**, the island sacred
by Pierre Loti as the "pearl of Egypt". When the High Dam
re all dismantled and rebuilt on another island, higher than
sanctuary was situated on the site where the annual miracle
the rebirth of life thanks to Isis who, with the power of love,
nd Osiris, was thought to take place.

LAKE NASSER

O
Abu Simbel

The **temple of Abu Simbel**, in the heart of the Nubian territory, almost at the frontier with Sudan, still defies the centuries. It was the most imposing construction of the greatest pharaoh in Egyptian history, Ramses II, who had it carved directly into the rocky mass of the mountain. The facade, 31 meters high, consists of four colossal statues of the seated Ramses II.

Stefano Benini

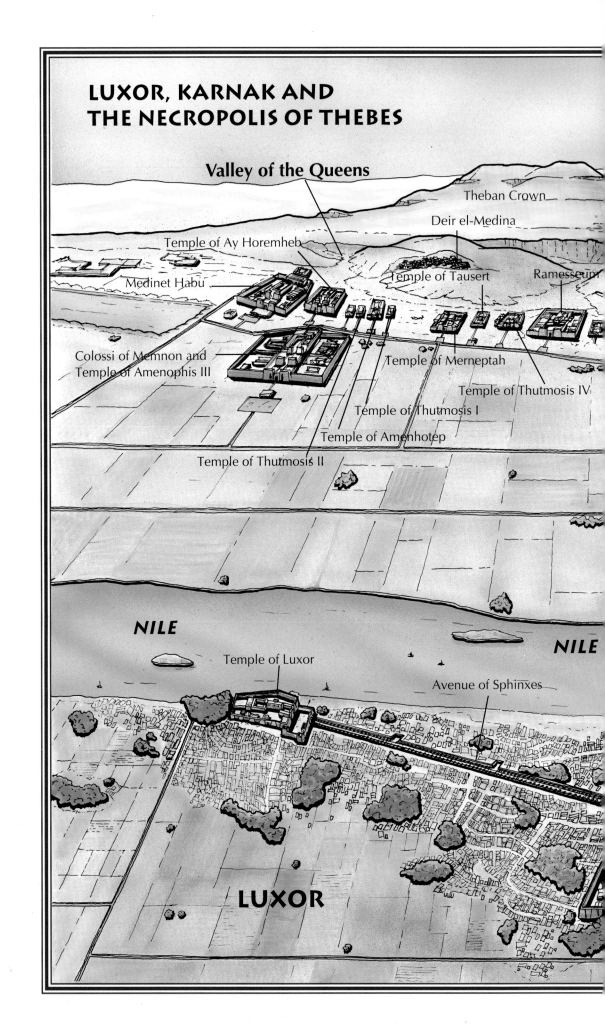

LUXOR, KARNAK AND
THE NECROPOLIS OF THEBES

Valley of the Queens

Theban Crown

Deir el-Medina

Temple of Ay Horemheb

Temple of Tausert

Ramesseum

Medinet Habu

Colossi of Memnon and
Temple of Amenophis III

Temple of Merneptah

Temple of Thutmosis IV

Temple of Thutmosis I

Temple of Amenhotep

Temple of Thutmosis II

NILE

NILE

Temple of Luxor

Avenue of Sphinxes

LUXOR

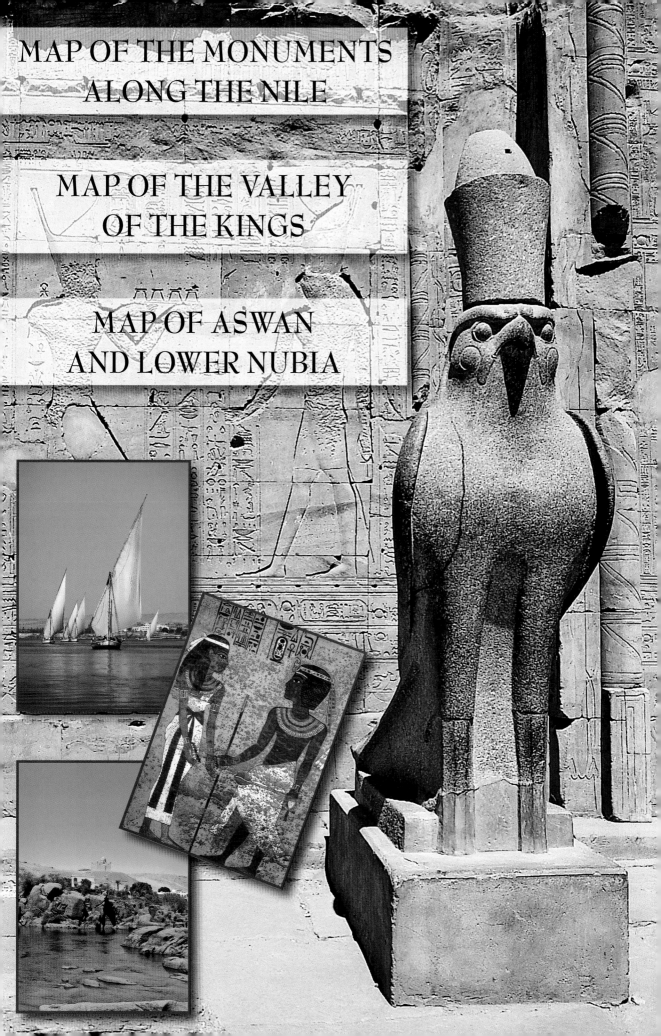

MAP OF THE MONUMENTS
ALONG THE NILE

MAP OF THE VALLEY
OF THE KINGS

MAP OF ASWAN
AND LOWER NUBIA

MAP OF THE MONUMENTS ALONG THE NILE

© All rights reserved. No part of this book may be reproduced without the written permission of the Publisher. Project and realization by Casa Editrice Bonechi. Under © protection.

MEDITERRANEAN SEA

The **Nile Delta** consists of that large triangle formed by the two branches of the river and the two principal routes, one leading from Cairo to Damietta, and the other which goes to Tanis. The Delta, with its cities of Tanis, Sais and Bubastis, was extremely important in Egyptian history. The landscape is still extraordinary, with its far flung stretches of rice and cotton. Then as now, numerous species of aquatic birds, such as egrets, flamingoes and pelicans gather on Lake Manzala.

The **Rosetta Stone**, which held the key to deciphering hieroglyphics, is a fragment of a black basalt stele. The original is now in the British Museum in London. The inscription consists of three scripts: 14 lines of hieroglyphs, 32 of demotic Egyptian and 54 in Greek. The Frenchman François Champollion was the man who succeeded in deciphering it in 1822.

Rosetta

Alexandria

Alexandria is the second largest city of Egypt, founded by Alexander the Great on the site of an ancient fishing village, and with a harbor that was protected by the island of Pharos. Only a few submerged fragments remain of the famous Lighthouse or Pharos, one of the Seven Wonders of the World, erected by Sostratus of Knidos: it was a terraced tower, 120 meters tall, and mirrors reflected the light of the fire of resinous wood burning at the top up to a hundred miles away.

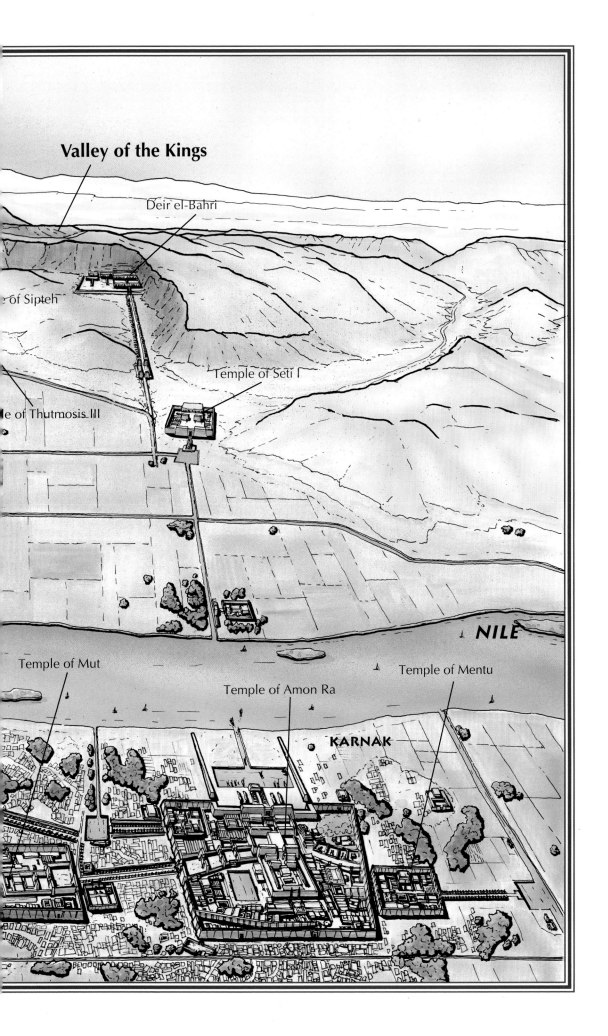

Valley of the Kings

Deir el-Bahri

of Sipteh

Temple of Seti I

e of Thutmosis III

NILE

Temple of Mut

Temple of Amon Ra

Temple of Mentu

KARNAK

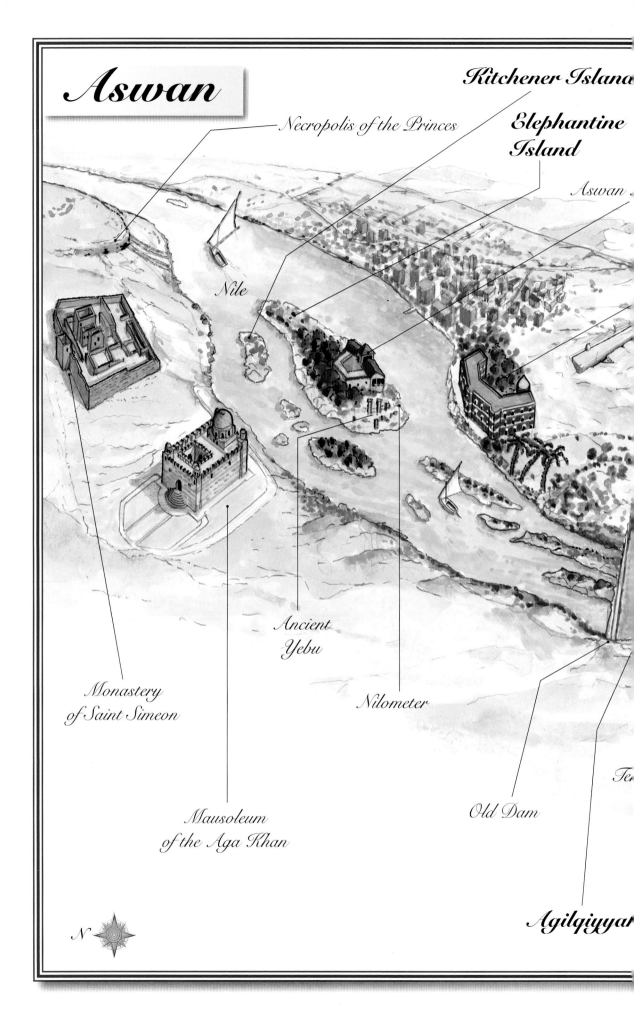

Aswan

Necropolis of the Princes

Kitchener Island

Elephantine Island

Aswan

Nile

Ancient Yebu

Nilometer

Monastery of Saint Simeon

Mausoleum of the Aga Khan

Old Dam

Te

Agilqiyya

N